# AROUND THE WORLD ON TWO WHEELS

# ANNIE IS BACK.

### Has Traveled Around the World on a Sterling Finished in Ivory and Gold.

## HER JOURNEY THE RESULT OF A BET.

#### A Short History of Her Adventures—Attacked and Robbed in France— Nearly Killed by a Road Hog In Stockton, Cal.—She has Gained $1,500 on Her Trip, and Expects to Make $3,500 More Before Reaching Boston.

#### ENTHUSIASTIC OVER HER STERLING, WHICH HAS COME THROUGH WITHOUT A SCRATCH.

Miss Annie Londonderry, the first woman to ride around the world on a bicycle, is back.

#### Her Mount was a Gold and Ivory Sterling.

Starting before she had even mastered the rudiments of cycling, she

So far Miss Londonderry's trip has been a great success. She has

#### Traveled Thousands of Miles

over the roughest country on her "Sterling" and speaks in the highest terms of praise of her machine.

In one of her letters to the Sterling people, dated from Yokohama, she writes, "I have ridden all through Japan, and my wheel is creating great excitement." In another letter, from Shanghai, she says, "I also wish to express to you the great satisfaction which your 'Sterling' has given to me."

Miss Londonderry is now back in America, and has been stopping some little time in California.

Outside of Stockton a few days ago she met with a bad accident. As she was riding along the driver of a buggy ran her down and ran over her.

#### She was Picked Up Unconscious

and carried into Stockton, where she lay in the hospital for two days. She coughed up a good deal of blood, and the doctors said she could never recover, but, talking of the accident, the plucky little woman said the other day, "Here I am, and, what is more, I intend to complete the journey."

While riding through Paris to Marseilles, Miss Londonderry rode nearly day and night, and when in the neighborhood of Lacone she was

*Map of the World, Showing Route Traveled by Annie Londonderry.*

has, with a pluck and resolution unusual in one of her sex, surmounted every obstacle, and although she left America

#### Without a Cent in Her Pocket,

she has brought back over $1,500.

About nine months ago two wealthy club men of Boston were discussing the modern woman, and one of these gentlemen, who was a woman hater, remarked very ironically that he supposed that the woman of the present age was able to do almost anything that was done by the masculine sex. His companion differed with him, and the discussion finally culminated in a bet of $20,000 to $10,000 that there was no woman living who could attempt the feat performed by Paul Jones. The conditions under which Miss Londonderry started were that she was to

#### Ride Around the World

in fifteen months; that she should stop at Havre, Marseilles, Colombo, Singapore, Hong Kong, Shanghai, Nagasaki, Kobe, Yokohama, and then return to America.

At each of these places she was to obtain the signature of the United States Consul, as proof that she had been there. She was to earn during her trip $5,000 in any honorable manner, with the exception of journalism, which is her profession.

#### Held Up by Three Masked Men

who sprung out from a clump of bushes by the wayside. She pluckily drew her pistol and was just about to shoot when one of them grabbed her from behind and took the pistol away. All they secured was three francs and they left her, swearing a variety of French oaths, as they had expected to get all the money which she had made in Paris.

So far, Miss Londonderry has been able to gain $1,500 by selling advertising space on her wheel, etc., and she expects to make the balance of the $5,000 between California and Boston by lecturing on the Chinese Japanese war.

While in Japan Miss Londonderry made the acquaintance of two war correspondents with whom she went to Port Arthur. Her two companions rode ponies while she rode her Sterling. She had, hard work, the roads were very bad, but she managed to keep up with the native ponies. She was

#### In the Thick of the Battle

at Gasan, and went over all the battlegrounds of last year's campaign in Corea.

During this trip the cold was intense, and the food so deficient that Miss Londonderry congratulates herself on getting out alive.

Her trip has proved what a strong and reliable mount the Sterling really is.

# AROUND THE WORLD ON TWO WHEELS

## Annie Londonderry's Extraordinary Ride

## PETER ZHEUTLIN

CITADEL PRESS
Kensington Publishing Corp.
www.kensingtonbooks.com

CITADEL PRESS BOOKS are published by
Kensington Publishing Corp.
850 Third Avenue
New York, NY 10022

All Kensington titles, imprints, and distributed lines are available at special quantity discounts for bulk purchases for sales promotions, premiums, fund-raising, educational, or institutional use. Special book excerpts or customized printings can also be created to fit specific needs. For details, write or phone the office of the Kensington special sales manager: Kensington Publishing Corp., 850 Third Avenue, New York, NY 10022, attn: Special Sales Department; phone 1-800-221-2647.

CITADEL PRESS and the Citadel logo are Reg. U.S. Pat. & TM Off.

First printing: November 2007

10 9 8 7 6 5 4 3 2 1

Printed in the United States of America

Library of Congress Control Number: 2007929065

ISBN-13: 978-0-8065-2851-9
ISBN-10: 0-8065-2851-6

*For my late father, Lionel Zheutlin, a kind and gentle soul.*

# Contents

# AROUND THE WORLD ON TWO WHEELS

# Prologue

*The maiden with her wheel of old*
*Sat by the fire to spin,*
*While lightly through her careful hold*
*The flax slid out and in*
*Today her distaff, rock and reel*
*Far out of sight are hurled*
*And now the maiden with her wheel*
*Goes spinning round the world*

—Madelyne Bridges, *Outing* magazine, September 1893

On the morning of January 13, 1895, an enthusiastic crowd, giddy with anticipation, lined the streets of Marseilles to see the arrival of a brave young American in her early twenties. As the petite, dark-haired cyclist pedaled into town with one foot—her other foot, wrapped in bandages, was propped on the handlebars—the Stars and Stripes flew in the breeze from an improvised mount on her bike frame. A loud cheer went up and people waved and shouted as she wheeled by. Dressed in a man's riding suit and astride a man's bicycle, she was accompanied by several Marseilles cyclists who had ridden with her from the village of Saint Louis. The riding party proceeded to the Brasserie Noailles where the local cycling club, the Cyclophile Marseille, hosted a luncheon in her honor. Feted in Paris for several weeks, she had braved bitter cold and snow to reach the south coast of France.

Annie Londonderry was already famous by the time she reached Marseilles. The French press had been writing about her prolifically since her arrival in France, at the northern port of Le Havre, on December 3, 1894. She had started from Boston seven months earlier in a daring attempt to become the first woman to circle the globe by bicycle, and, it was widely reported, to settle an extraordinary, high-stakes wager between two wealthy Boston businessmen.

While in Marseilles, Miss Londonderry endeared herself to the local population. She donated to a children's clinic several pieces of jewelry she had purchased in Paris. Admirers sent her countless letters at l'Hôtel de Provence, where she was staying. Unable to reply to them all, she set visiting hours, published in the local newspapers, when people could come to meet her. There, she sold photographs of herself, which she autographed, to help pay her travel expenses. She became a familiar, if curious, sight on the Cannebiere, riding up and down the boulevard, her bicycle and her clothing festooned with advertising ribbons, and handing out leaflets promoting the wares of perfume maker Lorenzy-Palanca, and the dairy cooperative of Alpes-Bernoises.

On Friday, January 18, a crowd filled the city's Crystal Palace to see her. When the famous cyclist appeared, dressed in a suit provided by la Maison Jaegel, a local boutique, the audience applauded wildly. As Miss Londonderry circled the room on her ivory and gold Sterling bicycle, an orchestra, conducted by the Maestro Trave, struck up "The Star-Spangled Banner" and "La Marseillaise," the French national anthem. In a brief speech, translated into French, she told the people of Marseilles they were "the elite of the French nation." The crowd roared its approval and threw flowers at her. She had, said one local newspaper, "captured the hearts of the people of Marseilles."

Two days later, thousands gathered to bid Miss Londonderry adieu as a drum and bugle corps and a delegation of local cyclists escorted her aboard a French *paquetbot,* the 413-foot steamship *Sydney.* Deeply moved by the outpouring of affection, she wept. Then Miss Londonderry and her Sterling bicycle sailed away through the Mediterranean toward the Suez Canal and points east.

But, unbeknownst to the people of Marseilles, the young cyclist from Boston with the Irish name was, in fact, Annie Cohen Kopchovsky (Mrs. Simon "Max" Kopchovsky), a Jewish working mother of three young children, ages five, three, and two. What the people of Marseilles also didn't know is that "Mlle. Londonderry" was not simply a cyclist on an around-the-world journey, but an illusionist possessed of what one American newspaper called "an inventive genius." She was, to be sure, making a trip around the world by wheel, though she made liberal use of steamships and trains, as well. But just as Londonderry was not her real name, with Annie Kopchovsky things were rarely as they appeared. There were even some who questioned whether she was a woman at all.

By the time she arrived in Marseilles, Annie was halfway through a traveling fifteen-month theatrical production starring herself, a veritable one-woman carnival on wheels who turned every Victorian notion of female propriety on its ear. An inveterate storyteller, consummate self-promoter, and masterful creator of her own myth, she turned her journey into one of the most outrageous chapters in cycling history, and herself into one of the most colorful characters of the gay 1890s.

For more than a century, the story of the audacious and charismatic Annie Kopchovsky and her attempt to circle the world by wheel has been lost to history. Who *was* this mysterious young woman on a bike? What was she like? How did she free herself from the social constraints that surrounded late Victorian women, and undertake such an adventure? Finally, how did an anonymous working-class Jewish mother from the tenements of Boston's West End transform herself into a new woman— the daring, internationally renowned globetrotter, Mlle. Londonderry? In short, what happened?

# Chapter One

# Going Woman

## ANNIE KAPCHOWSKY IS A POOR RIDER, BUT INTENDS TO DO THE EARTH*

*Good health to all, good pleasure, good speed,*
*A favoring breeze—but not too high*
*For the outbound spin! Who rides may read*
*The open secret of earth and sky.*

—Anonymous, *Scribner's Magazine*, June 1895

M onday, June 25, 1894, was a perfect day for baseball in Boston. The weather was fair, if somewhat overcast, but the hometown team, the Beaneaters, was in Louisville to play the Colonels. The big news this early summer day—news carried by telegraph cables to newspapers across the country and around the world—was the assassination the previous day in Lyon of French president Sadi Carnot at the hands of an Italian anarchist.

With the South End Baseball Grounds on Columbus and Walpole streets quiet, some who might have gone to the ballpark chose instead to ride the swan boats plying the lagoon in the Boston Public Garden. Others sat on benches, reading the news from France. Pedestrians strolled along gently curved walkways under the garden's graceful willows. If any of them had wandered the short distance to the gold-domed Massachusetts State House on Beacon Hill they would have been treated to an unusual sight. There, at about eleven o'clock in the morning, a crowd of five

---

* All chapter titles are headlines from newspaper accounts of Annie's travels. Kapachowsky is a misspelling.

hundred suffragists, friends, family members, and curiosity seekers gathered at the steps to see a young woman about to attempt something no woman had before—an around-the-world trip by bicycle.

Annie Cohen Kopchovsky arrived in a barouche accompanied by a friend, Mrs. Ober-Towne, and Mrs. J. O. Tubbs, head of the local chapter of the Women's Christian Temperance Union (WCTU). Her close friends, Pear Stone and Susie Wyzanski, were there to meet her. Governor Greenhalge was expected to preside over the proceedings, but sent word at the last moment that he could not attend, much to Annie's disappointment, no doubt. Though "the event lost something of the glamour that comes with state patronage," the scene was a festive one.

Annie was dressed in typical late Victorian attire: a long dark skirt, a dark blue tailored jacket with billowing leg-o'-mutton sleeves, a white shirtwaist with a striped collar and a neat bowtie, dark gloves, and a flat-topped hat, under which her dark hair had been tied up in a tight bun. "[S]he was short and lightly built," reported the *Boston Post*. "Her face was unmistakably Polish; her eyes, big brown and sparkling, her mouth wide but well formed and stamped with determination, her complexion olive, her hair dark brown, waving luxuriantly over a countenance full of expression."

To one side, Captain A. D. Peck of the Pope Manufacturing Company, maker of Columbia bicycles, stood watch over the Columbia "wheel" on which Annie would make her journey. Peck, an officer of the Massachusetts chapter of the League of American Wheelmen, a cycling organization, was dressed in his formal riding attire, including epaulets bearing the abbreviation "MASS," which allowed him to pass "as a State dignitary."

Mrs. Ober-Towne briefly addressed the crowd, declaring her conviction that "woman should have the same chances as men." The head of the WCTU spoke next. "May she set a noble example wherever she goes!" shouted Mrs. Tubbs, who also expressed the wish that Annie would "spread good tidings . . . among the Bedouins and the nations of the earth." She then introduced Annie to the crowd. Annie kissed all the women around her, asking each "if she had got her hat on straight," and announced she was making the trip to settle a wager between two wealthy Boston sugar merchants:

"I am to go around the earth in fifteen months, returning with five thousand dollars, and starting only with the clothes on my back. I cannot accept anything gratuitously from anyone." She turned her pockets inside out to show that she was penniless.

Mrs. Tubbs held up a copper coin and offered it to her. "A penny for luck!" she declared.

"I can't take it," replied Annie. "I must earn it."

"Take it as pay in return for speaking for the white ribbon, then," said Mrs. Tubbs, who pinned a white ribbon, the emblem of the WCTU, on Annie's right lapel.

Next, a representative of New Hampshire's Londonderry Lithia Spring Water Company stepped forward, handed Annie $100, and attached an advertising placard to the skirt guard on the rear wheel of her Columbia. The money was payment not only for carrying the Londonderry placard on her bicycle, but for Annie to use the surname "Londonderry" throughout the journey, as well. The latter served more than a commercial purpose; it had a practical one. It would ease her journey to travel under a name that didn't call attention to the fact that she was a Jew. And, more prosaically, she already had a keen awareness of the importance of publicity and a penchant for showmanship; "Annie Londonderry" would be far more memorable than "Annie Kopchovsky."

"Anyone else make a bid for space on the wheel?" she asked. There were no other takers that day, though there would be many down the road. "There was quite a crowd present to see her off," reported the *Chicago Daily Inter Ocean,* "the advertising man being particularly prominent."

As she prepared to mount her bicycle in front of the State House, her husband and three small children were nowhere to be seen, and she lamented to a reporter that her brother, Bennett, who *was* in the crowd, "didn't come up to say goodbye." Bennett may have thought his sister was *meshugineh,* Yiddish for "crazy," or he didn't expect her to get very far—or, perhaps, both.

As Captain Peck steadied her bicycle, she climbed into the saddle at last. Then, carrying only a change of underwear and a pearl-handled revolver, Annie Cohen Kopchovsky, now Annie Londonderry, "sailed away like a kite down Beacon Street." She would not return for well over a year.

It was "one of the most novel wagers ever made" said one Iowa newspaper: $20,000 to $10,000 that a woman could not go around the world on a bicycle as had Thomas Stevens a decade before. The wager was designed to settle an argument between two wealthy Boston men, but carried on at all levels of society in the 1890s, in homes, parlors, public meetings, work places, legislatures, rallies, and newspapers—indeed *everywhere*—about the equality of the sexes, a debate that carried well into the twentieth century and, one could argue, continues today. The requirement that the woman earn the formidable sum of $5,000 en route above her expenses made the journey not merely a test of her physical toughness and mental fortitude, but of her ability to fend for herself in the world. If she succeeded, she was to win the staggering sum of $10,000 in prize money.

Talking to reporters as she traveled, Annie often gave idiosyncratic descriptions of the wager. She sometimes said it prohibited her from earning money as a journalist, her chosen profession, and that she was prohibited from speaking any language other than English, even though the only other language she actually knew was Yiddish. One newspaper reported, fancifully, that "when riding she must dispatch a postal card to Boston every ten miles telling where and how she is, as well as the condition of the roads." Annie even told one El Paso newspaper that the wager prohibited her from contracting matrimony during the trip, not disclosing that she was already married.

ANNIE KOPCHOVSKY WAS, on the surface, as unlikely a candidate for the adventure she was about to undertake as one could imagine. Slightly built and a novice cyclist, she was a Jew, a married woman, and a working mother who was helping her husband, a peddler, to support a growing family.

It was a hectic household. When Annie left Boston in June 1894, she and her husband, Max, and their children lived in the same Spring Street tenement in Boston's West End as did Annie's brother, Bennett, his wife, Bertha, and *their* two young children, ages four and two. Max was a devout Orthodox Jew who spent hours studying Torah and attending shul. Bennett was an up-and-coming newspaper executive determined to make a success of himself at the *Boston Evening Transcript,* one of the city's many daily newspapers. Annie, though already the mother of three and only in her early twenties, worked as an advertising solicitor for several Boston dailies—a vivacious, bright, and attractive young woman and a skilled conversationalist, a woman who could charm even the most frugal customers into buying the newspaper space she had to sell.

She came to the United States in 1875 from Latvia as a young girl of four or five with her parents, Levi (Leib) and Beatrice (Basha) Cohen, and her older siblings, Sarah and Bennett. The Cohens were relatively early arrivals in Boston's Jewish community, for it wasn't until the 1880s that large waves of Jewish immigrants began arriving in America, many fleeing oppression in czarist Russia. Boston's Jewish community was relatively small, however, because the city had a reputation for virulent anti-Semitism. Many Jews remained in New York, where most, like the Cohens, first entered the country, or headed to the midwest or south to Baltimore, Savannah, and Charleston.

In the mid-1890s, about 6,300 of Boston's 20,000 Jews lived in the West End, the largest concentration of Jews in the city, but only a quarter of the neighborhood's ethnically diverse population. The West End was filled with new arrivals from all over Europe who tended to carve out small ethnic enclaves block by block. Spring Street was in the heart of the Jewish community, but within a few city blocks were clusters of Irish, Portuguese, Poles, Germans, Russians, and Italians, and a significant number of African-Americans, as well. It was one of the most ethnically mixed neighborhoods in America, a great churning place of immigrant life; a place where one would hear intriguing stories of faraway places.

In the early twentieth century, Mary Antin described the West End in her memoir, *The Promised Land,* and her experience, arriving as a young child, was not unlike Annie's:

> Anybody who knows Boston knows that the West and North Ends are the wrong ends of that city. They form the tenement district, or, in the newer phrase, the slums of Boston . . . the quarter where poor immigrants foregather, to live, for the most part, as unkempt, half-washed, toiling, unaspiring foreigners; pitiful in the eyes of social missionaries, the despair of boards of health, the hope of ward politicians, the touchstone of American democracy. . . .
>
> He may know all this and not yet guess how Wall Street, in the West End, appears in the eyes of a little immigrant from Polotzk. What would a sophisticated sight-seer say about Union Place, off Wall Street, where my new home awaited me? He would say that it is no place at all, but a short box of an alley. Two rows of three-story tenements are its sides, a stingy strip of sky is its lid, a littered pavement is the floor, and a narrow mouth its exit.

But I saw a very different picture . . . I saw two imposing rows of brick buildings, loftier than any dwelling I had ever lived in. Brick was even on the ground for me to tread on, instead of common earth or boards. Many friendly windows stood open, filled with uncovered heads of women and children. I thought people were interested in us, which was very neighborly. I looked to the topmost row of windows, and my eyes were filled with the May blue of an American sky!

Nevertheless, life in these tenements was hard and cramped. Though she was writing about New York, Gail Collins's description of tenement life could apply to Boston's West End, as well: "No one in the tenements had any privacy—apartments looked into one another across narrow airshafts, and women often carried on conversations with each other while working in the respective kitchens. A husband and wife knew that half the neighborhood could hear them arguing, or making love."

As Annie walked the West End's cobblestone streets, either going to and from work on Washington Street on the other side of Beacon Hill, to shop for necessities, or simply to escape the claustrophobia of a crowded household, she would hear conversations in as many as a dozen languages. The sound of horseshoes hitting cobblestone ricocheted through streets as horses pulled peddler's wagons past four- and five-story buildings, many with storefronts at street level and apartments above.

If the conversations in the West End created a veritable Tower of Babel, the odor of ethnic foods wafting from downstairs shops and upstairs apartments were similarly diverse. The smell of barreled pickles outside a Jewish grocery mingled with the aromas of tomato sauces simmering in Italian homes, cooked sausages from the homes of Poles, and borscht from the apartments of Russians.

Pedestrians ruled the streets. Women in shawls, long-sleeved blouses or bodices, and ankle-length skirts or dresses fondled fruit for sale and cast discerning eyes on cuts of meat and poultry hanging in shop windows. Boys in knickerbockers and caps hawked newspapers and chased one another down busy sidewalks, Men in topcoats and bowlers talked business and baseball; and the Orthodox Jews, identifiable by their long beards, black hats, and *payot,* long locks of hair near the ears, walked to shul. Kosher butchers abounded in the West End, as did small shops where clothing and shoes were manufactured and sold. The air, already tinged with the aromas of ethnic cooking was scented, too, with leather, fresh meat, and horse sweat. Heavy clothing worn year round, combined with limited facilities for bathing in crowded apartment blocks, meant the streets were filled with human odors as well. The West End was a crowded and smelly place, both for better and for worse.

Though some Jews became prosperous, tenement families like Annie's were the norm. Incomes were modest, with most laboring in small factories, retail shops, or, like Annie's husband, Max, as peddlers of second-hand clothes and other sundries. Consequently, many Jewish women worked as a matter of economic necessity, torn between what most saw as their principal obligation—raising families and instilling a love of Judaism in their children—and the need to feed and clothe those families. Precisely for this reason, material success was greatly admired and revered in much of the Jewish community. Although women especially were expected to devote themselves first and foremost to home and family, their striving for wealth was no sin.

In this regard, Annie was a *shvitser* (literally, one who sweats, a hard worker), a type of Jewish immigrant for whom America was seen as the place to make a fortune. She certainly had a *shvitser*'s mentality. "*Shvitsers* allowed nothing to stand in the way of their getting ahead," Jonathan Sarna of Brandeis University has written. "They shamelessly abandoned elements of their faith and upbringing, sometimes they abandoned their families . . . Everything they did focused sharply on the goal of making money and achieving success—that, they believed, was what America was all about."

Opportunities for men, even Jewish men, to realize their dreams of wealth were far greater than those for women, of course. With many traditional avenues unavailable to her, Annie hit upon an extraordinarily novel approach to chasing the *shvitser*'s dream. Nevertheless, her Jewish neighbors may have viewed with some astonishment her decision to leave her family for an adventure on a bicycle, for it is one thing to take a job across town to help support the family, and another entirely to leave a husband and three small children to take a dangerous journey from which one might never return. What possessed Annie to make such a radical choice?

As a young woman, Annie had already had her share of heartbreak and borne considerable responsibility for the care of others. She was eager to free herself from the narrow confines of family life on Spring Street and, at least for a time, to forge a new identity, one that would carry her to a better life.

On January 17, 1887, when she was just sixteen or seventeen years old, her father, Levi, died. Her mother died only two months later. Her younger brother, Jacob, was then only ten, and her sister Rosa was only eight or nine. With her older sister, Sarah, already married and living in Maine, Annie and her brother Bennett, twenty, became responsible for their younger siblings. Jacob was to die at age seventeen of a lung infection.

Annie married in 1888, the year following the death of her parents, and her first child, Bertha Malkie (known as Mollie), was born nine months later. In 1891, she had her second daughter, Libbie; and her third child, Simon, was born in 1892.

If Annie was at all conflicted about leaving her husband and children behind in 1894, there is no evidence of it; nor did she, later in her life, express regret about her decision to journey far from home on a bike. Indeed, later events would suggest she was not troubled in the least by her impending separation. "I didn't want to spend my life at home with a baby under my apron every year," she would often say.

With the cycling craze at its height in the mid-1890s and women, led by Elizabeth Cady Stanton and Susan B. Anthony, challenging the established social order, the bicycle represented to Annie a literal vehicle to the fame, freedom, and material wealth she so craved; her proposed journey could provide the opportunity to refashion her identity and create a new life for herself. But it was the sheer force of her irrepressible, flamboyant personality and her gift for drama that would transform Annie Cohen Kopchovsky, Jewish housewife and mother, into the globetrotter Mlle. Annie Londonderry, the most famous lady cyclist of her day, a woman celebrated around the world. For many immigrants, the chance to forge a new identity was part of America's promise: a chance to leave one life behind and create another. Annie was hardly alone in this regard, though she was wholly unique in how she went about it. Indeed, throughout the course of her trip, she would prove to be, among other things, a master of self invention.

THOUGH SHE MADE her "official" start from the Massachusetts State House on June 25, Annie remained for two additional days in Boston. She had formal photographs taken at the Towne portrait studio, photographs she would sell en route, and handbills printed explaining her venture. She made her final good-byes to her friends and young family and then, on June 27, left Boston at last.

For Max, who worshipped her, it must have been an excruciatingly painful time. The children, except perhaps the oldest, five-year-old Mollie, couldn't possibly have comprehended what was about to happen. However, Annie's ambitions came first. She had decided in February to make the trip, intending to leave in May. The death of her teenaged brother, Jacob, on the twelfth of that month, may have caused the delay. But her mind was set. The journey was on.

New York was Annie's first objective, and from there it was on to Chicago. She did not yet know that, by riding west, she would nearly doom her trip from the beginning.

TO NEW YORK and Chicago, Annie hewed to the cycling routes described in pocket-size tour books published by the League of American Wheelmen (L.A.W.), a national cycling organization founded in 1880. Cumulative distances, landmarks, road surfaces, terrain, and directions were laid out clearly. Thus, a cyclist would know whether she had miles of flat, paved road or impassable sandy hills, or, perhaps, a water crossing, ahead. Places to eat and hotels offering discounts to cyclists were noted. Furthermore, Annie sought the company of other cyclists, whom she was more likely to encounter on the L.A.W. routes.

When Annie left Boston on June 27, she rode out of the city through the area known as the Fens (from which Boston's Fenway Park derives its name) and the Jamaica Plain, Forest Hills, and West Roxbury neighborhoods of Boston. Here all the roads were macadamized, making for a smooth run on a bicycle, but they turned to gravel at Dedham a few miles further south. Gravel roads offered relatively good riding through Norwood, Walpole, and Wrentham. Annie rode through Attleboro and into Providence, where she stopped for the night, on paved roads.

The trip took her nine hours, an impressive day's work for a woman who had never ridden a bicycle, save for two or three brief cycling lessons in the days just before her departure. This was fairly typical of the days ahead. On her weighty forty-two-pound Columbia bicycle, dressed in long skirts and riding over roads that ranged from smooth asphalt to grainy sand, Annie averaged between eight and ten miles an hour on smooth roads, and a good deal less on poor roads, very slow by modern cycling standards. Nevertheless, "[b]icycling seems to have been a heaven-born talent with her," declared the *Atlanta Constitution*.

Annie spent the night of June 27 at a Providence hotel, earning the cost of her lodging plus "$50 extra by selling candy and lecturing." "My expenses will be met by clerking in a store as a drawing card, by selling photographs and autographs, and by lecturing on physical culture," she told the *New York Herald* when she arrived in the city a few days later. "I have studied medicine for two years, and have paid particular attention to the cultivation of physical beauty."

The roads south of Providence were poor, and the gravel gradually gave way to sand for many miles. In some spots the roads were barely passable by bicycle and she had to dismount and push her wheel along. But, when Annie did find a reasonable patch of road and was able to coast down some of the modest hills in southwest Rhode Island, she probably experienced a physical freedom unlike any she had known before—untethered, defying gravity. For a freethinking woman who had been chaffing for years under the burdens of marriage, work, and motherhood, it must have been exhilarating to glide down gentle hills on a bicycle built for one.

Annie crossed the state line into Connecticut at Stonington. At Darien, she picked up the historic Boston Post Road to Greenwich and crossed the Byram River Bridge to Main Street in Port Chester. On July 2, as temperatures climbed into the high eighties, Annie reached New York City.

---

## WHEELING 'ROUND THE WORLD
### MISS LONDONDERRY MUST EARN $5,000 BEFORE BOSTON SEES HER AGAIN

Mlle. Londonderry . . . arrived in New York early yesterday morning and went to the house of some friends at No. 208 East Broadway.

Mlle. Londonderry set out from Boston last Monday [June 25] . . . She says she has met the most polite and kindest treatment on the way to this city. Male and female bicyclers escorted her along stretches of her journey, and even the tramps she encountered treated her with the most distinguished consideration.

Mlle. Londonderry was a solicitor of advertisements in Boston. Her maiden name was Annie Cohen and she is married to a man named Kapchowsky [sic], who is in business in the city. She has three children. Her husband, she said yesterday, is perfectly willing that she should make the journey, otherwise she would not have undertaken it. It was suggested to mademoiselle that she might carry her children along with her on a bicycle built for four, but she answered that she had enough troubles of her own. The bicyclist's features are of the Slav cast, but her face is lit up by beautiful brown eyes.

—*The World* (New York), July 3, 1894

Annie knew the public was enamored with novel around-the-world adventures and the people who made them, and that once she had proven her mettle her efforts would likely be followed with great interest by the press and the public. She was also aware that publicity would be essential to her success.

"I think after I have been on the road for five or six weeks I can make more money," Annie told the *New York Herald,* "for then the world will see that I am really in earnest about this trip I have carefully planned for the past three months."

The word *globalization,* which typically describes the process of international economic integration largely wrought by the revolution in information technology, came into vogue late in the twentieth century. But the later decades of the nineteenth century were also a time of globalization, when advances in communications and transportation technology gave people the means to satisfy their curiosity about their world as never before, and made the world a more interconnected place than it had been just a few decades earlier. International travel was no longer available only to princes and aristocrats; it was becoming accessible to the middle class. Annie understood, as did almost every modern American and European, that at the end of the 1800s the world was, figuratively speaking, growing smaller.

The dramatic spread of the railroads connected once remote cities and towns. Great ocean liners shrank the distance between nations. When Krakatoa, the volcano in the strait between Java and Sumatra, exploded with cataclysmic force in August 1883, the electric telegraph and submarine cables carried the news worldwide within hours, long before the volcanic dust finally settled many months later. It was the first truly global news story that people all over the world learned about almost simultaneously. Though not built until the early part of the twentieth century, it had been conceived in the 1870s that the excavation of a canal across Central America, would literally shrink the world for ships. The Avenue of Nations at the World's Columbian Exposition in Chicago in 1893 featured representations of life in Algeria, Egypt, Turkey, Java, and Lapland, with an enormous international supporting cast, a veritable human zoo. Buffalo Bill Cody's Wild West Show starring sharpshooter Annie Oakley, a fixture at the exposition, toured Europe in the mid-1890s, giving Europeans a taste and a vision of the American West.

The nineteenth century, which began with Lewis and Clark's expedition in 1803–1805, ended with a series of around-the-world adventures that held the public in thrall. Thomas Stevens became the first man—the first *person*—to pedal around the world, leaving California in 1884 and returning almost three years later, having covered some 13,500 miles by bicycle. Josiah Slocum, originally from Nova Scotia, would become the first person to sail solo around the world, leaving Boston in 1895 on a thirty-seven-foot sloop he made himself, and returning three years and forty-six thousand miles later.

In 1872, Jules Verne captured the spirit of the age in *Around the World in Eighty Days,* a novel in which Verne's hero, the wealthy eccentric, Phileas Fogg, puts his fortune and life at risk in a wager that he can circumnavigate the globe in a mere eighty days. Seventeen years later, as a publicity stunt for Joseph Pulitzer's *New York World,* the journalist Nellie Bly, who would later come to figure in Annie's story in unexpected ways, set out to break Fogg's record. A contest sponsored by the *World* to see who could come closest to guessing the time it would take Bly to make the circuit drew more than 1 million entries at a time when the population of the United States was only 63 million people. Bly, traveling mostly by train and ship, made the trip in 72 days, 6 hours, 11 minutes, and 14 seconds, arriving back in New York to a hero's welcome on January 25, 1890. Almost certainly, when she was in her late teens, Annie had read of Nellie Bly's adventures, for it was hard not to be aware of Nellie's spectacular and much-heralded dash around the world, the defining story of her career.

Bly's trip so captivated the public that the famous game makers, McLoughlin Brothers, reissued and renamed their 1890 board game originally titled Race Around the World. It was now called Around the World with Nellie Bly, and the object was to see which player's game piece would be the first to traverse a map of the world. Such board games of geography and travel adventure were extremely popular with American consumers of the 1880s and '90s, another indication of how globalization was fueling interest in the world at large and in around-the-world journeys such as Annie's. Indeed, Bly, Thomas Stevens, and soon Annie Londonderry were the pop stars of their day, delighting armchair adventurers with published accounts of their adventures. For those who could not travel, these globetrotters offered vicarious thrills as they navigated through exotic locales, faced danger, and mingled with exotic peoples.

With the cycling craze and the women's movement for social equality in full swing in the mid-1890s, the public was ripe for an around-the-world cycling trip with a woman heroine of the wheel. All Annie had to do was prove that she was a serious contender, and not just a lady with large ambitions.

THOUGH SHE TOLD the *New York Herald* on July 3, 1894, she would be leaving New York within days for Washington, perhaps hoping for an audience with President Grover Cleveland, "then on to Honolulu and China," Annie spent nearly the entire month of July in New York, a strangely leisurely attitude considering the time limit imposed by the wager. She stayed with friends at 208 East Broadway and spent time devising a more practical riding costume: bloomers under a "short skirt coming to my shoetops. Then when the wind blows I won't have to stop to hold down my skirts. I find that my blue serge skirt kept getting in the way whenever I tried to make any speed and I would be obliged to stop and fix it, so I decided I must have something different." Annie's new suit was made of "dark blue henrietta cloth" with "a comfortable blouse waist." "She wears rubber sole shoes, no corsets and a jaunty cap to match her suit," described the *Atlanta Constitution*. "When the riding is hard and the skirt seems in the way it is easily pinned up."

As she tinkered with her cycling outfit, Annie also displayed a towering self-confidence. "In her opinion there is no reason in the world she should not go around the world in fifteen months, support herself and bring back $5,000 besides," reported the *New York Herald*. This was pure Annie, full of bravado and, seemingly, devoid of doubt. Asked by the *Herald* if she was afraid of tramps, she replied, "No, I do not think anyone would harm me, but when I leave New York I shall carry a revolver to protect myself in case of danger." As an urban housewife and mother, Annie had as much experience with a gun as she had with a bicycle, but if she had any doubts about her ability to defend herself, or to make a trip around the world by wheel, she never voiced them.

BY THE END of July, Annie was ready to continue her journey. July had been a month of blistering heat in New York City, and she departed on July 28, the hottest the city had seen in thirteen years. "Not a breath of cool air was to be had," declared the *New York Daily Tribune* the next day. "The fitful breeze came laden with humidity and hot as the blast from a furnace. The rays of the sun were almost insupportable and the sky had a coppery look, which was accentuated by the heat as it rose in waves from baked sidewalks." The temperature at midday soared to ninety-five degrees, and the humidity was a miserable 86 percent. Nevertheless, a crowd estimated at "several hundred persons, many of them street Arabs," gathered at New York's city hall to bid Annie farewell. She was attired in "[a] Nellie Bly hat . . . a linen waist and a blue skirt of conventional length." Then, at 12:35 P.M., "a deafening shout went up from the multitude," and Annie was on the road again.

"Her route lay through Broadway to Fifty-ninth Street, where a large crowd congregated and cheered the rider," reported the *New York Times*. "Old cyclists are of the opinion that Mlle. Londonderry will never finish the trip. Yonkers will be the first resting place." Luckily for Annie, she only had to cover eleven miles that day, for riding a heavy bicycle in long skirts through the oppressive heat was miserable. Washington had been dropped from her agenda as quickly as she had added it.

From Fifty-ninth Street and Broadway (Columbus Circle) Annie rode through Central Park, dense with summer green. The park was an oasis, a respite from the relentless thrum of the streets of New York. It was the place New Yorkers—at least those who couldn't get to the shore—fled to escape the oppressive summer heat and, hopefully, to catch a breeze.

Next Annie crossed the Harlem River on the Washington Bridge, a graceful two-arched span that afforded a broad view of the city looking south across Manhattan and the Bronx and headed north through Yonkers and over the Hudson Highlands opposite West Point. These were the largest hills of her trip thus far, and no doubt a formidable challenge with the heavy Columbia bicycle beneath her. But if she had a tough time on the uphills, Annie surely had a whale of a good time on the downs, though it may have taken her a while to learn how to control her unwieldy bicycle on steep downhill grades.

The Columbia was equipped with a "spoon brake" activated, like the brake on a modern bike, by a lever on the handlebar. The lever was attached to a plunger that forced a curved metal shoe into contact with the front wheel to slow it. But unlike modern bicycles, Annie's had no freewheeling mechanism, a device that allows wheels to spin while the pedals remain stationary. Rather, the pedals turned in direct relationship with the rear wheel. When the speed became too great she had to place her feet on coaster brackets mounted to the lower part of the forks, lest her skirts get caught up in the spinning pedals and cause a sure fall.

Once through the Hudson Highlands, Annie passed through Poughkeepsie, crossed the Hudson River at South Bridge, and rode into Albany.

It was early to mid-August and well over a month since Annie left Boston, yet she was a mere 150 miles west of where she had started, a distance an experienced cyclist could have covered in two days, even in the 1890s. The wager clock was ticking and she had barely made a dent.

Outside of Albany the roads deteriorated, and Annie found herself facing hilly roads of sand and clay for ten miles to Schenectady. Following side paths, roads, and the Erie Canal towpath, she traveled until the steeples and electric light towers of Utica came into view. While the Erie Canal towpath generally offered smooth, flat riding, teamsters driving mules and horses that pulled barges up and down the canal often didn't take kindly to cyclists, whose presence frequently startled the mules, and the teamsters often hurled epithets as the cyclists sped by. But the sight of a lone woman on wheels was a rarity and might well have been cause more for astonishment than anger. Annie crossed the Erie Canal, turned on to Genesee Street, and pedaled into the heart of Utica. Past Utica, the roads were excellent all the way to Syracuse.


BY MID- TO LATE August, Annie found herself between Syracuse and Rochester. She must already have begun growing weary of life on the road.

When she was unable to find a hotel or rooming house to put her up for the night, she sometimes slept outdoors, under bridges, or in barns—any place that offered some protection from the elements and tramps. Though the roads were good in central New York, the lack of ordinary household conveniences and the labor of going mile after mile, day after day on her forty-two-pound bike was tiresome. As washing her clothes was a rare treat, in the August heat they became quite unpleasant to wear. Even when she did find lodging where she could wash her clothes, there often wasn't time for them to dry completely before starting off again.

When drenched by downpours, Annie continued to ride in clothes that were soaking wet and therefore heavier; at day's end, she would be caked with mud. In dry weather, she ended the day covered with dust and dirt. She tried, she said, "to eat three square meals a day," but when she couldn't she ate apples. Annie also had to become accustomed to relieving herself in creative ways and not always in pleasant places. A proper toilet was one of the luxuries she most appreciated. All in all, the reality of the road may have been quite at odds with the glamorous life she had imagined when she left Boston. She had, it seemed, traded one form of drudgery for another.

THE ROUTE TO Rochester was a convoluted one involving countless crossings over the Erie Canal, under railroad tracks, over the tracks, and over the canal again. From Rochester, Annie followed the telegraph line through Coldwater, North Chili, and Churchville, where she picked up a cinder path between the railroad tracks to Bergen, a harrowing experience if one were caught between an east-bound and a west-bound train. Nonetheless, cyclists of the time often rode the path between double tracks because those paths dried before other roadways. In 1895, George T. Loher, a butcher from Oakland, California, rode a Stearns Yellow Fellow bicycle from his California home to New York City. In his journal Loher described such riding as "a dangerous undertaking, owing to the high speed of the trains as they fly along over the well-ballasted tracks."

By the time Annie reached Buffalo, she had ridden about 460 miles since leaving New York City and had been traveling for two months, yet was not even halfway to Chicago. She must have started to wonder whether she had underestimated the undertaking and overestimated herself.

The route out of Buffalo offered Annie beautiful views of Lake Erie, especially at Woodlawn Beach. The roads were poor along the telegraph line that cut across the Cattaraugus Indian Reservation, but once Annie crossed over Cattaraugus Creek to Irving the roads improved on the way to Fredonia.

On August 30, Annie passed through the small towns of Brocton and Westfield. "She seems to be possessed with abundant muscle and an equal desire for notoriety," reported *The Brocton Grape Belt*, and *The Westfield Republican* identified her as a Harvard student, an affectation she would soon begin to repeat with some frequency. She also told the *Republican* her month in New York would "not count" against the fifteen-month time limit.

Annie was now some thirty miles from the Pennsylvania line. The anticipation of crossing the state line was surely a psychological lift—once into Pennsylvania she had only to cut across the state's narrow northwest corner before reaching Ohio and the Midwest.

The roads between Fredonia and Erie were good, and the countryside between Erie and Conneaut, Ohio, as lovely as any Annie had seen so far. With excellent roads and side paths along the flat Lake Erie shore, the wheeling through this stretch of Ohio was as pleasant as she could have hoped for. Near Ashtabula, large farms stretched out along both sides of the road; the towns were prosperous with beautiful homes and tree-lined streets.

In early September, Annie reached Cleveland and knew she had to hurry to Chicago. The appearance of early fall weather brought days of more comfortable riding than those of August, but now she faced the daunting prospect of trying to cross better than two-thirds of the country before the frigid winter swept in. Annie crossed into Indiana near Butler and continued on to Kendallville and Goshen, following good roads and side paths all the way. Annie pedaled from Goshen to South Bend, and crossed the Illinois state line soon thereafter.

In June, she had been a working mother whose horizons went no further than the Charles River in Boston. By September, she was within reach of the great city of Chicago. Annie was now, no doubt, filled with mixed emotions. On the one hand, she had nearly made it to the first major destination of her trip. On the other hand, she was mentally and physically spent from days of rigorous riding and exposure to the elements.

ON SEPTEMBER 24, exactly one week after her husband had been sworn as a United States citizen in the federal circuit court in Boston, Annie pedaled into Chicago in cool, clear weather. Temperatures were in the midfifties, the breeze light from the northwest.

"Miss Annie Londonderry . . . is in the city," reported the *Daily Inter*

*Ocean.* "After two weeks in the city she will tour through the South leisurely, and then go on to San Francisco where she will embark for the Orient." Though the *Inter Ocean* described Annie as "in prime condition for continuing her travels," it underestimated the toll the ride had taken on her.

Cycling to Chicago had been no easy task for her. She began the trip with no physical conditioning and no cycling experience. Plus, she only discovered while pedaling it that the Columbia was too heavy and cumbersome for long-distance travel. Moreover, Annie's riding attire—the "short" skirt over bloomers she devised in New York—might have been suitable for a spin through the Boston Common or New York's Central Park, but it was worse than useless on the road; it was an impediment, unnecessarily heavy and bulky, especially for riding in hot weather.

So arduous was the journey west, Annie had lost twenty pounds "kicking her heavy cycle over the country."

Not only had the trip to Chicago been challenging, the prospect of losing the wager loomed before her. She was three months out. If she continued west, she would have no time to waste in Chicago, for the season was growing late, almost surely too late to attempt a ride across the vast prairies and mountains that lay between Chicago and California. If she tried the southern route, as the *Inter Ocean* reported she would, it would add a thousand miles to her journey. If she reversed course, all the cycling she had done thus far would amount to naught. Trying to win the wager now looked like a fool's errand, and Annie would have to choose from among these options, or a fourth: to abandon the effort altogether. But giving up would have dealt a blow to the hopes and aspirations of legions of women now campaigning to be seen as the equal of men. And, given Annie's bold spirit, she may have bristled at the idea of the smug men who wagered against her in Boston toasting her failure. Would her pride and determination outweigh her mental and physical exhaustion? Or would she be forced to return prematurely to the constrained life she had managed, at least for a short while, to leave behind?

# Chapter Two

# Female Paul Jones on a Wheel

*In olden times the women rode*
*As fitted one of subject mind:*
*Her lord and master sat before,*
*She on a pillion sat behind.*
*But now upon her flying wheel*
*She holds her independent way,*
*And when she rides a race with man,*
*'Tis even chance she wins the day.*

—A. L. Anderson

As Annie pondered her options in Chicago, the wager clock continued to tick. The journey there had consumed three of the fifteen months she had been given to circle the globe, and she was a mere thousand miles from where she had started. It was beginning to appear that the "sugar king" who wagered against her had made a good bet. But who were the men who conceived this novel enterprise and started her on the road to Chicago? How was Annie chosen to settle the matter? Was there, in fact, a wager at all? Or was some other scheme afoot?

The inspiration for Annie's journey likely came from an eccentric former Harvard student named E. C. Pfeiffer. In mid-February 1894, four months before Annie left Boston on her Columbia bicycle, Pfeiffer, using the pseudonym Paul Jones, set out from Boston on foot with nothing, not even a change of clothing, ostensibly on a wager of $5,000, to go around the world in a year, earning his way as he went. But on February 25, 1894, just two weeks after his departure, Pfeiffer had acknowledged his plan was a "fake." "He said that there was never a cent of wager placed on the trip around the world, that he simply originated the plan to make money and gain notoriety," said the *Boston Daily Globe*.

On the very same day the *Globe* reported Jones was a "fake," a small headline in the *New York Times* declared, "A Woman to Rival Paul Jones." Though Annie was not identified by name, she was clearly the subject of the story: "A Boston newspaper woman about twenty-seven years old, the wife of a Boston business man, will undertake to travel around the world, and at the end of fifteen months return to Boston with $5,000, after having paid all her expenses, The trip will be the result of a wager . . . and a part of the plan is to travel through cities on a bicycle and in bicycle costume."

On the day Annie left the Massachusetts State House, some newspapers likened her to the discredited Pfeiffer: "Emulating 'Paul Jones,' " said one headline; "Female Paul Jones on a Wheel," said another. The unmistakable implication was that Annie, too, might be a schemer.

If indeed a wager was the catalyst for Annie's trip, who was behind it? If it was all a publicity scheme, as some suggested, who, if anyone, was behind *that*? Or, had Annie, like Pfeiffer, simply devised the entire plan herself, using a bogus wager to add drama and intrigue to her undertaking?

On June 26, 1894, the *Boston Post* reported that, "Mrs. Kapchowsky [sic] says that she is backed by rich merchants, and refers to Dr. Albert Reeder." The name John Dowe appears in two newspaper accounts much later—once just before the end of Annie's trip and one shortly after its completion—as one of the bettors. Other than these few references, the men involved in the wager are never identified by name, but only as "two wealthy clubmen of Boston," "two rich men of Boston," "Stock Exchange men of Boston," or as "two rich sugar-men of the Hub."

No John Dowe is listed in any Boston City Directory of the mid-1890s. Was this merely a variant of John Doe, designed to point to no one in particular? Dr. Reeder, mentioned in several reports, is almost always described as an intermediary who held the wager stakes and who identified Annie as the woman to undertake the journey.

Albert Reeder's medical office was in Boston's Park Square and his medical specialty, as listed in the *Boston City Directory* for 1894, was the curiously named "curative movement." Today, curative movement often refers to the use of motor activities to stimulate parts of the brain to help develop body awareness. It is sometimes used therapeutically with patients with autism, Asperger's syndrome, and learning disabilities, though it has other applications as well.

Just what Dr. Reeder meant by the term is unclear, but there was in the 1890s a lively debate about whether cycling was beneficial or detrimental to a woman's health, and many physicians took sides. Some, mostly men, argued that the exertion involved in cycling was too much for the frail female physiology. Others took the affirmative side, often with the financial "encouragement" of bicycle manufacturers. Whether "curative movement" suggests Reeder was a player in this debate is uncertain, and there is no other evidence to suggest this is where his interest in a woman's around-the-world bicycle trip lay. Nor is there any evidence that hints at the reason for his involvement in Annie's journey or how the two knew each other.

The *Boston Post* suggested right at the start of Annie's journey that her claim to be on a wager was suspect: "There are those who say that Mrs. Kapchowsky [sic] is not doing this thing for a wager at all, but that remains to be seen." And the *Boston Journal* reported, "The crowd [at the State House] were incredulous about her receiving any such sum as $10,000 upon her return. Many expressed the opinion that it was simply an advertising scheme from start to finish." If Annie's gambit was indeed a publicity stunt or advertising scheme, only one person stood to benefit more from the trip than she did, and that person was Colonel Albert Pope.

Colonel Pope was a leading industrialist of his age and one of Boston's most prominent citizens. The Pope Manufacturing Company of Boston and Hartford manufactured, among other things, Columbia bicycles. There is one obvious sign of Pope's involvement: Pope supplied Annie's Columbia bicycle and his representative, Captain Peck, personally delivered it to the State House on the day of her departure. But whether Pope's involvement went beyond using Annie's trip to promote the Columbia brand is unknown.

Alonzo D. Peck was one of Pope's longest-tenured employees, working in 1894 as the senior salesman in Columbia's flagship store in downtown Boston. It was not unusual for Pope Manufacturing to give away bicycles for promotional purposes, but none of the hundred or more bicycles it gave away in 1894 was to be used for a purpose as audacious as Annie's.

And Peck was not simply a Pope employee. He was also the captain of the Massachusetts chapter of the League of American Wheelmen, an organization started by Pope in 1880 to promote cycling and lobby for the interests of cyclists, especially the improvement of roads, an effort that came to be known as the "good roads" movement. Incidentally, Pope had another motive here besides making roads more accommodating for cyclists. The Pope Manufacturing Company would soon be producing automobiles.

How Annie and Peck knew each other is unknown but, as an advertising solicitor for several Boston newspapers, Annie may well have known many people in the Pope organization, which devoted considerable resources to advertising the Columbia brand.

It was clearly in Pope's interest to see Annie on a Columbia. The mid-1890s was the peak of the American bicycle boom and consumers were buying bicycles in large numbers. In 1897 alone, more than 2 million bicycles were sold in the United States, about one for every thirty people. A quality bicycle could be had for under $100. "Wheels," as they were commonly called, were everywhere in the gay '90s, as were "wheelmen's clubs," well-organized associations with newsletters, receptions, weekly outings, uniforms, and special meeting rooms. Bicycle paths were clogged with traffic on weekends, and newspapers were filled with cycling news and special columns for "wheelmen." Hundreds of manufacturers were successfully profiting from the sale of the must-have vehicle. In all, some three thousand American businesses were involved, in one way or another, in the bicycle trade, including a bicycle shop in Dayton, Ohio, owned by two brothers, Orville and Wilbur Wright, who were using bike technology to tinker with another invention they were working on.

So popular was cycling that, by 1896, even Madison Square Garden proved too small to accommodate all those who wanted to display their wares at the Great Bicycle Exhibition. Balconies and three tiers of terraces for promenading above the Garden's floor were constructed to expand the exhibition space. When the Garden's electric lights were turned on, the effect, wrote one reporter, "was brilliant." People in masquerade, human freaks, and other means were employed to attract visitors to the displays. "A Chinaman presides on the platform of a wheel known by its yellow frame. An Indian with his war paint on; a swell; a giant negro; a dime museum midget; a quartet of jubilee singers; a fat boy; young men in racing costume; allegorical figures that suggest the names of standard wheels; [and] a rambling tramp" contributed to the circuslike atmosphere that drew huge crowds to the Garden.

Cycling in the last decade of the nineteenth century was nothing less than "a general intoxication, an eruption of exuberance like a seismic tremor that shook the economic and social foundations of society and rattled the windows of its moral outlook." Nowhere was this more evident than in the role of the "wheel" in the changing lives of American women. Indeed, the women's movement of the 1890s and the cycling craze became so inextricably intertwined that in 1896 Susan B. Anthony told the *New York World's* Nellie Bly that bicycling had "done more to emancipate women than anything else in the world."

Women, though taking to the sport as never before, represented an enormous, relatively untapped market Colonel Pope was determined to exploit. If a woman could make it around the world on a Columbia, the public relations value would be incalculable.

IT WASN'T ALWAYS easy for women to ride bicycles; the technology needed to evolve to pave the way for women such as Annie to seize the bicycle as a tool of personal and political power. Before the development of chain technology, which allowed a cyclist to transfer pedal power to the rear wheel, bicycle designers increased the speed by increasing the size of the front wheel to which the pedals were attached. The typical Ordinary, as these high-wheelers were known, had front wheels as large as five feet in diameter so the machine would cover more ground with each pedal revolution. It required extraordinary athleticism just to mount an Ordinary, let alone ride one, and accidents were common. Steering was difficult and even a small obstacle, a rut in the road or a large stone, could send the Ordinary pedaler, mounted many feet above the ground, head first over the front handlebars. Indeed, learning how to "take a header" safely was an essential skill.

In addition to facing these common hazards, women had the additional problem of mounting and riding an Ordinary in the long, heavy skirts that they were expected to wear in public. Though some women were racing Ordinaries as early as the 1870s, and a women's version of the bicycle existed that seated the rider lower and further back, an Ordinary required more strength and athleticism than most women of the time could manage, as they were not, as a general rule, otherwise engaged in athletic pursuits.

In the late 1870s, the first so-called Safety bicycles appeared. Safety bicycles had wheels of equal size and a chain drive (a few models had a chainless "shaft drive") that transferred power from the pedals to the rear wheel. At first derided by experienced wheelmen as designed for old men and women, the Safety quickly proved the superior design, both faster and more stable than the Ordinary, and remains the basis for bicycle design today.

Unlike the Ordinary, the Safety, ironically, was a bicycle ordinary people, including women, could easily ride. The Ordinary quickly became obsolete, and the Safety ushered in the cycling craze of the 1890s. "The safety bicycle fills a much-needed want for women in any station of life," said *The Bearings,* a cycling periodical, in October 1894. "It knows no class distinction, is within reach of all, and rich and poor alike have the opportunity of enjoying this popular and healthful exercise."

As CYCLING'S POPULARITY exploded, a new breed of woman was making her mark in the 1890s. The "New Woman" was the term used to describe women who broke with convention by working outside the home, or eschewed the traditional role of wife and mother, or became politically active in the suffrage movement or other social issues. The New Woman saw herself as the equal of men, and the bicycle helped her assert herself as such.

With the advent of the bicycle, women not only gained physical mobility that broadened their horizons beyond the neighborhoods in which they lived, but they discovered a new-found sense of freedom of movement, a freedom previously circumscribed by the cumbersome fashions of the Victorian era as well as by Victorian sensibilities. The women who raced Ordinaries in the 1870s often did so in risqué garments that exposed a daring amount of flesh. Arms and legs were often bare and the outfits were low-cut at the breast. Such scandalous dress was criticized by many who could not abide a spectacle that combined overt sexuality and physical exertion by women. Yet these women were the vanguard of a dress reform movement catalyzed in no small measure by the increasing popularity of the bicycle. They simply wanted clothing better suited to the pursuit than was their traditional Victorian garb. The restrictive clothing of the era—corsets, long, heavy, multilayered skirts worn over petticoats or hoop, and long-sleeved shirts with high collars, the clothing in which Annie began her journey—inhibited freedom of movement and seemed to symbolize the constricted lives women of those times were expected to lead. Such clothing was inimical to even modest forms of exercise or exertion. Cycling required a more practical, rational form of dress, and so the restrictive skirts and corsets gradually gave way to bloomers—baggy trousers, sometimes called a divided skirt, cinched at the knee. Although bloomers first appeared decades earlier, and a major social battle was waged over their propriety, the cycling craze practically mandated changes in women's attire for any woman who wanted to ride.

"[C]lothing for sports engaged a wide variety of women in a discussion about their relationship with their garments," according to women's history scholar Sarah Gordon. "At a time when mainstream women rarely challenged fashion's dictates, the novelty of sports offered an opportunity to rethink women's clothing."

Annie eventually formed strong views on the matter. "Miss Londonderry expressed the opinion that the advent of the bicycle will create a reform in female dress that will be beneficial," reported the *Omaha World Herald,* when the cyclist passed through there in August 1895. "She believes that in the near future all women, whether of high or low degree, will bestride the wheel, except possibly the narrow-minded, long-skirted, lean and lank element."

But dress reform was not a simple matter of practical adaptation; it rewrote long-standing definitions of modesty and femininity, and became a hotly contested moral issue. Cycling attire, and indeed the popularity of cycling among women, forever altered public perceptions of female athleticism and proper female behavior. The prim and proper gentility expected of women yielded to an acceptance that they, too, could exert themselves on the bicycle while dressed sensibly for the activity and not only retain, but even enhance, their femininity. Once hidden under yards of fabric, women cyclists shed their old skins and emerged, quite literally, as "new women."

In the course of her own journey, both geographic and personal, Annie would run the sartorial gamut as she transformed herself into a new woman: she started in long skirts and a traditional blouse and jacket, took to bloomers in Chicago, and later would eventually don a man's riding suit for much of the trip, an evolution that symbolized the larger changes in women's lives as expressed in the clothing they wore. Her choice of dress shocked some. For example, when Annie was in Phoenix in June 1895, one elderly woman was so shocked to see a female cyclist in "men's pants" that she ran horrified into a nearby shop, muttering about the "depravity and boldness of the nineteenth century girl." Cycling, and the dress reform that accompanied it, challenged traditional gender norms and "provided a space where women actively contested and rethought femininity," and there is no better example of the phenomenon than Annie.

That bike riding might be sexually stimulating for women was also a real concern to many in the 1890s. It was thought that straddling a saddle combined with the motion required to propel a bicycle would lead to arousal. So-called hygienic saddles began to appear, saddles with an open space where a woman's genitalia would ordinarily make contact with the seat. High stems and upright handlebars, as opposed to the more aggressively positioned "drop" handlebars, also were thought to reduce the risk of female sexual stimulation by reducing the angle at which a woman would be forced to ride.

Some critics warned the bicycle was harmful to a woman's health, and all kinds of arguments were thrown up to try and discourage women from taking to the wheel. The fragility and sensitivity of the female organism was a common theme. An article in the *Iowa State Register,* typical of the times, warned that exposure during cycling to wet and cold "may suppress or render irregular and fearfully painful the menses, and perhaps sow the seeds for future ill health." The manufacturers of various "cures" capitalized on fears that cycling could injure the kidneys, liver, and urinary tract, some even suggesting that what might begin as a minor side effect from the vibrations of the wheel could eventually lead to death. Warner's Safe Cure made these claims in advertisements designed to look like ordinary newspaper articles. In the September 21, 1895, editions of the *Chicago Times-Herald* and the *Kansas City Star,* for example, Warner's Safe Cure didn't just warn women; men, too, were said to be at risk, and Warner's was the cure.

But the constant warnings about cycling's ill effects on women throughout the early 1890s also brought forth pointed rebukes, such as this one in the *Chicago Daily News:* "When woman wants to learn anything or do anything useful or even have any fun there is always someone to solemnly warn her that it is her duty to keep well. Meanwhile in many states she can work in factories ten hours a day, she can stand behind counters in badly ventilated stores from 8 o'clock to 6, she can bend over the sewing machine for about 5 cents an hour and no one cares enough to protest. But when these same women, condemned to sedentary lives indoors, find a cheap and delightful way of getting the fresh air and exercise they need so sorely there is a great hue and cry about their physical welfare." Clearly, with the advent of cycling as a recreation for women, the gauntlet over woman's rights had been thrown down.

For leaders of the woman's movement, such as Elizabeth Cady Stanton and Susan B. Anthony, the battle over women's dress, waged in large part over cycling attire, was a critical part of the greater struggle for sexual equality and even the right to vote. "Why, pray tell me, hasn't a woman as much right to dress to suit herself as a man?" Anthony asked a reporter in 1895. "[T]he stand she is taking in the matter of dress is no small indication that she has realized that she has an equal right with a man to control her own movements." Stanton, sometimes referred to as "the first new woman," also forcefully defended a woman's right to dress as she pleased, a right asserted in the context of cycling. "Men found that flying coat tails were ungainly and that baggy trousers were in the way [when cycling] so they changed their dress to suit themselves and we didn't interfere," Stanton told a journalist in 1895. "They have taken in every reef and sail and appear in skin tight garments. We did not bother our heads about their cycling clothes, and why should they meddle with what we want to wear? We ask nothing more of them than did the devils in Scripture—'Let us alone.' "

Despite Stanton's admonition that men "let us alone" on the question of cycling attire, even the male-dominated medical profession weighed in. At the Mississippi Valley Medical Congress in Detroit in September 1895, cycling was endorsed as healthful exercise for men *and women,* but the delegates derided bloomers as "something outrageous" and "unanimously declared [the garment] to be an abomination and the cause of lowering their wearers in the eyes of spectators." No medical reason was cited. In Norwich, New York, in 1895, a group of young men signed a written pledge promising not to associate with any woman who wore bloomers and to use "all honorable means to render such costumes unpopular in the community where I reside." Their goal, never realized, was to build their movement into a "national anti-bloomer brigade." Their effort was courageous, said the *Chicago Sunday Times-Herald,* tongue in cheek, for "[t]he wearers of the bloomers are usually young women who have minds of their own and tongues that know how to talk," a description that would have fit Annie to a T.

The issue of women's cycling attire became fodder for cartoonists, as well. In the August 25, 1895, edition of the *Omaha World Herald,* a cartoon published during Annie's visit to Omaha was a caricature of Egyptian hieroglyphics; it depicted several Egyptian men at the "Rameses Club" watching with bemusement as a woman cycles by in baggy pajama-like trousers. "The New Woman of Ancient Egypt," says the top caption; "First Appearance of Bloomers on the Streets of Karnak," reads the bottom one. Another cartoon, published during Annie's visit to San Francisco, showed a woman whose loose-fitting bloomers had been filled with air by the rushing wind, her legs and hindquarters floating above the bike. But for her grip on the handlebars she'd have sailed away. "Her bloomers were too loose," stated the caption, implying that the woman, too, might be loose.

As Annie rode, she encountered all of these preconceptions and misconceptions about both the sport and its attire, and became a figure onto which men and women could project their hopes and their fears about changing gender roles.

THE SOCIAL CHANGES wrought by the bicycle were hardly limited to women's fashion, however. A woman with a bicycle no longer had to depend on a man for transportation—she was free to come and go at will. She experienced a new kind of physical power made possible by the speed of the vehicle. The bicycle imparted a parity with men that was both new and heady. In short, "more and more women came to regard the cycle as a freedom machine."

Indeed, mastery of the bicycle as a metaphor for women's mastery over their own lives was the message of Frances Willard's 1895 book, *A Wheel Within a Wheel: How I Learned to Ride the Bicycle*. Willard was one of the most famous women of her day, a leading suffragist and founder of the Women's Christian Temperance Union, which had a mass following of independent-minded, often politically active women. At age fifty-three, Willard resolved to learn to ride a bicycle because, as she wrote, she "wanted to help women to a wider world . . . from natural love of adventure—a love long hampered and impeded . . . [and] from a love of acquiring *this new implement of power* and literally putting it underfoot."

"The occasional denunciation of the pastime as unwomanly, is fortunately lost in the general approval that a new and wholesome recreation has been found, whose pursuit adds joy and vigor to the dowry of the race," wrote Marguerite Merington of cycling in *Scribner's Magazine* in June 1895. "Having reached these conclusions, the onlooker is drawn by the irresistible force of the stream. She borrows, hires, or buys a wheel and follows tentatively. Her point of view is forever after changed; long before practice has made her an expert she is an enthusiast, ever ready to proselyte, defend—or ride!" And ride they did. Between 1891 and 1896, it is estimated that the number of female cyclists grew between one hundred and four hundred times, with 1.3 to 3.2 million female cyclists in the United States, Great Britain, France, and Germany by the end of that period.

Annie was hardly the only woman taking to the highways on a bicycle. A few, such as Elizabeth Robins Pennell, had already made lengthy journeys by wheel. Pennell, a writer with a strong interest in women's rights, and her husband, Joseph Pennell, spent their honeymoon in 1884 riding a tandem bicycle from London to Canterbury. Later that year, the Pennells rode a tandem tricycle from Florence to Rome, arousing great curiosity along the way. Two years later, in 1886, the Pennells, now astride Safety bicycles, toured Eastern Europe.

Fanny Bullock Workman of Worcester, Massachusetts, also made long-distance tours by bicycle with her husband, physician William Hunter Workman. For ten years beginning in 1889, the Workmans toured Europe, Africa, and Asia by bicycle. Unlike Annie, however, Fanny Workman was independently wealthy and, like Elizabeth Pennell, always traveled with her husband. Mrs. Workman always rode in proper Victorian attire, a high-necked blouse with full sleeves and "voluminous skirts" under which she wore a corset and a complete array of undergarments. In the spring of 1894, as Annie prepared to leave Boston, the Workmans were cycling 1,500 miles across the inhospitable terrain of Algeria. The following spring, as Annie was making her way down the California coast, the Workmans were riding 2,700 miles through Spain.

In the summer of 1895, as Annie pedaled through the American West, another Boston woman, Mrs. J. M. Savage, was riding more than 5,400 miles in and around New England, including twelve "centuries"—rides of one hundred miles. By the following year, Boston women had formed no fewer than four cycling clubs of their own, since the vast majority of cycling clubs did not permit women members. Cycling was now a mass phenomenon and not the province of a few well-heeled women or even of the so-called New Woman. "[A]ll sorts and conditions of woman have enrolled themselves among [cycling's] devotees," said the *Boston Daily Globe*. "The timid woman has cast away her fear, the stickler for proprieties has overcome her scruples, and the conservative has become a radical advocate of the merits of the wheel—it looks as though the whole feminine world, which does nothing by halves and is ever ready to follow a popular fashion, had gone wheel mad." Indeed, as many famous women joined the ranks of cyclists, the actresses Sarah Bernhardt and Lillian Russell among them, it served to further accelerate the passion for cycling among women.

Although Annie wasn't among the first women to ride a bicycle, nor the first long-distance female cyclist by any means, until June 1894, no woman had ever attempted to cross the United States on a bicycle, let alone circle the world alone on one. In this regard, Annie was both a product of the times and in the vanguard of them, as well. For unlike Fanny Workman and Elizabeth Pennell, she rode without her husband and with a purpose much different than the comfortably situated Pennells and Workmans: she rode for money, for fame, and for freedom. And if Annie and the new Woman were about anything, they were about personal freedom.

WHAT ALL OF THIS meant for Colonel Albert Pope was a huge and growing women's market for bicycles, a market being competed for by hundreds of manufacturers. Being associated with Annie's trip, especially if successful, would be an enormous public relations coup. But, did Pope, or his company, do anything more than provide Annie's bicycle?

In late December 1894, one French newspaper reported that Annie had, "made an arrangement with a manufacturer who consented to initiate her into the sport [of cycling]. This man of industry, in return for the commitment that she would not ride any other brand during the entire course of her voyage, gave her a machine and 500 dollars." If the report is true then the "man of industry" was surely Pope and the "machine" was Annie's Columbia.

There was also precedent for Pope's involvement in around-the-world bicycle travel. He had provided the Columbia bicycle on which Thomas Stevens made the first successful around-the-world bicycle trip in the 1880s. Indeed, Pope had not only supplied the bicycle, he had funded the trip, albeit indirectly, by ensuring Stevens received payment for articles about his trip from another Pope entity, *Outing* magazine. (If the colonel had paid Stevens directly, it would have called into question Stevens's amateur status. Pope was eager for people to see cycling as a popular, amateur sport, not one limited to professionals.) Stevens, ever grateful for Pope's support, dedicated his lengthy 1887 book, *Around the World on a Bicycle,* to the manufacturer.

But, while it is clear that Pope had a hand in Annie's adventure, it likely amounted to little more than providing a bicycle to a young woman who had an obvious knack for publicity and might help him reap a public relations windfall. There was nothing to lose, from his point of view. But, there is simply no evidence that Pope or his company conceived or sponsored Annie's trip in any other way.

Annie would prove to be such a master at advancing her own goals, so adept at creating sensation, and so skilled at building her own legacy, it strains credulity to believe that this anonymous Jewish working mother of three small children from the tenements of Boston was somehow plucked from obscurity to settle a bet, *especially in Boston,* a city where, Supreme Court Justice Louis Brandeis once wrote, "anti-Semitism seems to have reached its American pinnacle." Furthermore, Annie wasn't active in the woman's movement, so how would she have come to the attention of bettors seeking to settle an argument over the capabilities of women? Annie was not the Billie Jean King of her time, but she was clever enough to read the social trends of the 1890s and to exploit them, quite brilliantly, for her own purposes. Thus, the most plausible explanation of Annie's radical decision to use a bicycle to trade one life for another is that she concocted the entire scheme herself, persuaded Pope Manufacturing to supply her wheel, and, like E. C. Pfeiffer, alias Paul Jones, used the story of a wager to sensationalize her trip.

Though her scheme already had a grandiose twist—she would attempt to be the first woman to circle the world by wheel—positioning her trip as taken to settle a wager about women was a brilliant device. First, it turned a bicycle trip into a dramatic race against time: Would Miss Londonderry meet the deadline? Would she win the bet and reap the $10,000 prize? Would she prove some male chauvinist back in Boston wrong and, in the process, cause him to lose a large sum of money? Plus, by making the wager one that rested on and tested the capabilities of the New Woman, Annie ensured that both men and women, whatever their views on sexual equality, would have a vicarious stake in the outcome. Newspapers of the day devoted enormous attention to the New Woman and her doings, and by setting her trip up as a test of the New Woman, Annie greatly heightened her media appeal.

Annie was not alone in her use of the wager as a device for attracting attention. Indeed, around-the-world wagers in which the traveler was to earn a fixed sum and return within a specified time were becoming so commonplace by the mid-1890s that, on May 29, 1895, the *Los Angeles Times* commented, "Scarcely a week passes in which some person does not turn up who is bumming his way around the world on some asserted big wager that he will do it in a certain length of time, and sometimes in addition that he will collect so much money on the road. This style of beating one's way . . . is getting very stale and tiresome." Then, in an obvious reference to Annie, for she departed Los Angeles headed east on May 28 or May 29 of that year, the *Times* continued, "Of late even the 'coming woman' has gone into this line of business. It takes a good deal of faith in human nature to believe that there are so many people back East who are ready to wager thousands of dollars upon the feats of individuals, when they can never ascertain whether those feats have been properly performed or not. The globe circler has got to be as much of a 'chestnut' as the bridge-jumper and the forty-day faster, whether he starts with a paper suit and a cent in his pocket, or with a dozen trunks full of clothes and his pockets full of first-class tickets."

Few, if any, who tried similar stunts came close to achieving the notoriety Annie did: some because the rigors of the journey proved too much, others because they lacked her gumption and talent for self-promotion. Whether newspaper editors and their readers truly believed she was traveling on a wager or not, Annie caught their attention wherever she traveled because she made such good copy and was creating a popular storyline that resonated with the public of the 1890s.

The wager, as Annie described it, placed her squarely in the middle of the broad public debate over women's equality even though she had no personal history as an active feminist. She was quite unabashedly and adroitly exploiting the women's movement of the time as a platform for her personal ambitions. From a modern perspective, however, Annie was certainly a feminist in her determination to fulfill her personal need for freedom and independence, and to realize her full potential as a woman by charting a truly radical course for herself unbound by social convention.

By setting herself up as a symbol of the New Woman, however, she was also assuming some heavy baggage: the hopes and aspirations of millions of women were riding on her handlebars. It might have been a burden had her motives been political. But because her motives were at first purely personal, this extra baggage would not slow her down. Rather, it ensured that as she went people would take notice, lend their support, and, in some cases, empty their pockets to help ensure her success. And, if there were times during the ride when she was about to give up, the fact that she was no longer riding for herself may have provided just enough motivation to keep her going.

## Chapter Three

# A Woman with Nerve

### A Riding Advertising Agency—Wears Bloomers and Rides a Man's Wheel

*Away on the road where the dusty clouds whirl*
*Away with a spirit ecstatic*
*Goes the cool-as-an-icicle, bicycle girl*
*Bestriding the latest pneumatic;*
*She heeds not the scoffers who scorn,*
*Though knickers her kickers adorn,*
*The cool-as-an-icicle, bicycle, tricycle maiden by no means forlorn.*

—London Judy, *Buffalo Illustrated Express,* July 29, 1894

When she reached Chicago in late September 1894, Annie publicly declared defeat. The Columbia was an albatross, her skirts were cumbersome, and she had worn herself out on the ride from New York. There was no way she was going to cross the Great Plains, the Rockies and the Cascades before the snow started to fly, and a lengthier southerly route was a daunting prospect, too.

Annie appears to have done very little pretrip planning, despite what she told the *New York Herald* in early July, and her decision to travel west was beginning to look like a fatal mistake. At the very least, her leisurely but arduous three-month journey to Chicago had done her in. "Mlle. Londonderry, who started on a trip around the world by bicycle a few weeks ago, has decided not to complete the journey," reported the *New York Times* on October 11. "She is now in Chicago and she has a new scheme. It is to make a record ride for her sex between Chicago and New

York. She will start on Sunday next. Her route is through Cleveland, Buffalo, and Albany."

A few weeks later, Annie explained how she felt on her arrival in Chicago: "When I left Boston . . . I rode a 42-pound wheel and was attired in skirts. The result was that when I reached Chicago I was completely discouraged [and was about giving up riding and walk] to San Francisco."

Her new goal of a record run from Chicago to New York was nothing more than a face-saving maneuver. For a woman as ambitious as she was, her new proposed journey was a trifle compared to the glory, not to mention the money, she had expected to earn when she started out from Boston in June, hoping to become the first woman to circle the earth by wheel.

FREE OF HER Columbia bicycle, Annie probably walked the streets soaking up the city's extraordinary energy. After all, she was young, attractive, free, and anonymous in the big city. She needed a break before heading back east. Chicago was noisy and smoky and often basked in the sweet, nauseating smell of the nearby slaughterhouses. The city was a whirl of human motion. Bright yellow streetcars competed with wagons, horses, bicycles, and the occasional automobile for road space. With nearly a million and a half inhabitants, and more arriving daily, Chicago was big and getting bigger every day. People came from everywhere—job seekers from Iowa and Kansas, businessmen from New York and Baltimore, lawyers from Philadelphia and Boston, and cattlemen from Texas and Oklahoma. African Americans from the South, carrying cardboard suitcases, and young women from farms stepped off trains arriving in Chicago from every direction. Once there, the newcomers peered through smoke-filtered sunlight, many without any notion whatsoever of where to go next.

Despite her announcement of defeat and her intention to try to set the Chicago–to–New York record, Annie wasn't a woman who gave up easily, and it wasn't long before she switched gears yet again. While in the Windy City, she met with the people at the Sterling Cycle Works, which had its offices and factory on Carroll Avenue. Sterling had a reputation for making extremely high-quality bicycles—bicycles that were, according to the company motto, "built like a watch." How Annie's relationship with Sterling originated is yet another mystery, but a deal was struck. "The Sterling Cycle Company came forward with an offer of a light 20-pound diamond [men's] frame machine in exchange for the ice wagon [Miss Londonderry] was riding, and also made a lucrative contract with her to carry the Sterling banner on the tour," according to the *Buffalo Courier.* The Morgan and Wright Tire Company, suppliers of tires to Sterling, "also entered into a contract to carry a 'good tire' streamer, and to-day [Miss Londonderry] has advertising contracts aggregating $3,500 in value. . . ." The trip that had seemed doomed upon Annie's arrival in Chicago was now on the verge of a revival.

The bicycle the Sterling Cycle Works provided Annie with was a specially painted men's Expert Model E Light Roadster, ivory with gold trim and the words "The Sterling" painted on the frame. With its wood rims and white pneumatic tires, the Sterling was an elegant-looking machine, and it rode beautifully, too. News stories published after Annie acquired the Sterling consistently said the bike weighed 20 or 21 pounds. If so, it was, as one newspaper reported, custom made, because the standard issue 1894 Sterling Light Roadster with wood rims weighed 26 pounds. Like the Columbia, the Sterling had only a single gear and no freewheel mechanism. But the Sterling lacked something Annie's Columbia *did* have—a brake. Still, compared with the 42-pound bicycle that had brought her to Chicago, the lightweight Roadster was a vast improvement and offered a glimmer of hope that the journey around the world could be made after all.

With a new bicycle and new corporate sponsors in Sterling and Morgan and Wright, Annie decided to carry on after all. Her around-the-world trip was back on, and now the Sterling Cycle Works, not Pope Manufacturing, would reap the public relations benefits. Sterling wasted no time capitalizing on the association. At the studios of J. Manz and Company, one of Chicago's leading engraving and advertising houses, a photograph of Annie with her Roadster was turned into an image that graced the pages of at least two cycling magazines on October 11, 1894, *Cycling Life* and the *L.A.W. Bulletin.*

There was another Annie helping to build the Sterling brand in 1894, too—Annie Oakley. As part of Buffalo Bill's 1894 Wild West Show, Oakley sometimes demonstrated her skills with a rifle while mounted on a 27-pound ladies' Sterling. "Miss Oakley is an ardent wheelwoman," described *The Bearings* on August 17, 1894, "and takes a daily ride of twenty miles. She wears a suit of tan, with a white skirt that fastens at the knee to a pair of neat leggings." A promotional trading card featured Oakley, aiming her rifle, on her bicycle. Together, the two Annies were pioneering sports-related marketing for women.


As THE CYCLING mania swept the nation, manufacturers sought to appeal to both men and women with liberal use of the female image to promote their wares, and these images were sometimes very provocative. Columbia, for example, illustrated some of its ads with a photo of a partially nude woman, both breasts bared and a glass of wine held high overhead, seated on a Columbia. Art posters, a popular advertising medium of the day, frequently depicted women in poses that sought to convey the liberating and exhilarating sensation of cycling. Sometimes showing them scantily attired, at others more formally dressed in long skirts or bloomers, these images often suggested flight, literally and figuratively.

Poster artists, too, were caught up in the craze and were eager to use their talents in the bicycle trade. By the turn of the twentieth century, "more posters were created for bicycles than for any other product." The ubiquity of women in cycle posters, and beautiful, feminine women at that, conveyed the message that cycling was something quite ladylike and not, as some suggested, inappropriate or manly. Many images depicted woman triumphant. A French poster for Déesse Cycles, for example, depicted a very feminine winged angel in a translucent wisp of a gown floating above a throng of cyclists, the Eiffel Tower in the distance, holding a man's bicycle high over her head. Even when more formally attired, the women in the cycle posters of the 1890s were always depicted as confident, in control, and very much out in the world. Bicycle manufacturers weren't simply selling bicycles; they were selling freedom, prestige, and a new lifestyle.

The commercial illustrations in magazine ads were much the same, though more modest in execution. Many depicted women getting the better of men. One Columbia ad of the mid-1890s shows a woman, smiling and upright, easily climbing a hill astride her Columbia while her male companion is wiping his brow with a handkerchief and walking his bicycle up the hill behind her. In other ads, men and women are presented bicycle touring together, sometimes in exotic locales such as Rome, images that suggested that bicycle riding could also be the path to love. Sterling frequently used an illustration, both in print advertising and on lapel pins (another popular advertising medium of the day), of two women, one in an ankle-length skirt and the other in a rather low-cut blouse and short skirt, trying to master the art of bicycle riding. Incongruously, the scene is a beach near the ocean's edge, about the last place one would try and learn to ride a bicycle.

But until 1894, when Annie Oakley appeared on a Sterling trading card and Annie Londonderry's image appeared astride *her* Sterling, it appears that all of the woman in cycle ads were simply idealizations or models. The use of real women known for their athletic skills, whether as marksmen or cyclists, was new as was the notion of a product endorsement by a female athlete.

What appears to be entirely original to Annie Londonderry were both the use of a female athlete's fame to promote a product unrelated to her sport (Londonderry Lithia Spring Water), and Annie's use of her bicycle and her body as a platform, literally, for advertising all manner of products from bicycle tires to perfume. Though various male cyclists, mostly racers, promoted bicycles and related equipment, employing a woman for that purpose was unprecedented. Indeed, the photograph of Annie taken on June 25, 1894, which shows the placard of the Londonderry Lithia Spring Water Company on her bike frame, may be the first image ever taken that documents the marriage of female athletes and sports-related marketing.

UNLIKE OAKLEY, who rode a women's Sterling, Annie Londonderry's riding a men's Sterling meant that she had to ride in the increasingly popular bloomers, for riding a men's bicycle in long skirts was utterly impractical if not impossible: because of its top tube connecting the handlebar stem to the seat post, skirts would pile up in front of the rider, making for a very awkward ride. Why Annie didn't begin the trip in bloomers, which would have made the first part of her trip immeasurably more comfortable, she explained to a reporter: "I could not quite bring myself to wear the bloomers some women cyclists wear. Although I've cheek enough to go around the world, I've not enough cheek for that."

Although they had been around for decades, bloomers were still so risqué it was newsworthy when a city or town saw its first female rider wearing them. But it is surprising that a woman as independent and audacious as Annie was at first too modest to wear bloomers. Though she had been wearing them *under* her skirts so she could lift her skirts when necessary and not expose her undergarments, it was only when she acquired a men's bicycle and was forced to change her riding attire that she overcame her resistance to bloomers as outerwear.

The combination of the new Sterling bicycle and her new riding clothes made cycling an entirely new and far more pleasurable experience for Annie, and both changes contributed to her decision to continue with her journey. Nevertheless, she still faced the reality of geography and the lateness of the season, which compelled her to make a radical decision. She would indeed try and circle the globe, but she would do so by pedaling *back* to New York and making her way around the world going east. The likelihood of Annie's making the trip within the fifteen months to which she was publicly committed looked remote indeed, but she was determined to try. She would sail for Le Havre on the French liner *La Touraine,* scheduled to depart New York on November 24. After sailing to France, Annie's proposed route would take her "from Bordeaux southward through Italy and Greece and on to Constantinople, thence by steamer to Bombay, riding across India to Calcutta, by steamer to Japan, riding through that country and taking the steamer to San Francisco . . ."

ON THE MORNING of October 14, at ten A.M., Annie mounted her ivory and gold Sterling at the Columbus Fountain in front of Chicago City Hall. The send-off was surely gratifying. Members of Chicago's "lady cyclist" club joined her at the start to ride as far as Pullman, Illinois, and "all along the route down Michigan [A]venue unattached cyclists joined the procession until by the time the end of the boulevards was reached several hundreds were in line . . ." said the *Chicago Inter Ocean.*

As encouraging as it was to see the swarm of cyclists around her, it must have been daunting for Annie to realize that her long, hard trip from Boston to Chicago was for naught and to contemplate making a circuit of the earth in just eleven months. To win the purported wager and claim success, she would now have to circle the globe and return to Chicago by September 25, 1895.

The trip back to New York promised to be easier, if colder, than had been her trip west. She was now on a faster, more comfortable bike. Her freedom of movement was greatly enhanced by bloomers, and she was familiar with the route and could call on any number of acquaintances she had made going west should things get tough. Even her recent weight loss worked in her favor: between her new bike, new clothes, and new body, Annie and her gear weighed at least forty pounds less than when she left Boston, a huge difference. She was also a stronger and far more experienced cyclist than she had been when she'd begun her journey in June. Barring mechanical problems, a long stretch of severe weather, or a serious accident, Annie would be able to make New York in time to sail for France and continue her trip around the world.

Once Annie pedaled out of Chicago, she began garnering a lot of attention from the newspapers, mostly through a public relations campaign of sorts that she had devised herself. Intercity phone service was virtually nonexistent in 1894, so to ensure people would be anticipating her arrival, she routinely sent telegrams or telegraph messages ahead to the newspapers and cycling clubs to generate interest. The newspapers of those times and their readers alike had insatiable appetites for sensational, even outlandish, stories, and Annie was only too happy to give them what they wanted. Indeed, it was during her trip back to New York that her "inventive genius," her gift for showmanship and her flair for the dramatic, truly started to emerge. With her men's bicycle, bloomers, and advertising streamers flying from her clothing and bike frame, Annie was a virtual one-woman show.

On October 15, the day after leaving Chicago, she reached South Bend, Indiana, where she was joined by a woman named Jessie Padman, also on a Sterling, for part of the trip east. How Annie met Mrs. Padman is unclear, though Mrs. Padman, who was described by one newspaper as "an admiring friend" of Annie's, may have sought her out, given her growing fame. They planned to ride together for several days, until reaching the vicinity of Toledo, Ohio.

Then as now, October in the Midwest typically brought ideal cycling weather. Annie and Mrs. Padman most likely encountered weather that was not too hot but not yet cold while cycling through orange-hued trees and the golden light of autumn.

The two women left South Bend at ten A.M. on October 17 and arrived in Elkhart an hour later, where the *Elkhart Daily Truth,* as would most newspapers covering her journey, commented on Annie's physique and her clothing: "Miss Londonderry is unusually vivacious, and to add to her charms she wears the bloomer costume, which exquisitely becomes her petite figure. She has now traveled 1,580 miles, 1,400 of which she has traveled in the regulation feminine attire."

At two o'clock, after a brief stopover in Elkhart, the women headed for Goshen, where they "attracted considerable attention by their appearance in bloomers of a tight fitting pattern." Annie and Mrs. Padman called at the offices of the *Goshen Daily News,* introduced themselves, and explained that the former was on her way around the world. The *Daily News,* like some of the Boston press that covered Annie's farewell, was skeptical: "It is quite likely that such a world-circuiting tour is not at all contemplated, but that the scheme is simply a supposed ingenious device of the manufacturer of the bicycle used to advertise the wheel."

The following day, Annie and her companion passed through Ligonier and once again "soon became the objects of much interest not because they were at all good looking for they were not and not from any reason that they were expert riders but from the fact that they wore a new fangled and some what [sic] abbreviated bicycle dress and the further fact that one of the ladies, Miss Londonderry, is on her way around the world."

After dinner in Ligonier with Mr. Edward Sisterhen, the local Sterling agent, the riders, accompanied by two local cyclists, rode to Wawaka, making the short trip in thirty-one minutes. Later the same evening, Annie and Mrs. Padman arrived in Kendallville, where the town's pharmacist and Sterling bicycle dealer, Paul Klinkenberg, hosted them.

In Kendallville, Annie was questioned about her romantic life. "Miss Annie Londonderry, a plucky and good looking lady cyclist, arrived in the city from the west," said the *Kendallville Weekly News.* "To a reporter here who inquired if there were any danger of her falling in love with some handsome cyclist and abandoning her venture, Miss Londonderry pleasantly replied that she was too intent on gaining the distinction of being the only lady rider who had ever encircled the earth on a wheel to entertain any marriage propositions."

Here, for the first time, but certainly not the last, Annie elided the truth about her marital status. She didn't lie, but she didn't leap at the opportunity to correct the assumption in the question that she was unmarried, either. Although she surely resented the condescension implicit in questions about her marital status and marriage prospects, Annie would be asked such questions often. Here she was, attempting to go around the world by bicycle, something no woman had ever tried, and reporters, most of them men, were asking her whether her heart might get the better of her head. And if she spoke of her marriage, questions about children were sure to follow. Leaving a husband was radical enough; leaving him with three small children was, quite simply, socially and morally unacceptable in 1890s America. Even the most ardent suffragist might have raised an eyebrow.

Indeed, it probably never even occurred to most reporters that Annie might be married. Surely no self-respecting husband, especially one with three young children, would permit his wife to undertake a journey such as this. By ducking the question, as she did in Kendallville, Annie avoided having to explain how and why she had left her husband and children behind. It was easier to simply deflect questions about her marital status and move on.

ON THE AFTERNOON of Friday, October 19, Annie and Mrs. Padman passed through Butler, Indiana, near the Ohio state line. "It seems rather shocking to see young ladies dressed in such a manner," opined the *Butler Record* of their bloomers, joining the chorus of stunned observers.

Because of bad roads, Annie had planned to avoid Toledo. However, she apparently accidentally rode off course and wound up passing through the town anyway, where she was quite a curiosity.

Apparently alone and wearing her "sky blue bloomer suit" Annie "shot down Jefferson Street like a streak of blue and white" and stopped at the Jefferson House hotel. When she went in to register, she left her white Sterling at the "center of a curious crowd of people who inspected it as intently as though it were a baby elephant." Then people followed her into the hotel to inspect her signature in the hotel register as some of the more inquisitive grilled the desk clerk about her. Annie later appeared in the dining room in a plain gray dress and "was allowed to eat her dinner in peace" before several local cyclists joined her in the parlor.

The *Toledo Commercial* also took careful notice of Annie's riding outfit, which she continued to tinker with during her journey, noting that the trousers had been taken in "tighter than the ordinary divided skirts so as to offer no resistance to the wind."

Slowly but surely, Annie's riding clothes were evolving into something a man would wear. "Don't you attract considerable attention with your novel costume?" asked the reporter. "Oh yes," she replied, "the people all along these little country towns flock by the hundreds and stare at me as though I had escaped from a circus." Which was, of course, precisely the point.

\* \* \*

AFTER SPENDING the night in Toledo, Annie rode to Fremont, Ohio, covering the nearly forty miles in four hours, and spent the night before heading east.

When she passed through Norwalk, Ohio, on the twenty-third, she stopped long enough to chat up a reporter who noted that it was "the bad weather in this country at this time of year" that had caused her to reverse course in Chicago. The interview also revealed yet another way Annie supported herself monetarily while on the road: "Wherever she stops she sells silk handkerchiefs in order to obtain enough money to buy her meals. She says if she gets hard up she will do almost anything that is honorable—sometimes selling papers. . . ."

ON THURSDAY afternoon, October 25, Annie wheeled into Cleveland, proclaiming she had just set a new record for lady riders for the run between Elyria and that city, covering the approximately twenty-six miles in one hour and forty-two minutes. "[A] remarkably good performance," said one local newspaper. But, as would be the case for most of her trip, there was nothing to support the claim other than Annie's word.

Annie's first stop in Cleveland was Eberhart & Wright, a bicycle store on Euclid Avenue that sold Sterling wheels. She remained in the city as a guest of Mr. Wright, through Sunday morning, October 28, before continuing her eastward journey. Each night, Annie made an appearance at which she sold souvenir pins at twenty-five cents a piece, first at the Cleveland Wheel Club, then the Lakeside Clubhouse, and finally at the Cleveland Athletic Club.

THE WEATHER had been unseasonably warm, though occasionally rainy, as Annie, joined by a cyclist identified only as Mr. Bliss, covered the approximately two hundred miles between Cleveland and Buffalo in four days, arriving in Buffalo at five o'clock on the afternoon of the thirty-first. Here again, she was enjoying the freedom of the New Woman. Bliss would not be the last male rider to accompany Annie for part of the route, and her companions likely assumed Annie was both single and available. But she knew how to handle herself and seemed unconcerned with the impression that might be created as a lone woman traveling in the company of men.

She is a "clever and intrepid little wheelwoman" and a "bright and vivacious little person, possessed of any amount of grit and pluck," and her journey "one of the most perilous and remarkable trips ever undertaken by a woman," said the *Buffalo Courier* on Annie's arrival. Asked by the *Courier* if she wasn't taking "a mighty big risk in traversing portions of savage lands," she replied: "Well, $10,000 is a large amount, and I know that I am taking a big risk, and may never again see my native land, but then the grim shadow of death is ever at one's elbow, and my chances for not getting through safely are not sufficiently great to deter me from making the experiment." Of course, at this point the most savage land Annie had seen was New York City, but that was beside the point. She was in the process of creating both a drama and a farce, and she was quite conscious of the impression she wanted to make. Though she was often very impulsive in conversation, she was also very deliberate about stage-managing her traveling one-woman show. The reporter's question called for a dramatic answer and Annie provided it.

This skill for relating calculatedly colorful detail permeated many of her interviews. In addition to boasting to the *Buffalo Express* of her Elyria-to-Cleveland run (her time, she said, was only fourteen seconds off the record), she claimed to have ridden 110 miles in nine hours during a rainstorm, though she didn't specify where she had accomplished that feat. By now she had already amassed a growing collection of amusing anecdotes, some of dubious veracity, about her travels and she shared them at every opportunity.

During her brief stop in Elkhart, Indiana, some two weeks earlier, Annie told the *Buffalo Express,* she had been threatened with arrest for wearing bloomers, and had to apply to the chief of police for a permit to go about the town. "The chief of police eyed me from head to foot and when he got to the foot he seemed satisfied and gave me the permit," said Annie. "In about a half an hour I got $3 out of the men in the town by selling my brownie pins, but the women nearly dropped dead."

Although it is doubtful Annie had planned her route around the world by the time she reached Buffalo, she said that she would be cycling along the shores of the Mediterranean into Turkey, across Persia and thence to India. Her proposed itinerary was ever changing, but it was clear even by the time she reached Buffalo that she was determined to go around the world and had figured out how to support herself on the road.

## ROUND THE WORLD—A RIDING ADVERTISING AGENCY—WEARS BLOOMERS AND RIDES A MAN'S WHEEL

Miss Anna Londonderry, who has acquired considerable fame in connection with her contract to circle the globe on a wheel, riding at least 15,000 miles of the distance on the road, arrived in Buffalo yesterday afternoon and rode to the rooms of the Ramblers [a cycling club], where she answered the correspondence awaiting her. To an *Express* reporter Miss Londonderry told of her . . . experiences since she left Boston . . . "Why, I am actually gaining in weight right along, and now I weigh 125 pounds," she said to the reporter . . .

Miss Londonderry is . . . only 23 years old . . . and in her riding trape presents a very attractive appearance . . . The young woman is a sort of a riding advertising agency. She wears ribbons advertising various goods and will receive $400 for one firm's ad that graces her left breast. On her right bloomer leg she carries $100 worth of advertisements and she has just closed a contract to cover her left arm. She says her back is for rent yet and she hopes to get $300 for it. She must not beg a cent and makes enough money to pay for her board by selling little souvenir Brownie pins and other souvenirs of the trip.

She has never had to sleep out of doors except once and that time she was dead broke and slept in the cemetery at Amboy, a little village near Ashtabula. Miss Londonderry spent three years at Harvard and has studied medicine for a time, and will resume her studies when she returns from her trip. She is of German descent and speaks German and Swedish. . . . she says that so far she has met with the greatest respect all along the line and has not once had occasion to make use of the pearl-handled revolver which she drew from a pocket in her bloomers.

—*The Buffalo Express*, November 1, 1894

Although she told the *Express* that she had to sleep out of doors only once on her trip, she had another story for the *Buffalo Courier.* "[S]leeping in barns, haystacks, and under rail fences was a common occurrence, and the raiding of orchards and farms was necessary to sustain life and strength," said the *Courier.*

Just how much outdoor sleeping Annie actually did is not known, but one thing is certain: her claim to have attended Harvard and studied medicine was fanciful, and on many occasions she clearly delighted in testing the gullibility of reporters, especially men. She would often repeat her Harvard claim along the way, a small addition to her growing legend. And the further into her trip she got, the taller the tales she would tell.

In Buffalo, Annie decided that even bloomers didn't provide enough comfort, though they were an improvement over skirts. At the boys' department of a Buffalo clothing store she purchased a pair of pants for five dollars, cut several inches off the legs, and secured the bottoms, knicker-bocker style, with elastics. She also donned black stockings, gaiters, and a blue yachting cap to go with her tweed coat and vest, which the *Buffalo Illustrated Express* dubbed "an extraordinary and exceedingly unfeminine costume." Indeed, she was now dressed as a man. "An innate modesty impelled her to appeal to the reporter as she posed before the photographer for a picture for the *Express,* regarding her general appearance. 'Do I look dreadful,' she asked. 'Is this rig immodest?' " No doubt she was hoping the answer to the second questions was yes.

Annie attended a Halloween Ball and stayed overnight in accommodations provided at the Ramblers Bicycle Club. (It was not uncommon for cycling clubs of the 1890s to have their own meeting halls with overnight accommodations.) The weather on Halloween had been wet, but when she left Buffalo for Rochester the next day, the skies had cleared and temperatures were in the low fifties. The roads were too muddy for cycling, however, and she was forced to ride her Sterling along the New York Central Railroad tracks toward Rochester. The seventy-five-mile trip was quite a slog, as suggested by the *Rochester Democrat and Chronicle:* "Belated pedestrians on Lyell Avenue were somewhat surprised about 1 o'clock this morning to see an object closely resembling Billy Grimes [presumably a local drunk] doing his cellar-door act, flitting along the middle of the street towards State street. The object continued on its way eastward stopping at the Central-Hudson station, where it was corralled by Officer Stein. The officer was at a loss to make out what it was at first but finally discovered it to be a woman. She was dressed in blue bloomers, blue jacket and a blue cap." The story continued, "She was pushing a white enameled bicycle ahead of her when she appeared in the station. The officer conducted her to the Hotel Atlantic where she registered as Miss Anna Londonderry, of Boston."

The *Rochester Post-Express* described Annie's arrival in similar terms, and noted that the cyclist was something of a roving billboard: "The young woman presented a bedraggled appearance. She wore many flying ribbons, which on close inspection were seen to be advertisements for factories, medicine, dry goods and every variety of proprietary articles. Her coat was covered with advertisements and her bloomer costume was similarly adorned." When Officer Stein "recovered his breath," said the *Post Express,* he demanded an explanation for Annie's rather outlandish appearance, to which she replied: "My autographs cost 25 cents a piece. If you want one I should be glad to give it to you."

She is "prepossessing in appearance" and "extremely bright and animated in conversation," wrote a reporter who later met Annie for a chat at the Novelty Manufacturing Company on Exchange Street. During their talk, several wheelmen stopped by to meet her and she received them "with as much tact and graciousness as though she were in full dress in a ball room instead of being attired as she was in an ugly looking riding costume and wearing muddy shoes."

On her arrival in Rochester, Annie was "looked upon as a suspicious character in having a diamond frame wheel" and a "riding habit, which she acknowledged as being far from conventional even from the point of view of those who favor the bloomer."

"I am going around the world and with that object in view I cannot afford to let conventionalities impede my progress," she said. "Consequently, I have grown accustomed to this costume and do not now mind the stare of people."

When asked what she would do with her winnings, Annie wittily responded, "Why, I'll marry some good man and settle down in life."

On Friday evening, November 2, Annie attended receptions at the clubhouses of two Rochester cycling clubs, the Century Cycling Club and the Lake View Wheelman's Club, and prepared to leave for Syracuse, where her visit was much anticipated: as early as October 30, the Syracuse newspapers began writing of her impending arrival.

ON THE MORNING of Sunday, November 4, in the company of three Rochester wheelmen, H. W. Rulifson, H. Bachman, and C. J. Appel, Annie pushed off for Syracuse, ninety miles to the east, intending to arrive in Syracuse that night. The weather had been unseasonably warm in upstate New York, with gentle winds and temperatures reaching the mid sixties. But, unfortunately for Annie and her party, Sunday's weather turned. It became cold, with temperatures in the thirties and forties and brisk westerly winds. The roads were less than ideal. Annie and her party had "a hard struggle over poor roads from Rochester," and were compelled to spend the night in Jordan, New York, about fifteen miles west of Syracuse. The group finally arrived in Syracuse at 9:30 A.M. on Monday, November 5, where Annie checked in to the Globe Hotel.

" 'IS IT A GIRL?' was the query of pedestrians in South Salina Street this morning when Miss Anna Londonderry dismounted in front of Reuben Wood's Sons' store and displayed her shapely form in a men's bicycle suit," reported the *Syracuse Courier* upon Annie's arrival. At Wood's, a purveyor of sporting goods, Annie, spattered with mud, was seen "laughingly describing her trip to a knot of local 'cyclists."

Public fascination with Annie was clearly growing, as was the rather tangled web of stories she imparted to those she spoke with—often changing her story from state to state, and even town to town. "Miss Londonderry is an intrepid woman and backed by plenty of courage and muscle she will complete a circuit of the globe in the time specified if such a thing is possible," said the *Syracuse Standard.* Calling Annie's trip "one of the most perilous and remarkable trips ever undertaken by a woman," the *Syracuse Post* quoted the cyclist as describing her ride from Boston to Chicago as "a horrible nightmare." "Starting without a cent of money, she plodded along, [often] meeting with scant courtesy, even from her own sex," stated the *Post,* though Annie had said just the opposite in Buffalo a few days earlier. "The little woman had no means of earning money, except selling autographs and these had as yet not acquired a market value."

Annie worked for a few days as a clerk in the bicycle department of

Reuben Wood's, mainly to lure customers. The Centuries Cycling Club of Syracuse hosted a reception in her honor and arranged for some of its members to pace her toward Utica when she resumed her trip east. She left for Utica, fifty-three miles east, on the morning of November 10.

In 1893, H. H. "Dead Broke" Wylie set a record for the Chicago to New York run on a Sterling bicycle equipped with racing tires: ten days, four hours, and thirty-nine minutes. He earned the nickname "Dead Broke" because he traveled without money. Traveling as Wylie did became known as the "dead broke" plan, and when Annie arrived in Utica the *Utica Sunday Journal* announced the arrival of "A 'Dead Broke' Girl":

"The latest phase of woman's development and woman's enterprise along a unique line struck this city at 3:45 P.M. yesterday in the form of a charming and striking young lady attired in men's bicycling costume and 'treading' a twenty pound Sterling wheel in gallant style in very ungallant weather. Miss Annie Londonderry is the name of the daring young woman who is undertaking a bicycle trip around the world . . . She believes she can [do it], and with the grit and enterprise of modern femininity has determined to do it, or die in the attempt."

Annie arrived in Utica, as she had in Rochester and Syracuse, weary from traveling in bad weather. "I've made only forty-eight miles to-day, from DeWitt [just east of Syracuse]," she said. She then proclaimed she had on several occasions "ridden the century," or one hundred miles. "But the roads are so bad they made me tired," Annie continued. "I've had to try the railroad tracks, the highways being simply impassable, and it's hard work. I've never ridden a bicycle before!"

As she spoke with a reporter, Annie opened a parcel containing a new riding suit. " 'How do you like my new suit? Isn't it a dandy? I received [it] to-day from one of my advertisers in Buffalo, and am going to don it henceforth, though sometimes I'll wear my skirts—as I did from Boston—when I'm not riding.' " She explained that she chose her unusual clothes because they were best suited to riding, but that they also "helped her as a drawing card" as well.

"I have been treated handsomely wherever I've been," said Annie, "especially by cyclist clubs, and always royally by the press—and the newspapers are a very great help. [I] experienced a little difficulty between Buffalo and Rochester when a tramp placed a railroad tie on the tracks and dumped [me] into the ashes." Because she was riding with three men between Buffalo and Rochester, this story doesn't ring true, though she later repeated it, with some variations, when she got to France in December.

Annie's exaggerations didn't stop with her own stories. While in Utica, she was asked about the disappearance of an around-the-world cyclist from Pittsburgh named Frank Lenz, who had not been heard from in some time. She said she had heard a rumor that Lenz's traveling companion had left him sick somewhere in Asia, but she didn't know if the report was true. Never at a loss, she then ventured her opinion that Lenz was all right, though she had absolutely no way of knowing, and that "he was keeping close for a purpose that had a business idea in it." In fact, Lenz was already dead, though it was not publicly known yet, murdered by bandits near the modern-day border of Turkey and Armenia.

During her stay in Utica, Annie sold tie pins to the Utica Cycling Club and gave a lecture about her travels. *The Sunday Journal* urged readers to attend her departure from Utica: "Everybody ought to be present to give Miss Londonderry a hearty send-off. The sight will be worth seeing." But if there was any crowd turnout at the Utica city limits on November 11 to watch members of the cycling club escort Annie out of the city, they were sorely disappointed. The only people who saw her leave town were those at the train station at 8:51 P.M., when Annie boarded a train bound for Albany. It would not be the last time she played fast and loose with her means of travel, for she was often just as cavalier about her means of transport as she was with her stories. After all, she was now living life on her own terms, not the wager terms she made up and often modified along the way when it suited her purposes. Nor did she go to great lengths to conceal her actions, relying instead on her boundless self-confidence and colorful stories to distract attention from careful scrutiny of her day-to-day movements.

How Annie reached New York City from Albany is anyone's guess. There are no reports of her in Albany or at any point between that city and New York, suggesting she may have again taken the train. However, with *La Touraine* scheduled to depart for Le Havre on November 24, she certainly had time to make the trip by bicycle. In the event, sometime in mid-November, Annie was back in New York City, a city she hadn't expected to see again so soon when she pedaled down Broadway in the intense July heat. Nearly five months into her trip and with ten to go on her wager clock, she prepared to set sail for France, where the spectacle that was Annie Londonderry would become even more spectacular.

# Chapter Four

# Le Voyage de Miss Londonderry

*When Springtime's buds are flowering through the land;*
*While Summer's bloom is strewn on every hand;*
*And through Autumn blows*
*Or the chilling Wintry snows,*
*She drives her airy wheel so free and grand.*

—Ariel, *The Bicycling World,* February 16, 1894

On November 24 in New York City, Annie rolled her Sterling up the gangplank of one of the fastest and finest ocean liners of the day, the French Line's *La Touraine,* bound for Le Havre on France's north coast. Five hundred thirty-six feet long, and weighing over 9,000 tons, *La Touraine* was the sixth-largest ship ever built, capable of carrying 1,090 passengers at a speed of nineteen knots across the Atlantic. Also known as "the steady ship," *La Touraine* had a reputation for managing exceptionally well in rough seas. Equipped with a world-class kitchen staffed by trained French chefs, the vessel was often called "a piece of France itself."

*La Touraine* passed the southern tip of Manhattan and the Statue of Liberty. The last time Annie had sailed through New York harbor, she was a little girl on her way to America from Eastern Europe and Lady Liberty had not yet been built. From the harbor, the French liner slipped through the Verrazano Narrows and into the Atlantic. The air was mild, the breeze light from the west, and a slight haze lingered off Sandy Hook.

Annie loved being the center of attention and, during her time on the ship, she exercised her powers of self promotion by charming the passengers. She regaled everyone she met—Dr. C. W. Chancellor, the United States consul at Le Havre, the Baron and Baroness de Sellières, the Prince and Princess Ruspoli di Poggio Suasa, and Mr. and Mrs. Potter Palmer, socialites from Chicago, among them—with tales of her adventures. She may also have taken her ivory and gold Sterling for a few turns over the deck, or around the ship's ballroom, to the delight of her new friends. Once she had made herself known to the passengers, she "earned 150 francs lecturing."

*La Touraine* arrived at Le Havre on December 3, 1894, her daughter Mollie's sixth birthday. Annie's arrival was completely unheralded and without fanfare; she was listed among the ship's arrivals in a local newspaper simply as "A. Kopchovsky." She immediately rode into a bit of bad luck: French customs officials impounded her bicycle and her money was stolen. "I was in a predicament, for I was not permitted [by the terms of the wager] to speak French and I found it difficult to make myself understood in English," Annie later wrote in the *New York World,* though she didn't know French at all. Fortunately, Annie's new acquaintance, Dr. Chancellor, came to her aid and "printed a large placard which explained in French the object of my visit and asking for an opportunity to earn some money." Unable to persuade customs officers to release her bicycle, she negotiated for the Sterling to be shipped to Paris, where she traveled by train to stay with a Paris agent for the Sterling Cycle Works, Victor Sloan, and his wife, until its arrival.

The Paris where Annie arrived on December 4, 1894, was that of Camille Pisarro, Louis Pasteur, Henri de Toulouse-Lautrec, and le Moulin Rouge, perhaps the world's most famous nightclub, then *and* now. Almost every night Toulouse-Lautrec was at le Moulin Rouge, sketching the bohemians who came to smoke, drink, carouse, and watch the dancers. Sophisticated, cosmopolitan, and artsy, Paris was a modern world capital of some 2 million people, its skyline graced by the new Eiffel Tower, built just six years before. The salon, evenings of conversation among the city's intellectual, cultural, and artistic elite, was a fixture of the local social circuit, as was the café, where artists, writers, and poets would pass their days and nights talking over coffee and cigarettes.

The bicycle, too, was a prominent fixture of Parisian life in 1894. Indeed, earlier development of the vehicle decades before had proceeded roughly in parallel in France and the United States, with the French calling their machines *vélocipèdes* (literally, "rapid feet"). "In a short time you will see the country roads and the parks filled with people wheeling along upon vélocipèdes [and] the great ladies of the land will unblushingly don man's dress, or something alarmingly like it, and jump astride their apparatus," wrote Arsène Alexandre, a Paris writer, in 1895. So popular was cycling among the women of Paris that half a dozen tailors in the city specialized in bicycle costumes for society women. Bicycle "fever" was "at its height" and its popularity transcended class lines. "I have used the expression bicyclemania," continued Alexandre, "and in view of the facts is it anything short of that? No class of the community is free from the passion, the workers as well as the butterflies."

In short, France was primed for a heroine of the wheel, when in rode Annie on her ivory and gold men's Sterling. News of Annie's arrival in Paris wasn't reported in Boston until a month later. "Miss Londonderry . . . is now in Paris," reported the *Boston Daily Globe* on January 5, 1895. " 'She,' as the French papers say, 'is the object of much interest.' Deservedly, for when one has no money and no clothes one is, as the racing boys say, 'a poor beggar!' "

Annie's family probably knew of her arrival in France earlier than the *Globe* reported it. Though none of her letters or cables home have survived, she surely would have been writing home from time to time, if only to reassure her family that she was all right. It may have been remarkably brash for her to have left her husband and children, but she didn't abandon them altogether and would return to them when her trip was finished.

When Annie arrived in Paris, she immediately became the object of a great deal of interest and speculation in the press. "She seems made only of muscles and nerves and in spite of her petite size gives the impression of remarkable energy," said one French newspaper. This was one of the more flattering descriptions she would read about herself while in France, for although the French people embraced her with great enthusiasm and warmth, their journalists didn't think much of her appearance.

Though Annie was often described in American newspapers as a highly attractive woman, the French saw her quite differently. Because she was muscular from cycling and wore a man's riding suit, she didn't conform to French notions of femininity. After referring to France's "fragile and delicious" young maidens, one Lyon columnist wrote:

Truth be told, Miss Londonderry is not of their race, not even . . . their sex. She belongs to that category of neutered beings, single women without a husband or children, that social evolution and the increasing difficulties of existence [have] given birth to especially in America and in England.

Such women . . . resemble neutered worker bees whose superiority of labor is a result of infertility. And the suppression of love and maternal function so profoundly alters in them any feminine personality that they are neither men nor women and they really constitute a third sex.

Miss Londonderry belongs to this third sex. It is enough to see her masculine traits, her muscled physique, her athlete's legs, her hands which appear strong enough to box vigorously, and everything masculine which emanates from her energetic being, to establish that it would be difficult to apply the legendary verse of Mr. Legouve: *"Fall at the feet of this sex as you would to your mother!"*

Though this was the most venomous attack on Annie's femininity, many French reporters commented on what they saw as masculine traits. "[O]ne would be tempted to believe that Miss Annie Londonderry, with her boyish charms, is really a young man who assumed a female name in order to draw attention to her reckless enterprise," wrote one such observer. "Mannish, bright eyes, dark, tan, a bony and energetic face," said *Le Figaro*. She "has none of the physical charms of a woman," opined another Paris newspaper. "Of average height, very slender, Miss Londonderry could easily be taken for a young boy rather than a woman, and she doesn't have any coquettish mannerisms of a woman." Annie didn't appear slender to another reporter, who described her as "definitely not pretty, but, on the other hand, has a Herculean build."

Although the French press spilled a torrent of positive ink about Annie and her journey, lavishing her with praise for her gumption and her guts, many reporters simply could not believe that a woman on so independent a journey and dressed as she was could have any of the feminine attributes they so prized in women. Even her capacity to love was questioned. In Lyon, Annie was asked if she had left behind in Boston a romantic interest. She looked perplexed at first and then laughed heartily, a laugh the reporter interpreted as incredulity that she would have any interest in romance at all.

Once again, while in France, Annie changed her story to suit her mood or situation, painting a confusing picture of her background to match the confusing picture of her sexuality being painted by the press. Her repertoire of tall tales was limitless. In various interviews she described herself as "an orphan at a very young age" (not so); a law student (not true); a doctorate of law (not true); a medical student who earned money "dissecting cadavers" (not true); a businesswoman (true; she was an advertising solicitor); an accountant (apparently not); a reporter for several newspapers (unclear); a wealthy heiress who had inherited "a substantial fortune" (untrue); and the founder of a newspaper which she sold just before embarking on her journey (not true). Annie even claimed to have invented a method of stenography and boasted, disingenuously, that she was the cousin of a United States congressman and the niece of a United States senator. It's impossible to discern her motive in making these varied and, in some cases, outlandish claims. She often seemed to take delight in pulling the legs of reporters, almost all of whom were men at the time, and in testing the limits of their credulity. But the sheer randomness and grandiosity of some of her claims hints at an almost pathological aversion to telling a straight story, though she was never delusional—she knew exactly what she was doing and appears to have enjoyed the game, almost daring reporters to find out who she really was.

## LE TOUR DU MONDE
## [A TOUR OF THE WORLD]

About a month and a half ago, we had a visit from two young English journalists . . . who, having left their country without a penny in their pocket proposed to go around the world by foot earning their living during the trip. One must admit that the attempt did not lack originality.

Now here is a young American woman who has undertaken to accomplish the same feat, but who, more practical and more 1900s than her competitors of the ugly gender, wanted the bicycle to be part of the feat. And so she left her native Boston . . . to pedal courageously forward, to tempt luck and to attempt the unknown.

On departure she only had a penny and many ordeals were awaiting her but didn't daunt her. Her adventures? We would need an entire book to describe them. Attacked by a negro in New York whom she shot and nearly killed next to a railroad track where she had fallen off her bicycle onto the rails at the moment a . . . train was coming with phenomenal speed. It was truly a miracle that she escaped a terrible death and saved her bicycle.

—an unidentified Paris newspaper, December 1894

Here again was Annie, the master storyteller, at work, creating a larger-than-life portrait of herself: the courageous heroine narrowly escaping death to make her journey around the world. The entire story about being attacked "by a negro," shooting him, and nearly being run over by a train is almost certainly apocryphal, a piece of pulp fiction used to build her legacy. Annie repeated this story to several French newspapers, saying the incident occurred between Rochester and Syracuse, a stretch, considering at that time she was riding in the company of three wheelmen from Rochester. Nor was the story reported in any of the two dozen or so accounts of her travels in the Buffalo, Rochester, Syracuse, and Utica newspapers.

Despite the questionable veracity of the stories she was spinning to European journalists, or perhaps *because of them,* Annie found French soil fertile for making money. By her own account, she was "quite the rage [in Paris] as an advertising medium." Various bicycle sellers engaged her at the Salon du Cycle, a huge bicycle exhibition held in Paris, to promote their wares, as did the director of the Vélodrome d'Hiver, where Annie was to compete in a five day indoor bicycle race against two of France's best male riders, Tricot and Chevreuil. The race was canceled before it began, however, purportedly because use of the indoor track for five consecutive days would interfere with the training regimen of many racers.

Annie also lectured in Paris, though she did so in English. "Not one in a hundred could understand," she wrote. "Every few minutes I would shout 'Vive la France!' Then how they did cheer! It was positively inspiring. *I found out what they liked and gave them plenty of it.*" (emphasis added) This would be Annie's modus operandi throughout her trip; she knew how to win over both a crowd and a single reporter, and this type of showmanship contributed to her livelihood on the road.

THOUGH ANNIE later wrote that she stayed in Paris two weeks, it was closer to three and half weeks. Before leaving Paris, the American consul presented her with a silk American flag, one she would deploy as a prop to make her dramatic entrance into Marseilles a few weeks later. "He told me to keep that flag prominently displayed wherever I went and that it would always protect me."

ANNIE LEFT PARIS on December 30 at eight thirty in the morning from the Porte-Dorée Café on avenue Daumesni, riding down the rue Coquillière. Among those now accompanying Annie were Victor Sloan, the Sterling dealer with whom she stayed during her time in Paris, and his brother, James.

To help her find her way south, Annie sewed a small piece of cloth into her bicycle jacket with a message written in French: "Miss Annie Londonderry from Boston (America) is traveling around the world on her 'Sterling' bicycle, built like a watch, with only a penny. Please show her the way to Marseilles." She wouldn't need it, however, because the Sloans were just the first in a series of escorts organized by France's ubiquitous cycling clubs, escorts that traveled with her, in relay fashion, nearly every mile of her journey from Paris to Marseilles.

The trip out of Paris was an awful one, twenty miles of mud-covered roads in rain to Lieusaint, where Annie and her party arrived at 11:45 A.M. for a forty-five-minute break to rest and dry off. Then the "half-frozen riders hobbled on their course." By early afternoon they had arrived in Melun, where she posed for photographs before heading off again about 2:30 P.M. Joined by two additional local cyclists from Melun, they then rode through the famed oak and pine forests of Fontainebleau by the Seine. *L'Abeille de Fontainbleau,* the local newspaper, noted that the woman who had passed through town on her white Sterling was "known under *the pseudonym* of Miss Annie Londonderry," one of the few French newspapers to report that Londonderry was not her real name. Annie had given interview, reportedly in Paris just before her departure from that city, in which she said, "By the bye, you know Miss Londonderry is only my pseudonym; my real name is much prettier and better known, but I can't let you know it at present. You will know it if I succeed." Of course, Kopchovsky was neither prettier nor better known than Londonderry, but the statement was pure Annie, designed to be an intriguing tease. Around 5:30 P.M., "spattered with mud and soaked to the bone," she arrived in Nemours and bid farewell to the Sloan brothers. She spent the evening at l'Hôtel de l'Écu de France, where the proprietor provided a change of warm clothes, no doubt a relief to Annie, who had ridden some fifty cold and rainy miles that day.

She was on the road again at 9:30 A.M. the next day. A sizable contingent of local townspeople came to see her off, and two employees of a local bike shop rode with her through the bitter cold and falling snow to Souppes, a few miles south. The bad weather made for slow progress, and by New Year's Eve Annie was in or near Montargis, a mere twenty miles or so south of Nemours and about sixty miles south of Paris.

The dawn of the new year brought little change in the weather. On New Year's Day, Annie continued south on the national highway to Cosne-Cours-sur-Loire, where she arrived "in a very good state, but covered in mud." From there, she wrote to *Le Vélo,* a French cycling journal, of the warm hospitality she received in that town, which included gifts that she accepted in exchange for sharing stories of her journey, per the terms of the purported wager, which prohibited her from accepting anything gratuitously. One in particular, a box of chocolates, she described as "superb." Annie spent the night at the home of the Hourds, "a hospitable family . . . who offer[ed] her lodging [and] a meal."

Her progress was slow again the next day. After she arrived in the small village of la Charité-sur-Loire, the local consul of the Union Vélocipédique de France (U.V.F., the Velocipedic Union of France), Monsieur Nicart, persuaded Annie to take the train some 170 miles to Lyon "because of the deplorable state of the routes."

Annie stayed at l'Hôtel de l'Univers in Lyon, where she regaled a reporter with her story of being attacked by "a negro" in New York State, which she altered slightly from other tellings. In this version of the story, she hadn't fired any shots, but she was portrayed as heroic nonetheless. "Miss Annie Londonderry, with unusual energy and a vigorous push, rid herself of the negro. She just had enough time to get up and throw herself and her bicycle aside as the train went by at full steam." She left this city on January 6, in the company of three Lyon wheelmen. Again, the weather was dreadful. It was snowing and the temperature was well below freezing. Just as the group was ready to depart, however, Annie had a mishap and suffered a minor injury to her leg, delaying her party for an hour. The group then pedaled on to Vienne, where the president of the local bicycle club provided a luncheon; then they continued south and spent the night in the village of Saint Rambert.

Annie left for Valence in the company of a new group of cyclists. The roads on the way to Valence were poor, the weather was still cold, and her ankle was sore from the accident in Lyon. She arrived in Valence at eleven o'clock in the morning, completely fatigued, though one of her riding companions told a local newspaper he was "stunned by her valiant enthusiasm."

"Her endurance is remarkable," said the *Journal de Valence.* Apparently unaware that she had taken the train from Cosne-Cours-sur-Loire to Lyon, the *Journal* continued: "She took only four days to go from Paris to Lyon never sleeping more than two hours a night. Her routine is such, that from Saint Rambert to Valence, where, by the way, she was only pedaling with one foot, the cyclist accompanying her had a hard time keeping up."

Had she read the story in the *Journal,* Annie would not have rushed to correct the misimpression she had ridden all the way from Paris to Lyon. She seemed to have an intuitive understanding that people's assumptions about her and her journey would often play to her favor. Like any good illusionist, she encouraged people to see what they wanted to see, or thought they saw; and the French, in particular, wanted to see a heroine of the wheel.

Just as Annie never disabused people of the assumption she was single (a logical assumption about a woman circling the world on a bicycle in those times), she would never have come forward to say that she had taken the train to Lyon if people assumed she had ridden, even though there were many, including Monsieur Nicart of the U.V.F., who knew differently. If the *Journal* had asked her directly, she likely would have told the truth, but with a creative explanation. Later in her journey, she sometimes explained away stints by train by stating that the wager had a rail allowance of a fixed number of miles, or permitted train travel with the advance permission of the bettors if conditions made riding impossible, which permission she would obtain by telegraph. Since Annie almost certainly concocted the wager story, there was no one back in Boston to contradict her creative variations of the wager terms.

Annie registered at l'Hôtel de la Tête d'Or in Valence and a Dr. Magnanon was summoned to see her. He diagnosed the injury to her leg as an inflammation of the Achilles tendon. As a result of her injury and the bitterly cold weather, Annie delayed her departure from Valence. Her Sterling was put on display at a local bicycle shop, to be admired by the curious public. "It is a man's bicycle," reported the *Journal.* "Seeing this specimen, we see to what degree of perfection the builders of the New World have attained." While at the hotel, Annie received a note, certainly one of many such notes received over the course of her journey: "A lady great admirer of your courageous travel will come and see you tomorrow between twelve and half past one. Pray do wait for her." Her celebrity was, by now, secure.

While she recuperated, Annie held court at the hotel and met with local journalists. "In general Miss Londonderry likes French men but couldn't say as much for French women," said the *Journal de Valence.* "In Paris she was very shocked to see that women smoked. During her stay in the capital people proposed to her to have a contest against cyclists of her own sex, but she declined having judged them not worthy of competing with her. She competed well against the finest of Parisian male cyclists and did not appear to be struggling to compete with any of the racers."

Because there are no reports in the Paris newspapers of Annie's having competed with male cyclists, let alone Paris's finest, the *Journal* reporter may have been especially credulous, for she was the likely source for the story. Indeed, as noted, her scheduled five-day race against two male racers in Paris had been canceled so as not to interfere with the training schedules of the French cyclists.

Typical of Annie's impulsive conversation were her comments about Frenchmen and women. What slights, real or perceived, she may have suffered at the hands of Frenchwomen she never said but, by hinting that she liked Frenchmen but not the women, she may have been coyly trying to disabuse people of some of the perceptions that flowed from the many reports about her masculine appearance and her uncertain sexuality, while at the same time boasting of her skills on the bike. (Modesty was not in her repertoire.) As for being "shocked" that Frenchwomen smoked, it's hard to imagine that Annie, who had few qualms about dressing in men's cycling clothes and making a general spectacle of herself, would find smoking a shocking affront to femininity.

At 9:00 A.M. on the morning of January 10, a crowd gathered at l'Hôtel de la Tête d'Or as Annie left Valence with eight other cyclists, including a gentleman by the name of Paul Seigneuret. Because of her injury, she and Seigneuret shared a tandem, while another rider rode Annie's Sterling. Seigneuret intended to escort her to the village of Montélimar, but soon found himself twice as far down the road in Orange, having fallen under Annie's spell. She was a woman of enormous charisma, charm, persuasiveness, and self-assurance, and repeatedly demonstrated, both during her bicycle trip and later in her life, an uncanny ability to hold people in thrall. Seigneuret was hardly alone in succumbing to her vivacious and captivating personality.

"To explain to you how, having departed to accompany Miss Annie to Montélimar, I went to Orange, will be difficult because I am not aware myself," wrote Seigneuret two days later in an account of his trip with Annie written for the *Messager de Valence*. "[B]ut, what is certain, is that I saw myself almost en route to Marseilles and that I had the promise of a trip to Bombay using my bicycle, from this city to Calcutta. Do not believe this is a tall tale . . . I say this in all seriousness."

By the time the riding party reached the village of Paillasse, en route to Orange, the entire group save for Annie and Seigneuret, had had enough of the cold weather and snow-covered roads and "steered their handlebars toward the station." Three of the riders met up with Annie and Seigneuret a bit further south, in Loriol. She and Seigneuret continued on together, with two others, to Montélimar. The roads improved, but "the wind create[d] heaps of snow, especially on the descent of Saulce," wrote Seigneuret.

Though her Achilles tendon continued to bother her, so much so that she was pedaling with only one foot, Annie managed the large hills near Montélimar quite well. Indeed, she and Seigneuret kept up a brisk pace of about twelve miles per hour. Her injury notwithstanding, Annie's enthusiasm, joy, and joie de vivre were undiminished. "She possesses an unheard of energy, laughs continuously and does not stop singing," Seigneuret wrote. "On the hills, she pushes her pedal leg with her hand and breaks out in laughter once she has ascended the slope. She is always gay and we arrive at Montélimar without even noticing the route."

After lunch at l'Hôtel de la Poste in Montélimar, the group, now four strong, departed for Orange. Despite rough conditions, Annie's buoyant personality kept the group's spirits afloat. As the party ascended a steep two-mile slope at Bel-Air, they were forced to dismount and walk to the top before beginning a fast descent into the village of Donzère. On the way down, one of the riders lost control and was pitched into a snowbank. "[W]e [saw] a snow-covered head poking out of a hole in such an amusing way that we didn't even notice his legs which were desperately kicking in the air," wrote Seigneuret. Even a near collision didn't dampen Annie's spirits: "[W]e avoid[ed] the accident and, with a burst of laughter from Miss Londonderry we [got] back on our route."

Beyond Pierrelatte, a village south of Donzère, the roads were smooth and clear of snow, and the party continued to Orange. Over their final dinner that evening, Annie playfully implored her companions to accompany her to America via Bombay, Calcutta, and Yokohama, but finally settled on a promise, never fulfilled, to return to Valence in 1896 for a reunion. After dinner, the Valence cyclists boarded the train for the trip back north, leaving Annie to begin the next leg of her trip on her Sterling—and to entertain a new group of escorts.

Annie spent the night of January 10 in Orange, just north of Avignon. The next morning, two members of the Avignon cycling club met her there and the Cercle Musicale, most of whose members were cyclists, played for her enjoyment, no doubt making her short journey to Avignon a festive one.

When Annie reached Avignon just before 11:00 A.M., with her two new companions, the city was well primed for her brief visit. Two days before, a local newspaper had already trumpeted, "Miss Londonderry will pass through Avignon on her bicycle tour of the world!!" and the organizers of Annie's visit were "redoubling their zeal so that nothing is overlooked." "Hip! Hip! For the courageous bicyclist," proclaimed *L'Echo du Jour,* another Avignon paper, one of many that served as a chorus of cheerleaders as the American cyclist made her way south. She was, by now, a bona fide hero in France.

At a reception hosted in Avignon by a Madame Boyer, Annie was given a well-heated room "stocked with drinks to strengthen her." Then, just four hours after arriving in Avignon, Annie was off again with Monsieur Geo, one of the Avignon cyclists who had met her at Orange. They reached Salon de Provence, some thirty miles southeast of Avignon, later that same day.

Marseilles, Annie's final destination in that country, was now just a few hours' ride away. But this last leg of her French sojourn proved to be the most perilous, at least by Annie's account.

"One night I had an encounter with highwaymen near Lacone [Laçon, about thirty miles north of Marseilles and about ten miles southeast of Salon de Provence]," Annie later wrote in the *New York World.* "I think they were waiting for me, for they knew I had been earning money in Paris.

There were three men in the party, and all wore masks. They sprang at me from behind a clump of trees, and one of them grabbed my bicycle wheel, throwing me heavily. I carried a revolver in my pocket within easy reach, and when I stood up I had that revolver against the head of the man nearest me. He backed off but another seized me from behind and disarmed me. They rifled my pockets and found just three francs. They were magnanimous enough to return that money to me. My shoulder had been badly wrenched by my fall, *and my ankle was sprained,* but I was able to continue my journey. Several wheelmen of the Lacone Club rode out to meet me, and when they understood the cause of my injuries they would not let me travel alone while I remained on French soil."

Despite the trauma of the night before, on the morning of January 13 Annie made her triumphant arrival in Marseilles. "Great preparations had been made for my reception in Marseilles, but I cut a sorry-looking figure when I reached the city," she wrote. "My ankle was so badly swollen that I could not use it, so I was forced to ride into the city with my injured foot in bandages hanging over the handle-bar and pedaling with the other. I was escorted to the hotel by a long procession of cyclists, and the streets were lined with people who were anxious to see the American lady who was riding around the world on a bicycle. My Stars and Stripes were hung from a staff attached to my handle-bar, and it was heartily cheered."

While the dramatic encounter with highwaymen near Marseilles quickly became a staple among Annie's many stories, repeated regularly to reporters along her route, it was never mentioned in the Marseilles newspapers, near the scene of the alleged crime, nor, in fact, in *any* French newspapers. There was, of course, another explanation for why Annie pedaled into Marseilles with one foot and the other in bandages propped on her handlebars: the inflammation of her Achilles tendon diagnosed in Valence. But there was little glamour in an inflamed Achilles tendon. Surviving a dramatic robbery was much better copy and served to enlarge her already growing legend, and nowhere had it grown as large as it did in Marseilles.

Indeed, she had become such a star by that time that, during an appearance at the city's Crystal Palace, Annie received a glorious ovation as she rode her Sterling through the crowd. Telling the people of Marseilles they were "the elite of the French nation" endeared her to the Marsaillais even more, as they loved being told their countrymen to the north were less hospitable and more vulgar. Annie regaled the local papers with anecdotes from her trip and continued to pour on the flattery, working her audience like the seasoned performer she now was. According to one local newspaper, "When she left for Marseilles, Parisians who had only given her a lukewarm welcome, didn't hesitate to warn her: 'You will be poorly welcomed in the South! Prepare yourself for a cruel deception.' It was with a childlike joy that Miss Londonderry declared that the Parisians were bad prophets. She thinks that she has never experienced such sincere warmth and respectful kindness as that which surrounds her in our city."

"Maybe Paris got up on the wrong side of the bed when I was there," said Annie. "In Marseilles, people have shown such cordiality that I'm overwhelmed with emotion."

INDEED, MARSEILLES *was* good to Annie. Not only was she given a hero's welcome, local merchants eagerly helped her earn money to continue her trip. Monsieur Lorenzy-Palanca, a Marseilles perfume maker, initially offered her money directly but, citing the prohibition on gifts established by the wager, the cyclist replied, "nothing stops me from doing work for any amount you offer me." True to her word, the next day Annie was out and about the streets of Marseilles, distributing handbills for the Lorenzy-Palanca company from her Sterling.

Annie received so many letters in Marseilles from well-wishers hoping for a word with her that visitation hours at her hotel were posted in the local paper. Indeed, her celebrity had grown so large, that on January 20, the day of her departure for points east on the steamship *Sydney,* thousands turned out by the docks to bid her farewell. The throng "resembled a huge swarm of ants," reported *Le Petit Provençal.* "The Soufre pier was equally invaded. Along the quay, privileged hundreds came to make their good-byes to the intrepid . . . Miss Londonderry." For all her outward bravado and, at times, emotional detachment, Annie was deeply moved by this outpouring of affection and her eyes "filled with tears." France had embraced her and she returned the embrace.

As the *Sydney* maneuvered through the port, American and French flags flying from her stern, the captain passed as close as possible to the pier so the crowd could soak up one last long look at their heroine. The crowd cheered and Annie waved her final farewell. France would never see her again.

# A Girl Globe-Trotter

## Annie Londonderry Circles the Globe on a Wheel— Attacked by Highwaymen in France—Wheeling Across the Battlefields of the Oriental War She Gathered Materials for a Lecture Tour

*On that simple machine she rode like a winged victory,
women's rights perched on the handlebars, and cramping modes
and manners strewn on her track.*

—Fairfax Downey

The time between Annie's departure from Marseilles in January 1895 and her return to the United States was filled with harrowing adventure, frequent danger, and endless drama.

Annie rode her Sterling through Alexandria, Port Said, Jerusalem, and Aden. She rode across the "Hindustan Peninsular" from Bombay to Calcutta, a trip made miserable by insects. In India, she hunted Bengal tigers, sometimes in the company of German royalty. Nearly killed several times by "Asiatics" who mistook her for a flying squirrel, some believed her to be an evil spirit, or a even a Martian. She rode overland from India to the China coast, often wearing local clothing over her own to keep from being molested. Caught up in the Sino-Japanese War of 1895, she traveled to the front lines with two journalists and a missionary, fell through a frozen river, took a bullet in the shoulder that caused a full month's delay in her trip, rode over fields littered with the dead, and was thrown into a Japanese prison where she saw a Japanese soldier kill a Chinese prisoner. She endured freezing nights on "Corean furnace beds" heated by coals, and made her way by bicycle across the Korean peninsula to

Siberia, where she "observed the workings of the Russian system of treating political prisoners."

It was a remarkable series of adventures and an extraordinary amount of cycling, especially for a woman who left Marseilles on January 20, 1895, and departed Yokohama on March 9, 1895, just seven weeks later. In fact, while all of this high adventure in the jungles of India, at the war front in China, and in the bitter cold of Siberia was unfolding in her fertile imagination, Annie was instead onboard the *Sydney,* skipping like a stone across the water. When she left Marseilles in late January, she had just eight months to make it back to Chicago if she was going to claim victory in her wager. She needed to find a fast away across Asia—and to obscure the fact that she had taken such an extraordinary liberty with her means of travel.

During the course of Annie's around-the-world journey she logged thousands of miles by bicycle, and it could be argued that she was genuinely the first woman to cross the American continent by bicycle, even if she hopped the train from time to time. But her accounts of the Asian leg of her trip are virtually another story altogether. Even if she had ridden nonstop, it would have been impossible for Annie to have crossed India and cycled overland to the China coast in seven weeks.

Annie often lived on the edge of reality and fiction. Simply put: when it suited her, she made up parts of her own story. Her real goal wasn't to circle the globe on a bicycle, but to become rich and famous in the attempt, or at least in what appeared to be an attempt. And if she was going to lay claim to having cycled around the world, she needed to deliver a colorful account of her travels between Marseilles and Yokohama, one more interesting than she undoubtedly had during her time at sea. Upon her return to the States, in her lectures and for the trip account she later wrote for the *New York World,* she told amazing, literally incredible tales of bandits, war, and derring-do that would appeal to American audiences—even if they had little more than a grain of truth in them, or perhaps none at all—and she evinced no concern about whether her contradictory stories were adding up.

AFTER LEAVING Marseilles on January 20, the *Sydney* sailed east toward the Suez Canal. Its first port of call, on January 25, was Alexandria, on Egypt's north coast. A day later the *Sydney* stopped at Port Said, a major coaling station for ships passing through the Suez Canal. Annie wrote in the *New York World* that she visited Jerusalem, where, it appears, she amassed a collection of about a dozen lantern slides of the Holy City that she used in her lectures about the trip. To reach Jerusalem from either of these cities, she would have had to have taken a boat to the ancient port of Jaffa, near modern-day Tel Aviv, and a forty-mile, three-hour overland journey on a narrow gauge railway to the Holy City. It seems improbable, but Annie could have made it to Jerusalem and back to the *Sydney* if she had left the ship in Alexandria and rejoined it in Port Said the next day.

Annie had a strong Jewish identity; the opportunity to see Jerusalem, even if briefly, would have had strong appeal. However, her many slides of Jerusalem do little to confirm her presence there, for the slides were made by a commercial photographer and could have been purchased elsewhere.

After refueling at Port Said, the *Sydney* continued its voyage east to deliver the French mail. At one P.M. on the afternoon of February 7, the vessel, having sailed through the Suez Canal to Aden, reached Colombo, Ceylon (now Sri Lanka). Apparently, Annie was not the only female cyclist among the *Sydney's* approximately eighty passengers, and women on bicycles were not a common sight in 1890s Ceylon. "A great deal of amazement was caused among the natives in the Fort [the center of colonial Colombo was the area near the city's fort] this afternoon, by the unusual site of three lady cyclists in reformed dress—tights, knickerbockers and jacket—peddling [sic] their machines along the streets," said the *Ceylon Examiner.* "These were from the French steamer 'Sydney,' which came in during the afternoon; and crowds kept following them, and surrounding shops and other places they went into. They seemed amused to see the crowds watching them; and after a time proceeded on board." Annie found time to take a "30 mile spin" around Colombo with members of the local cycle club later that day.


THE *SYDNEY* left Colombo the very next day for Singapore. On February 14, the *Singapore Straits Times* reported on Annie's brief stop there. The tone was more skeptical than she had come to expect from the generally admiring French press, but she would soon have to get used to such attitudes and worse when she returned to the United States. It would only be a matter of time until some journalists would begin to take note of her remarkably fast time passing through Asia, especially for someone supposedly riding a bike.

---

# A WOMAN ON WHEELS
# 50,000 FOOLS AT MARSEILLES

About two years ago a gentleman, who, not inappropriately, had been dubbed in America "the boss dead beat," passed through the East on a journey around the world. He started from Copenhagen centless, to beg or borrow, or if dire necessity compelled, work his way around the world to win a wager, variously stated and variously explained. An indulgent public took this young man by the sleeve and led him comfortably on his way. He was furnished with the best of food and the most comfortable lodgings; his progress was watched with interest and recorded by the press. We believe that he succeeded in his task with but trifling difficulty, for the great steamship lines seemed to think the advertisement which this unmitigated young humbug gave them was worth the passage ticket which they presented. He had what Mark Twain's bad boy would describe as a "bully time." . . .

And now we have chanced upon another crank from that land of marvellous [*sic*] wagers and remarkable exploits. This time it is a woman; a woman arrayed in an advanced costume smacking of the feminine attire of the next century. Last evening on the balcony of [her hotel] . . . [she was] the object of curious interest. A short woman, with a not unpleasant face, and a back at once suggesting to a Sherlock Holmes, by the deductive theory, she was addicted either to a sewing machine or a bicycle. Her costume removed the doubt. An easy fitting, low-cut blouse of pale blue, knickerbockers of dark serge, black stockings on well shaped legs, and white shoes denoted the modern cyclist. Her face was sunburnt, and there was a latent will power, not to say aggressive independence, in its lines which prepared one to know that the lady was not an ordinary tourist.

The cyclist was introduced as Miss Londonderry and when she spoke one would have known at a considerable distance that she hailed from the land of the stars and stripes . . . [S]he cycled to Paris and there appears to have had a "high old time." *La belle France* was at her feet. Her photographs were bought for 200 fr. a-piece. Advertisers found it a paying business to give her 100 fr. a day to distribute prospectuses. Smith's soap and Jones' pills were labeled all over the machine at 25 cents a spoke. She sampled somebody's milk, gave a certificate of its excellence, and pocketed 200 fr. She wore another enterprising firm's boots and testified to the durability. She donned all kinds of patent arrangements, and received substantial bonuses . . . And when she took reduced passage from Marseilles to Yokohama there must have been 50,000 people on hand to give her a royal farewell. But we fancy she exaggerates. Some women do.

Singapore has been reached, therefore, by the easy method of a French mail [a reference to the *Sydney*] on the cheap . . . To the chagrin of the wagerers she will be in Boston once more . . . with the $5,000 legitimately earned according to the terms of the contract. Miss Londonderry then, fortunately for journalism, retires on her laurels, and writes a book. Miss Londonderry has had experiences, of course, but they are reserved for the volume which a waiting world is bound to buy. She carries a revolver and a small chemist's shop. The revolver she has used twice in the free land of America. The drugs are to analyse Bink's milk and Juggins' soda water. Her trip, has on the whole, been a pleasant and profitable outing. As [Miss Londonderry] told us, "I have been treated most beautifully; it is wonderful to find the sympathy and courtesy of the people?" It is indeed!

These individuals seem to be coming—the experiment having proved such a success—in a regular procession. Another man has started on his way, clad in a newspaper, and may in due course find his way to Singapore. It is reasonable to protest vigorously against this latest phase of beach combing—but is it of any use?

—*Singapore Straits Times,* February 14, 1895

Another Singapore newspaper, the *Free Press,* was a little more charitable, but just a little. "Astonishment, curiosity, and amusement were created last evening by the advent of the New Woman . . . To [the M.M. *Sydney's*] brief stay in port the community is indebted for its glimpse of the dress of the Woman of the Future, and a peep at the Woman herself."

That Annie was utterly unabashed about using her sexuality to help promote the wares of the advertisers who commissioned parts of her body as a billboard was clear in Singapore. "Miss Annie Londonderry . . . the lady cyclist who might have been seen walking about town yesterday evening and cycling around Teluk Ayer and the roads near the Borneo Wharf this morning, has dispensed with any superfluous outer garment or skirt above the knee and wears a pair of knicker-bockers calculated to effectively display a pair of advertisement garters, advising everybody to 'Ride Somebody's tyres' or perhaps to wear 'Untearable Twills,' " said the *Free Press.* "The textual accuracy of the quotations is not vouched for, our representative (who is a modest man and fears to be misunderstood) not caring to appear as if gazing too intently in that quarter."

The *Free Press* noted that Annie was "but lightly" touching Asia on her around-the-world tour, and gently chided her for her naïveté about the region. "Miss Londonderry said . . . that she would have liked to cycle from Singapore to Hongkong, if time permitted, and asked as to the nature of the roads, which shows how easy it is to be in Malaya and not know anything about it. She is a very chatty person, and does not mind showing how she stops her cycle when going down hill, using her foot as a brake, the machine . . . having none."

As she had in Colombo, Annie tried to enlist some local Singapore cyclists for a bicycle tour, but to no avail. "No doubt the local cycling club would have been delighted—but, at all events, they did not know of the advent of the 'nervy' young lady, who appears quite capable of holding her own on the road and full of 'grit'—extending nearer the finger tips than is usual with her sex," said the *Free Press.* Then, a gentle parting shot: "But that is perhaps due to the fact that the *Sydney* has been coaling."

FROM SINGAPORE, the *Sydney* sailed to Saigon. Annie, acting as her own press agent, sent a telegraph message from Singapore to the *Progres de Saigon,* one of the city's major newspapers, to tell of her impending arrival there on February 16.

She found a more sympathetic reception in Saigon than the one afforded her in Singapore, and two admirers in Gaston Amelot, editor of *Le Courrier de Saigon,* a French-language newspaper, and a Monsieur Mouline, also of *Le Courrier.* So taken was he with Annie, Mouline penned an ode to her on a small piece of paper, three by four inches, to the left of which he sketched a woman on a bicycle atop a globe, which in turn sits on a pedestal from which the American and French flags are flying. On the pedestal, the words *Le Courrier de Saigon* are written.

The ode, dated Saigon, February 17, 1895, was a tribute to Annie's daring, courage, and tenacity. It is fourteen lines long and, read vertically, the first letters of each line spell out MISS LONDONDERY, with one *r* missing. Though the anagram disappears when the poem is translated, it reads:

> *Ladies and Gentlemen, Hurrah for the cyclist!*
> *Idol of a growing public*
> *If France believes in a fearless traveler*
> *We should offer her our warmest bravos*
> *The fashion today is to pedal on a path*
> *However, Miss Londondery [sic], in a delectable speech*
> *Invites us to celebrate her artistic voyage*
> *Do we have to hold back our enthusiastic praise?*
> *Should we deny the audacity of this woman*
> *Deny her beautiful courage and her boldness*
> *In a century where everything is somber and depresses the*
>     *soul*
> *As I question you, I hear you say*
> *Nothing is as beautiful as a deserving talent*
> *And the treasure of a radiant smile.*

*Le Courrier de Saigon,* it appears, was serving as a collection agency for donations to help Annie continue her journey. On February 18, the newspaper reported that Monsieur Mouline, the poet, had added $23.50 to what had already been donated by "friends of *Le Courrier de Saigon*" and that $85 had been collected at the theater the night before. When, at a performance of a play called *Voyage de Suzette,* arrangements had been made for Annie to make a cameo appearance with her Sterling. "The Cyclewoman, Miss Londonderry, was to appear in the ninth act and everybody was looking forward to seeing her," wrote theater critic Harry Cappa. "Unfortunately she was not able to appear due to nails sticking out of the stage floor. She had to be satisfied with a public appearance with her bicycle and holding a French flag and giving a little speech in English that the spectators seemed to be listening to with deep interest."

Annie, never shy and retiring, used the opportunity to ask the audience directly for donations, something Cappa found rather bold but appropriate under the circumstances. "I can't say that she doesn't have a lot of energy and tact," he admitted, "but, equally, under these conditions, I am also the first to subscribe to these tactics in order to do my jaunt around the world."

ANNIE AND the *Sydney* left Saigon on February 18 or 19, with a positive send-off from the *Le Courrier:* "All who had the good fortune of studying her from near were able to see that this charming girl isn't a comedian or an adventurer, not even as eccentric as some people claim, but an accomplished, courageous and strong-willed intrepid woman that imposed on herself the will to reach a specific goal and nothing will come in her way to achieve the pursuit of her ideal . . . Miss Londonderry is in the process of proving to the whole world that the American race is the most tenacious and strong-headed of the universe, and, furthermore, that women are able to sum up the courage and energy that very few men would be able to stack." It is striking that Annie engendered such different responses in different cities, generally meeting with approval in France and its colonies and skepticism in parts of the British Empire. Whether she was viewed as a hustler making a buck, as in Singapore, or as a becoming young woman making a statement, as in Saigon, it's clear that Annie made an impact wherever she traveled. In reality, she embodied a piece of every description given to her—a beguiling combination of P. T. Barnum and Nellie Bly, a bold New Woman emblematic of the pursuit of sexual equality, but with a decidedly cunning twist.

As ANNIE MADE her way from Europe across Asia, the tone of journalists at home, like those in Singapore, was becoming decidedly less flattering. At first, the negative press focused on her shameless self-promotion and the commercialization of her trip. Later, those paying attention to her timeline would begin to question her entire enterprise, some going so far as to label her a fraud.

"Miss Annie Londonderry as an attraction is hardly a success," reported the *Pittsburgh Chronicle-Telegraph.* "It certainly is bringing down the level of legitimate touring when one sees a woman working her way around the world and so far degrading herself as to be put on exhibit, so to speak, dressed in a fancy costume with circulars and advertisements sewn all over her dress." Another sour note appeared in *Cycling Life,* which had been covering Annie's progress in short news briefs: "Glib and vulgar is Annie Londonderry. Her aim is to be notorious."

But Annie cared little about the negative press. From her point of view, the more ink she got, the better. At one point, before reaching Asia, she responded to a critical column, though precisely which column is not known, in this way: "Did you see the scorching the reporter for the cycling column of a daily paper gave me? Wasn't it great? Just what I wanted. Thought he was worrying and mortifying me. I'm going to write up some beautiful 'roasts' of myself and send them to some of the leading dailies, and I'll get all the free advertising and notoriety I want, and everybody will be on the lookout for me. Then people will flock to see me and buy my cheap souvenirs, over which they can lift their hands in thankfulness that they have not the courage to make of themselves wheeling advertisements for the sake of husband and children, and at the same time envy me my hardihood and business sense."

Not only was this a rare acknowledgment by Annie that she was both married and a mother, it addresses a subject never hinted at elsewhere—either by the cyclist or those following her story—that she was making the trip to support her family. Indeed, Annie usually went out of her way to suggest she was unmarried. But she was very savvy, and very modern, when it came to understanding the power of the press: if fame is your goal, there is no such thing as bad publicity.

Indeed, fame, money, and an escape from the ordinary, were Annie's real quest and her real achievement. Already evident by this point in her journey, was her extraordinary skill at finding a way to make that dream come true. She may have been cavalier and cunning, with the dash of a snake-oil salesman, but in the space of seven short months she had radically changed the circumstances of her life. She was no longer an anonymous working mother living in a Boston tenement; she was a global celebrity, albeit an increasingly controversial one.

They loved her in Marseilles and Saigon, but back in the States some were less than enamored of Annie and her methods. She couldn't have cared less as long as people, and particularly the newspapers, were paying attention.

\*   \*   \*

ON FEBRUARY 21, Annie's hop-scotch tour of Asia continued as the *Sydney* arrived in Hong Kong. Here she demonstrated just how skilled she was at talking rings around any subject. "Miss Londonderry describes herself as a journalist," reported the *Hong Kong Daily Press,* "but says that according to the terms of her bet she is allowed neither to work nor beg. On our venturing to express our disapproval of people traveling around the world without money the young lady asked what was the good of traveling *with* money, and went on to explain that with money you could do anything, but that her object was to show what could be done without money. We did not try to argue the point with her." Just a day or two in Hong Kong and Annie was off yet again, cycling but little and riding the waves a lot.

When she reached Shanghai a few days later, Annie wrote the Boston City Press Association from Astor House, a hotel on Shanghai's famed Bund that runs along the north bank of the Suzhou Creek: "I left Boston last June on trip around the world without money. I have succeeded in getting so far and I feel sure to win my $10,000 wager." Then she added, cryptically, "My cycle is my only protection."

On February 25, Annie wrote a note to the editor of Shanghai's *Celestial Empire* newspaper, asking him to call on her at Astor House. When he arrived, he found Annie in knickerbockers and a blouse, eager to spin her tale. She "at once informed her interviewer that she was a journalist and was at that time engaged in writing to twenty-two newspapers, for which she was allowed to correspond." Not a single such dispatch from Annie has been found, however. She also claimed that she had been accompanied into Marseilles by "a brass band and ten thousand people" and that at every place she had visited "she had been taken up by the press and 'boomed.' " She made it clear she expected the same in Shanghai so she could "secure the balance of her passage to Japan." One can only imagine the look on the face of her interlocutor; Annie was a woman of astonishing directness and said the most outlandish things without batting an eye. She wasn't so much asking for help as insisting upon it as her due. "Assuring the lady that he would have great pleasure in assisting to any scheme she might arrange whereby this could be done, our representative left. Up to going to press no further notice has arrived, so we are unable to say how the lady fared," said the *Empire.*

\* \* \*

THE WAR BETWEEN China and Japan waged over control of Corea (as it was then spelled) in 1894–95, had been a dominant story in the American press for months before Annie arrived in the area. War was declared on August 1, 1894, while Annie was pedaling toward Chicago, and by November of that year, as she made her way back to New York, China's defeat already seemed certain with the fall of Port Arthur. By the time Annie arrived in the vicinity of Port Arthur, sometime after February 25, 1895, the war was winding down. The smaller but better equipped Japanese forces had overwhelmed the Chinese, the Japanese navy had routed the Chinese navy at Weiheiwei Harbor and taken the town, and signs of the siege were everywhere.

It was a war notable for its savagery, with both sides engaged in decapitations, mutilations, and the cold-blooded slaughter of civilians.

Annie saw the war as a human tragedy—she vividly described its horrors in her story for the *New York World*—but she also was quite candid about seeing the war as an opportunity. She decided to make herself an eyewitness to the war so that upon her return to America she could earn money lecturing about it. Indeed, a substantial number of the slides in her lantern slide show depict scenes of the war: Japanese soldiers on horseback, hand-to-hand combat between Japanese and Chinese soldiers, great naval battles in the Yellow Sea, and prisoners of war. For American audiences, Annie would be their eyes and ears, bringing home a firsthand account of a distant and bloody war. In the process, not incidentally, she would further build upon her image as a daring and dashing heroine undaunted by great risk. What American audience, whose only news came from ink on newsprint, and few of whom had ever ventured abroad, wouldn't be enthralled by the stories Annie had to tell from the front?

Annie's account in the *World* was filled with hyperbole and utterly fantastic stories very similar to those she delivered in her lectures:

> [W]hen I reached Shanghai I heard of the danger of traveling through that country. I had unwittingly approached the very seat of hostilities. I was warned to get out of the country as quickly as possible, but my American spirit was up, and I was determined to see the fun. I knew that here was a glorious opportunity for me to collect material that would yield a good

financial return when I reached my own country, for that was my only hope of raising the stipulated $5,000.

So I determined to go to the front, and I went. I knew that I could fill any hall in the United States with the announcement that I was an eye-witness of battles in China. The result proved that I was right, for I easily completed the amount as soon as I reached this country. From Shanghai I went to Nagasaki and met two war correspondents bound for the front. I received passports from the Japanese Government and accompanied them. We landed near Port Arthur with the second Japanese Army. Wei-heiwei was their objective point. We followed. I shall never forget the horrible scenes I witnessed at Port Arthur. We arrived there after the butchery, but the dead remained unburied. I saw the bodies of women nailed to the houses, the bodies of little children torn limb from limb. Everywhere there was evidence of the most horrible butchery and mutilation of the dead. At Wei-heiwei the slaughter had been worse than at Port Arthur. When we passed through Chefoo the streets were filled with the dead.

I was an eye-witness of the battle of Gasan. It was the first I had seen, and I don't want to see another. The fighting continued from 9 o'clock in the morning until 4 o'clock in the afternoon. The Chinese had laid some mines for the destruction of the Japanese Army, and then by some mistake the Chinese Army occupied that identical position. The stupid men in charge of the mines exploded them at that moment and caused a frightful slaughter of their own people. Fifteen hundred Chinamen were killed and only twenty-two Japanese. Great chasms fifty feet in depth were formed by the explosion. They proved to be burial places for the dead. It was a horrible experience.

I crossed the Pontoon River accompanied by a Japanese guide and a British missionary named F. A. Moffatt. The river was frozen over, but when near the shore the ice broke and we fell in. While in that predicament a party of Chinamen appeared on the opposite bank and fired at us, killing the Japanese guide, and wounding both Mr. Moffatt and myself. I was shot in the shoulder. Both of us reached the shore alive, but Mr. Moffatt died from the effects of his wound a few days later.

That same day we were captured by the Japanese and were thrown into a cell, and left without food for three days. Mr. Moffatt would have lived if he could have received proper medical attention. The cell was merely a hut with lattice-work sides. There was no protection from the bitter cold and I suffered keenly. While thus imprisoned a Japanese soldier dragged a Chinese prisoner up to my cell and killed him before my eyes, drinking his blood while the muscles were yet quivering.

I appealed to the American Consul, but he paid no attention to my call. Then I requested the French official to secure my release, and he sent a troop of forty soldiers. I was released in a hurry. Before leaving for Japan I took a run up to Siberia, and saw the prisoners working in the mines. I saw one string of forty prisoners arrive. They had walked 1,400 Russian miles.

Was *any* of it true? Almost certainly not. By February 15, at least ten days before Annie could possibly have arrived in the area, the Chinese had reportedly surrendered the port of Weiheiwei, but information was sketchy. "Admiral Ting sent a flag of truce to the Japanese Admiral offering to surrender all the men-of-war, arms, and fortifications," reported the *North China and Supreme Court & Consular Gazette* on that date. And on the twenty-second, the *Gazette* reported, "Weiheiwei has now completely surrendered."

Annie's claim to have been at Weiheiwei, or indeed anywhere else in the war zone, is further undermined by the fact that after leaving Shanghai, most likely on February 26, the *Sydney* arrived in Nagasaki, Japan, on February 27, Kobe on March 3, and Yokohama on March 4—where Annie was listed among the ship's passengers. The only time she could have made it to the war front would have been between February 26 and March 3, assuming that she didn't sail on the *Sydney* to Nagasaki but managed to get to the front by other means before rejoining the vessel in Kobe for the passage to Yokohama. Yet, she later wrote she had been in Nagasaki. In short, it is virtually impossible that Annie spent any time at the battlefront. Likewise, her claim to have reached Siberia (the only evidence is a lantern-slide photograph of Vladivostok in her collection) simply could not be true because she arrived in Yokohama on March 4 and left on the *Belgic* for San Francisco five days later. Though the majority of her tale was clearly impossible, she certainly managed to conjure dramatic and sensational accounts of those days, accounts she would use to entertain American audiences in the spring and summer of 1895.

BY THE TIME Annie arrived in Yokohama in early March, skepticism about her claims was, justifiably, on the rise. According to the *Japan Weekly Mail,* she was traveling the world *"with* a bicycle." "The advanced lady appears to have availed herself of the services of the M.M. steamer *Sydney* from the Far East," said the *Weekly Mail,* "but as she has several months in which to accomplish her task, she will doubtless put in her real bicycling in the States, starting from San Francisco . . . We hope she will accomplish her undertaking, but at the same time we must again express our astonishment at the open-handed manner in which the public support these undertakings . . . [T]he game seems extremely profitable for all those who care to take it up; and so long as it pays, so long will it find ready votaries."

Before setting sail for San Francisco, Annie had a run-in with the American consul in Yokohama, John McLean, to whom she appealed for help in raising the money for her passage home. She didn't have a high opinion, in general of the American diplomats she met and decided, a few months later in El Paso, to bare her grudge. An El Paso reporter played Annie's gripe to the hilt:

> The general run of American consuls were proven a sorry lot, sort of last run of shad. American consuls live in the finest houses and cut the biggest swell, but when it comes to putting themselves to any trouble to assist American citizens, particularly if they be women tourists, why it seems as though they don't just 'give a dern.' Of course there are bright exceptions, but the average lot gave Miss Londonderry the dead cold shake, and didn't want to be bothered. What business had a woman a galivantin' 'round the wu-r-rld for enyheow on a boike? . . .
>
> The American consul at Yokohama, John McLean of New York City, proved a lovely specimen. He seemed to take about as much interest in his fellow citizens as he would in a dead cold griddle cake. Miss Londonderry wished his advice and cooperation in raising 85 yen to pay her passage from Japan,

and all she could get out of this old stiff was that his wife was away, and he was, ter hum, taking care of things, and—oh, he could not be bothered at all. She could go out and rustle, leaving this misrepresentative of the glorious b-u-r-r-d of fray-dem at home, with his feet cocked up on his desk and complacently smoking his briarwood pipe.

The French consul at Yokohama, a model of politeness and a thorough gentleman, immediately interested himself in mademoiselle. And it was through his courtly generosity and timely assistance that 250 yen were raised in short order for La Petite Mademoiselle and she went on her way rejoicing.

Miss Londonderry found another superfoine riprisintative of a jimieratic administrashun at Hangchow who wouldn't help her at all because he said she had no business in thim parts, and ought ter have staid at home; and the same interesting state of affairs obtained at Nagasaki . . .

At Yokohama the ratty old buzzard who acts, or rather misacts as American consul there, wanted to charge Miss Londonderry $3 for a passport and at other places she was given to clearly understand that the American consul was not out there for his health, but for something else.

Without the help of American consul John McLean, on March 9, 1895, Annie boarded the *Belgic* in Yokohama for the voyage home to America. Four hundred twenty feet in length and 2,212 tons, the ship was equipped to sail or to steam, its deck punctuated by three towering masts and a single smokestack. Unlike *La Touraine,* this vessel was a workhorse with a top speed of fourteen knots, one that often carried legions of Chinese and Japanese immigrants looking for work in America.

As she sailed for home, Annie continued to hone the stories of her extraordinary escapades, tales she would soon relate to audiences thirsty for a taste of her adventures. For people in small towns and cities in California, Arizona, New Mexico, Texas, and Colorado, her vivid descriptions of adventures in places they could only imagine, literally illuminated with her slides of the extraordinary and the exotic, promised an evening of grand entertainment. "I found out what they liked and gave them plenty of it," Annie had said of her popularity with the French. She was about to do the same for her countrymen back in the United States.

## Chapter Six

# Annie Is Back

### Has Traveled the World on a Sterling Finished in Ivory and Gold
### Nearly Killed by a Road-Hog in Stockton, Cal.

*If there's any symbol for the transformation that had occurred in the lives of American women as they approached the twentieth century, it ought to be the bicycle.*

—Gail Collins, *America's Women:*
*400 Years of Dolls, Drudges, Helpmates, and Heroines*

On March 23, 1895, the day after Libbie Kopchovsky turned four, the *Belgic* completed its transpacific voyage. With the cannon battery at Fort Point off its starboard, and the Marin Headlands off to port, the ship passed through the Golden Gate and, much to Annie's relief, arrived in California. "[W]hen I reached San Francisco I felt as if my journey had ended," she wrote. "I was glad enough to get away from the land of rats and rice, and into a country where one could get a decent bed."

Nine months after leaving Boston, Annie was back in America. But she was no longer a lone adventurer with a personal agenda; in the course of her journey, she had become a symbol of an entire generation of women, and a pioneer in the struggle for women's equality. The day after Annie landed, a major feature in the *San Francisco Examiner* headlined Annie as "The New Woman on a Tour."

"Annie Londonderry has proved that a woman can make her way three-quarters around the globe riding a bicycle wherever that was possible, and making money as she went," said the *Examiner* somewhat generously. But the newspaper also noted, relying no doubt on Annie's say-so, that the wager allowed "considerable latitude to the conditions [of travel]. [It allowed] the woman to make a great deal of the trip by steamer . . . The remainder of the trip has to be taken entirely on her bicycle."

But Annie wasn't entirely disingenuous about her journey thus far. She was well aware that questions might surface about her fast passage through Asia and, to the *Examiner,* at least, she didn't claim to have ridden across India or overland to the China coast. Rather, she explained that in Alexandria, Port Said, Jerusalem, and Aden she made only "short tours near each of those places and then started for Singapore on the same steamer." Though the wager required her "to *report* at Colombo, Singapore, Hong Kong, Shanghai, Nagasaki, Kobe, and Yokohama," it *"did not matter how I reached those places,* so long as I made the circuit and secured the signatures of the Consuls at each of the cities as proof that I had accomplished the purpose of the trip," a rather odd statement given that the purpose of the trip was, ostensibly, to ride around the world on a bicycle. "If she succeeds she is to receive the purse that prompted the journey," continued the *Examiner, "and another victory will be scored for the new woman."* (emphasis added to these three extracts)

However ambiguous her descriptions of her means of travel, in San Francisco Annie *was* staking her claim as the first woman to go around the world by wheel. The "buxom young woman" who arrived on the *Belgic,* "claims the distinction of being the first bike rider of her sex to attempt to circle the sphere," reported the *San Francisco Chronicle.* "She shook the dust of the classic Massachusetts metropolis off her tires several months ago, and with a degree of self-assurance somewhat unusual to her sex, ventured to 'beat her way' around the world."

The *Chronicle* was not much taken with Annie's appearance, in any sense of the word. "Miss Londonderry is short and stout and takes pride in the fact that she sacrificed personal appearances for comfort during her journey. She looks it. She was not mistaken for an Oriental princess when she stepped down the gangplank of the *Belgic,* and she professed to be somewhat disappointed that the populace, headed by several brass bands, had not turned out to welcome her as had been the case, according to her diary, in other great cities." In regard to the latter, the newspaper pointed out that Annie's arrival in San Francisco was unexpected. Given her skill as her own publicity agent, however, that seems unlikely. Though in France she had achieved media coverage and adoration, her tepid welcome in San Francisco demonstrated that she still had a lot of work to do to achieve similar notoriety at home. Although newspapers often shared stories (the major story in the *Examiner* on her arrival, for example, also appeared in full in the *Washington Post* some three weeks later), this wasn't an age of mass communication and instant celebrity. And the vast territory of the United States was not as easy to conquer, figuratively speaking, as a small country such as France. In America, Annie would have to start building her fame all over again and the considerable newspaper coverage she received in San Francisco was an excellent start.

Though Annie told the *Examiner* she had taken the steamer to Singapore, on the very same day she told the *San Francisco Call* and the *San Francisco Chronicle* entirely different stories. She informed the *Call* she had ridden across India, and she boasted to the *Chronicle* that she had made "a long, fatiguing journey over land to the Chinese coast." Whether these claims were simply meant to add drama and intrigue to her story, or were a response to skepticism expressed by the reporters about her claim to be cycling the world, cannot be determined. More likely, Annie didn't care. Often very impulsive in conversation, there is *nothing* in the record that suggests any defensiveness on her part at any time, or any attempt at any time to set the record straight on a point where there might have been confusion. She made no effort to stick to a single, consistent, intact story.

In San Francisco, the first of several remarkably precise but questionably accurate accounts appeared of how many miles the cyclist had traveled. In terms of the world's surface, she had transversed close to 20,000 miles by this point. However, Annie's Sterling, unlike the Columbia she rode from Boston to Chicago, had a cyclometer, an odometer-like device, which was difficult but not impossible to tamper with. She, or rather, "her bike [had] traveled, in all, 7,280 miles," according to the *Call*. This clearly refers to the mileage supposedly covered by the actual vehicle in motion; anyone standing near it could have read the cyclometer easily. Seven thousand miles at San Francisco is reasonably consistent with Annie's later claim, in the *New York World,* to have ridden precisely 9,604 miles by bicycle during her entire journey, for the indirect route she would take back to Chicago from San Francisco was approximately 3,000 miles. But even adding in the approximately 1,000 miles Annie rode on her Columbia, she certainly had covered less than 7,000 miles by bicycle when she reached San Francisco. The trip from Boston to Chicago and back to New York had been about 2,200 miles, and the journey from Paris to Marseilles about 400, some 170 of which she covered by train.

She had been at sea for most of the time since leaving France. As she continued from San Francisco across America, the mathematics of Annie's cyclometer and various news reports about it would become even more conflicted.

The miles she had traveled were not the only currency by which Annie's trip was being measured, however. She was still bent on establishing that she was fulfilling the other important requirement of the wager—that she earn $5,000 en route. In San Francisco, she also described how she decided to earn money lecturing about the war, stating that to that point she had sent only $1,500 "to Boston to be placed to my credit. I was looking toward earning the money between San Francisco and the Atlantic coast and to do it I must have some means of entertaining the public."

That Annie was in earnest about making money by lecturing about her experiences, the captain of the *Belgic* learned firsthand on the voyage from Yokohama. "She is fully capable of taking care of herself as Pilot Newton Jordan discovered when he began quizzing her on the *Belgic*," said the *San Francisco Call*. "She recited to him some of her adventures and then told him if he wanted to hear more he would have to pay for it." But, like the mathematics of her mileage, the various figures of Annie's earnings are also impossible to reconcile. Well before she reached San Francisco, there were reports that she had earned considerably more than $1,500. In Buffalo in November 1894, for example, it was announced she had already earned $3,500, principally in advertising contracts. These inconsistencies of her reported earnings would also become of increasing interest to the press as Annie entered the home stretch of her journey and sought to lay claim to winning her purported wager.

It was during her time in San Francisco that she tested the war stories she would use throughout her travels. She told the press she took a steamer to Nagasaki, where she met two correspondents bound for the front and landed near Port Arthur with the second Japanese army. "The two men rode on ponies while I used the bicycle. The roads were very poor and it was hard work, but I managed to keep up with the rest, and was in at the fight at Gasan . . . I like the two correspondents, was not allowed very close to the actual line of battle, but I saw enough of it to know what the horrors of war are . . . It took us a week before we reached Che Foo, and I thought we would never accomplish the journey. The cold was intense, and the food we could scare up was not sufficient for one person, let alone three." But, as noted, there is simply no way Annie spent a week reaching Chefoo (modern-day Yantai, across Korea Bay from Port Arthur); at best she was in the vicinity of Port Arthur for no more than three days, and most likely aboard the steamship *Sydney* the entire time.

ANNIE SPENT about two and a half weeks in San Francisco, staying at least part of that time at the Palace Hotel, where she prepared to continue her journey. At Taber Studios on Polk Street she had a formal portrait of her Sterling taken; and somewhere in the surrounding hills, stage-managed a photo of bandits accosting her at gunpoint, a slide she would use, along with others she had purchased along the route, to illustrate the lectures she would give as she made her way east. The photograph with the bandits was pure Annie—a fanciful but dramatic backdrop against which to spin her tales of high adventure. During her time in San Francisco, she began organizing and labeling the lantern slides she had collected and carried with her, in two lacquered boxes acquired in Asia. She also answered mail waiting for her in San Francisco, some 4,200 letters by one account, 147 of them "proposals of marriage from men of wealth and nobility," a number she could have made up, of course, but not implausible given her growing fame.

While Annie prepared for the rest of her journey, some in the European cycling community who had feared she had been killed somewhere between France and Asia, were just learning that she had reached Saigon safely. On March 29, 1895, four days after her arrival in San Francisco, a Paris newspaper reported, "Miss Londonderry, whose fate we have been very much worried about, has been located. It seems that she left Saigon to continue her tour of the world." And a few days later, a German cycling journal reported, with some relief, that "a postal message from Saigon" brought news that "Miss Londonderry, about whose fate the worst was feared, left this town by bike and continued her trip around the world bravely." Perhaps her fellow Americans were not yet following her every step, but others abroad were.

BEFORE SHE RESUMED her journey, Annie met Mark Johnson, a cyclist from San Francisco's Olympic Club, and they decided to ride south together. Though her cycling companions typically rode with her for a few days, Johnson was the exception. He rode with her the entire four-hundred-mile stretch to Los Angeles. It took them more than *five weeks* to make the trip—quite a long time for such a short distance. Had they walked, they could have made it to Los Angeles in half the time it took them to get there by bicycle. Though this was not the first time Annie had ridden in the company of a lone male rider, Johnson was clearly no ordinary escort. When the pair reached Santa Maria on May 10, a month after leaving San Francisco, the *Santa Maria Times* reported that Johnson was going down the coast with Annie "just to learn the road." Perhaps. But if so, he appears to have been a very slow learner. The point doesn't need to be belabored, but these were two young, athletic people cycling through some of the world's most spectacular scenery at the height of the lush and sensuous California spring. For a woman racing the clock around the world, Annie certainly lacked a sense of urgency during this leg of her trip. Perhaps it was Johnson's company that caused her to "[pass] through Morgan Hill . . . a whooping."

Annie and Johnson left San Francisco on their bicycles on April 9 or 10, reached the east side of San Francisco Bay, and spent the night in Tracy, some fifty-five miles east. She was expected in Stockton the next day to deliver a lecture.

But the very next morning, near tragedy struck. While riding downhill on the narrow Niles Canyon road, a runaway horse and wagon rounded a bend and ran Annie and Johnson off the road and into a barbed wire fence. "The couple were going at a four-minute clip [a four-minute mile, or fifteen miles per hour] down grade along the canyon road, when, just around a curve in the narrow road, they saw a runaway team coming towards them," reported the *Stockton Evening Mail.* "There was little time for thought, but Johnson, who was in the lead, called out to his companion to follow him. This she did, and as the team went whizzing past, the bicyclists were crowded against the side hill and both struck the same obstruction at the same time. Johnson relaxed his muscles and landed limp, so that he was not as badly shaken up as Miss Londonderry, who put her arm out to try and break the fall. In doing this she was badly shaken up and injured internally. Her face suffered severely and is now black and blue."

Annie, in typical dramatic fashion, would later say the accident had knocked her unconscious and kept her bedridden for five weeks, coughing up blood. But, according to the *Stockton Evening Mail,* "Her bicycle was damaged but it was patched up and she proceeded to Livermore where a physician was consulted. He took from her lip several small pieces of rock that had been pressed through the skin. The plucky little woman refused to stay over at that point and have her injuries attended to, as she was anxious to be on hand in Stockton tonight to deliver her lecture."

True to her word, despite "[a] black eye, a scarred face and a badly bruised body," Annie delivered her lecture in Stockton on the night of the eleventh against the advice of Dr. Lilla Miller Lomax, a thirty-seven-year-old physician in Stockton.

---

## MISS LONDONDERRY'S LECTURE

"Annie Londonderry," the clever young bicyclist who is touring the world, lectured to a large crowd at Mozart hall last night. There was not one vacant seat. The audience was composed almost entirely of men and the majority of them seemed to take more interest in Miss Londonderry—who is a shapely young woman—in her abbreviated cycling habit than they did in the stereopticon views that were thrown on the canvas.

—*Stockton Daily Independent*, April 12, 1895

---

By the next day, Annie was feeling the ill effects of her accident. She was taken to Dr. Lomax's home, which doubled as a clinic, and placed in her care. A reporter for the *Stockton Evening Mail* visited Annie there and reported she was suffering "a high fever and was in great pain." Nevertheless, Annie held forth, quite expansively, on cycling, its benefits for women, and proper riding attire, once again illustrating her very advanced views for a woman of the 1890s.

"You want to know what I think about the bicycle for the physical development of women?" she asked the reporter. "Well, I know from experience that there is nothing better than a wheel to build a woman up. When I started out on this trip I weighed 105 pounds, and now my weight is 140. [Like her mileage and her earnings, Annie's reports of her weight are suspect as she had, purportedly, lost a good deal of weight en route from Boston to Chicago. Perhaps she gained it back, this time in muscle.] The exercise has not made hard, bunchy muscles, such as you often see on athletes among men, but has made good, pliable muscles that have developed me all over and have rounded out every curve.

"[I]f the wheel is used as it should be the exercise can never be injurious to women," Annie continued. "As a rule women ride on a drop seat and will keep their corsets on when taking a spin. They could not do anything that would hurt them more. The corset should be discarded, and nothing but a thick sweater used. This fits tightly about the form, keeps the body in shape and absorbs the perspiration that must come through taking such exercise. The fact that women will wear corsets when riding is the reason so many suffer from the exercise. It is against all reason to box one's self up when making any such exertion as is required in riding. Tell the women to discard their corsets, and they will get some pleasure and health out of cycling." Though feeling quite ill, Annie had much more to say that night on the subject of women and the wheel.

"There is another thing I would like to point out to my fellow riders of the weaker sex. They should not ride on a drop seat, but on a diamond wheel, such as is ridden by men. The position of the rider on the other seat is not a correct one nor conducive to health. On the wheel ridden by men the position is correct, and exercising on it cannot hurt anybody. The doctor who says it will harm the ordinarily healthy woman doesn't know what he is talking about. I have studied medicine some, and I know what I am saying is true.

"Not only should women ride the wheel, but they should not wear heavy, baggy bloomers that make the work a torture and do not look nice. They do not have to go to the other extreme, either, and look unwomanly. There is just as correct a costume for bicycling as there is for the ladies' habit in riding horseback, and to wear what is not the correct thing looks just as much out of place on a bicycle as on a horse. A heavy sweater, a neat pair of bloomers, leggings and a natty cap constitute proper costume. It looks simply ridiculous to see a woman peddling [sic] on a wheel wearing a heavy dress and a sailor hat.

"If women will exercise properly on a wheel they will have nicely rounded figures, bright eyes and healthy 'cheeks, and will feel well the year 'round," Annie concluded. "My work on the bicycle since I started on this trip has developed me wonderfully."

This monologue is revealing of Annie's towering self-assurance and of the degree to which she now saw herself as someone who had lessons to impart to millions of women. In Stockton, from her sickbed, she was expressing the sense of well-being and strength the bicycle had delivered to her personally and her view that one could be both feminine and physically active at the same time. She was not only advocating for cycling, and the benefits it could deliver to women, but for something more—the liberation of women from their corsets, both literally and figuratively. She was practically imploring women, in her direct, opinionated way, to take up arms, so to speak, through the bicycle. Not bad for a woman struggling to speak through pain and a fever.

ANNIE RECUPERATED for a few days in Stockton, climbed back on her bicycle, and, with Johnson and an escort of San Jose cyclists, reached San Jose on the evening of April 18. "Miss Annie Londonderry . . . has traversed [her] stipulated course with nearly two months overtime to her credit, and almost three-quarters of the journey done," reported the *San Jose Daily Mercury.*

Asked about her accident, Annie revved up the myth-making machine. "Outside of Stockton a few days ago, I met with a horrible accident," she said. "As I was riding along a driver of a buggy ran me down and ran over me. I was picked up unconscious and carried into Stockton, where I lay in the hospital two days. I coughed up a good deal of blood and the doctor said that I could never recover, but here I am, and what is more, I intend to complete the journey."

On Saturday, April 20, San Jose hosted a large bicycle meet. Annie announced the winners and handed out the prizes, a sign of her growing celebrity, especially in cycling circles. Asked about her route back to Boston, she said she would ride south to Los Angeles, across the south to New Orleans, and then on to Boston.

ON APRIL 25, a few days after leaving San Jose, Annie and the ubiquitous Johnson arrived in Salinas from the north. By coincidence, Tom Winder, a newspaper editor from Warsaw, Indiana, reached Salinas by bicycle the very same day from the south. Winder was on what the *Salinas Weekly Index* called "the longest ride ever undertaken on a bicycle," a 21,000-mile journey along the entire coast and border of the United States that Winder was hoping to complete in three hundred consecutive days of riding. Winder, too, had a spouse and children at home and, like Annie, ostensibly, he was chasing prize money: $1,000 put up by the manufacturer of his bicycle. By the time Annie and Winder met in Salinas, she was in the middle of her six-week, 400-mile, San Francisco to Los Angeles jaunt, while he, in just six weeks, had covered an astounding 3,000 miles.

Winder's opinion of Annie was less than complimentary:

> Here I met the famous Anna Londonderry . . . Miss Londonderry's trip has been a remarkable one from the fact that she went entirely around the world on steamboats, *according to her own story,* excepting a ride from Havre to Marseilles, France on her wheel. Miss Anna is a hustler for sure. She is some 50 days ahead of time, and has been in California for two or three weeks, and only has to get $3,400 more when she will have the $5,000. She tried lecturing out here, but the venture proved a dismal failure and Londonderry was quite gloomy and discouraged at the time I saw her. She intends to write a book, so I thus early put the public on its guard. (emphasis added)

This would not be the last time Annie would be described in such unflattering terms.

As elsewhere, in Salinas the description of Annie's 'round the world route had some fanciful entries. The *Index* reported she had ridden through England and Spain, though she had been in neither, and also reported incorrectly that Annie was thirty years old, the speaker of several languages, and of French descent.

TOM WINDER and the *Singapore Straits Times* weren't the only skeptics to think Annie was a traveling sideshow making her way around the world more on a whim than a wheel, and gulling a lot of people along the way. As she and Johnson made their way south, touring several of California's Spanish missions, public doubts about Annie's claim that she was riding around the world by bicycle began to proliferate and some of her press coverage turned sharply negative. Words such as "allegedly" and "supposedly" were beginning to appear with some frequency in connection with her claims to have been cycling around the world.

In April, *Cycling Life,* which had begun to write sarcastically of Annie's unabashed interest in notoriety, wrote, "Smart girl, Annie Londonderry, but much too fresh to be touring the world as a representative of American womanhood in any shape or form. It is told of her that before she would taste of a patent milk preparation of a Yokohama man, or even signed a testimonial as to its efficacy, she insisted upon receiving 200 yen."

*Cycling Life* made clear that it placed little stock in Annie or her stories. "Folks will pity Annie Londonderry upon learning that she was once compelled to sleep in a graveyard without other protections than her anatomical advertisements. To read of the hair-breadth escapes of this young woman, to say nothing of the hair-breadth escapes of the people who make her acquaintance, makes our eyes bulge with astonishment. She says she came within an ace of fighting and bleeding at Port Arthur." Others in the cycling community complained that Annie wasn't good for the sport or for women: "She is not elevating either cycling or her sex," wrote the editor of one British cycling magazine.

Others joined this critical chorus: In late April, the *Sandusky Register,* whose reporter had met Annie when she rode through Norwalk, Ohio, on the first leg of her trip, reported Annie had reached San Francisco from Japan, "and as she left Marseilles, France sometime in January her trip across Eastern Europe and Asia must be considered a record breaker from a cycling standpoint. What are you giving us, gentle Annie?" The *Chicago Tribune* also observed that Annie was making remarkably good time: "According to original plans, [Miss Londonderry] should be in the wilds of some savage country instead of delivering lectures on the west coast."

And there was more. On May 3, the *Olean (New York) Democrat* reported that Dr. and Mrs. H. D. McIlrath of Chicago had set out "to girdle the globe on bicycles." "Men globe girdlers are by no means a novelty, for Thomas Stevens, Thomas G. Allen and William L. Sachtleben have demonstrated that a plucky rider may pedal a bicycle entirely around the earth," said the story. "The woman globe girdler has not thus far proved her right to the title by riding the necessary 25,000 miles. Miss Annie Londonderry is now completing an alleged bicycle ride around the world, but has made such astounding time through Europe and Asia that her riding must have been done on steamers and railroads."

To be fair, even the undisputed holder of the title "first human to circle the world by bicycle," Thomas Stevens, didn't cover anywhere near 25,000 miles by wheel—he rode 13,500 miles—and only by figuring out a way to ride on water could a cyclist hope to cross the oceans in a single, direct circumnavigation of the earth. But, it is surprising that *more* observers hadn't already drawn the same conclusions about Annie's "astounding time through Europe and Asia on land." Her "secret" was hiding, if it was being hidden at all, in plain sight. After all, she told the *San Francisco Examiner* that she had sailed to Singapore on the same steamer that took her to Suez from Marseilles and that she was permitted to make much of the trip by water. Furthermore, in early May, *The Bearings* and *The Referee,* two cycling magazines, carried an advertisement featuring Annie accompanied by a map of her route, a narrative of her adventures, and her testimonials to the virtues of the Sterling wheel. The map, unlike the cyclist's own varying descriptions of her itinerary, was an entirely accurate, if crude rendering of the route she actually traveled, though the map shows her starting from Chicago where the Sterling Cycle Works was located. It would have been clear to anyone looking at the map in the Sterling advertisement, how Annie had made such fast work of Europe and Asia. However, most readers and reporters alike ignored such details.

By dint of her ability to engage the imaginations of others with spellbinding tales filled with adventure and drama, Annie was able, when desired, to elide the fact that she had not traveled from France to Asia by land. Like any good illusionist, she worked through misdirection. People *wanted* to believe in her, and for the most part did.

BY THE VERY END of April, Annie and Johnson had reached Paso Robles, north of San Luis Obispo, about halfway between San Francisco and Los Angeles. The *Paso Robles Record* reported Annie expected soon to be in Mexico. According to the *Los Angeles Times,* however, she had been laid up with "the grip," or flu, in San Luis Obispo for a week in early May, the result of a soaking while crossing several streams in the area. But the same story also reported that Annie had made daily runs of one hundred miles on three consecutive days from Watsonville, just north of Salinas, *and well north of San Luis Obispo,* on her way south to Santa Barbara. Unless Annie and Johnson were simply riding these grueling "centuries" through the California hills for fun, or riding in circles, the report is implausible, for it is only a little more than two hundred miles from Watsonville to Santa Barbara. Had the cyclists ridden three hundred miles south in three days from Watsonville, they'd have been well *south* of Santa Barbara by May 12, not thirty miles *north,* as they were in Los Olivos. And how Annie managed both to have the flu for a week and do three centuries between May 1 and May 10 makes one or the other story implausible. Indeed, neither report may have been accurate.

Annie and Johnson arrived in Santa Barbara on the night of May 13, two days before a major bicycle racing event, one the *Santa Barbara Daily Independent* predicted would bring "the biggest day in wheelmen's circles that Santa Barbara ever saw." On May 15, Annie, sporting a dark tan, was on hand for the races. At the invitation of the organizers she rode her Sterling several times past the grandstand, but did not race a timed mile, disappointing some who had come to see her. The *Independent* took a generous view of her decision not to race, declaring "nothing less than the earth" suited Annie for a course. She delivered a short lecture about her journey and made a good impression on her Sterling. "She is a good rider," said the *Independent,* and "a plucky woman. [I]f she does not succeed in her undertaking it will not be on account of any fault of hers."

THE TWO CYCLISTS finally reached Los Angeles in the early morning hours of Saturday, May 18, walking the final twenty-four-mile stretch when Annie's Sterling suffered a tire puncture. She was "nearly exhausted" when she checked into the Hollenbeck Hotel. She had covered 114 miles in the previous twenty-four hours.

The Los Angeles Annie visited in 1895 would be virtually unrecognizable today. Nearly ten million people live now in Los Angeles County but, in 1895, Los Angeles was a sedate desert oasis of some forty thousand souls and Hollywood was merely the name of a place, not an industry. Indeed, it wasn't until late 1895 that the first motion picture camera—*le cinématographe*—was invented, in France, by Louis Lumiere, who saw no commercial promise whatsoever in the medium. Cable cars, paved sidewalks, and palm trees were features of the L.A. cityscape, but it was still only a small town when compared with Boston, New York, or Chicago. Annie remained in Los Angeles for ten days with "plenty of time at her disposal," during which she lectured at the Los Angeles Athletic Club, using her slides to illustrate her talk. She also contemplated the course of the next leg of the trip, considering direct routes to Albuquerque, Salt Lake City, or El Paso, and the fact that "the worst part of her journey lies before her, across the Colorado Desert [in Southern California, west of the Colorado River]."

At some point during her stay in Los Angeles, Annie said good-bye to Mark Johnson, though there is no record of their parting. If there was any subsequent correspondence between the two, she didn't save it.

\*    \*    \*

ANNIE EVENTUALLY decided to head for El Paso, almost due east. She left for San Bernardino on May 28 or 29, escorted by several Los Angeles cyclists. Today, this fifty-mile stretch is a continuous stream of urban sprawl, but in 1895 it offered Annie a ride through sparsely settled hills and valleys. When she arrived in San Bernardino, where she stayed at the Stewart Hotel, Annie had, according to the *San Bernardino Daily Sun*, earned just $1,625 of the $5,000 above expenses she was to accumulate as part of the wager. This amount is consistent with the $1,500 she reported having earned to date in San Francisco, but again considerably less than she had supposedly earned by the time she reached Buffalo the previous November.

Though the men of Stockton found it hard to take their eyes off Annie during her lecture there several weeks before, she didn't catch the fancy of a reporter who met her in San Bernardino. "Good looking? Not very. Bright, expressive eyes, which are keenly observant are the distinguishing feature," he proclaimed in the *Daily Sun*. "A young lady who is in the saddle most of the time, cannot be expected to pay much attention to style and there is not much to admire in a white sweater, a light brown skirt and a boy's coat and cap to match. Yes, she is interesting; evidently well educated, charming in conversation, and makes a good story out of any one of a hundred incidents in her journey, which has thus far carried her three-fourths of the way around the globe."

At this time, another sour note about her trip found its way into print, this time in the *Los Angeles Times*. "Annie Londonderry, who is supposed, from her own story, to be going around the globe on a bicycle . . . arrived [in San Bernardino] yesterday, and is working the town for what she can earn to add to her exchequer," said the *Times*. "Just at present all the loose change is flowing into the Fourth of July fund, and there is not much on hand to assist in advertising globe-girdlers, though she may realize enough to pay her fare on the Southern Pacific to Yuma, and thus avoid the dangers and dust of wheeling through the desert sand."

JUST BEFORE NOON on Friday, May 31, Annie reached nearby Riverside, where she stayed as a guest of the local wheelmen.

While in Riverside, either Annie or a reporter taking great literary license concocted a truly odd and patently false story about how she'd acquired her first bicycle: She purchased her bike frame for three cents from one manufacturer, the other components from various other manufacturers, then after assembling the bicycle herself, started out from Boston in a twelve-cent suit "made of cheese-cloth and paper."

However it came about, this tale of assembling the bicycle by parts is an appropriate metaphor for her entire journey, which had been undertaken with little or no advanced planning and put together with equal parts guts, gumption, and guile. Annie was winging it in many ways. And just as she arrived in various towns covered in advertising ribbons, banners, and baubles, she adorned her stories with colorful but not always genuine accessories.

Annie made a favorable impression in Riverside. "She says she has sawed wood and done other work of a similar nature since starting her trip," said the *Daily Press,* "and from her make-up she looks as if she might make a pretty good hand at almost any manual labor . . . Smart as a whip and an excellent conversationalist." She also proved her cycling prowess at the race track. On Saturday, June 1, she gave a riding demonstration before a large crowd at Riverside's Athletic Park and raced the clock several times. She rode one-eighth of a mile on a March brand bicycle in 0:14¾; a tandem mile in 2:28; a quarter-mile in 0:33¼, and on the Sterling, an eighth in 0:15½. These times suggest what was called a "flying start"—cycling records were kept for both flying and standing starts—but they are impressive nevertheless, all requiring speeds of close to thirty miles an hour, albeit over short distances. Whatever the doubts about her around-the-world claim, Annie had become a powerful and skilled cyclist in the months since leaving Boston as a complete novice.

But a woman racing a bicycle, as she did at Riverside, was still considered by many a disgraceful spectacle. Even *The Bearings,* one of the premier cycling magazines of the day, found it objectionable. *"The Bearings* has always been opposed to anything of this kind and it has not been the only paper which felt this way," stated a July 25, 1895, editorial. "We do not see how any self-respecting woman can so far forget herself as to appear before an audience to race. The spectacle of . . . females straining every muscle, perspiring at every pore, and bent over their handle-bars in a weak imitation of their brothers is enough to disgust the most enthusiastic of wheelmen." Can there be any doubt Annie would have had a few choice words for the editors of *The Bearings?*

On Sunday morning, June 2, in the company of several lady and gentleman cyclists for the first several miles, Anne cycled eastward across the California desert toward Yuma, 165 miles away.

The desert between Riverside and Yuma was forbidding territory. The names of the towns, settlements, and train depots that existed, or barely existed there in 1895, are indicative of the harsh landscape: Thermal, Volcano Springs, Cactus, and Mesquite among them. Hot by day and sometimes frigid at night, it was a landscape suitable for rattlesnakes and scorpions but not cyclists. Because this leg of her journey lacks local newspaper documentation, how Annie crossed the desert may only be speculated. That she was following the Southern Pacific tracks to Yuma is clear, and she wrote that a train engineer named Ziegler stopped his freight to offer a ride but that she refused. She also wrote that upon arriving in Yuma she was refused a drink of water by a woman at whose home she stopped. That last story may be apocryphal, but she would tell it several times.

Annie would later say that crossing the Southern California desert was the most difficult part of her trip. Multiple reports surfaced that her Sterling had broken down in the desert some sixty miles west of Yuma, forcing a five-day trek across the sand pushing or carrying her bike. But the *Los Angeles Times,* again playing skeptic, was dubious: "She started from [Indio] afoot, ostensibly to walk to Yuma, but if certain railroad men were asked how she crossed the desert, 'they would wink their other eye.' "

This much is certain: when Annie finally reached Yuma, she was no longer in the United States, as Arizona would not become a state for another seventeen years. Annie was now in the Wild, Wild West, a place known for colorful, larger-than-life characters, and this Jewish mother from Boston was about to become one of them.

# Chapter Seven

# Tour on a Bike

## Miss Annie Londonderry Coming to El Paso After a Trip Through Europe and Asia, the Lady Is Bound for Her Home on a Bike

*I had made myself master of the most remarkable, ingenious, and inspiring motor ever yet devised upon this planet.*

—Frances Willard on learning to ride a bicycle.

No one really knows how Annie Londonderry, the "circumcycler" as the *Daily Star* of Tucson called her, entered Arizona Territory in early June 1895. Did she cross the border by bicycle, on foot, by train, or perhaps even by hot air balloon? One thing was for certain: the longer she was on the road, the more fanciful her accounts of her travels became.

"In speaking of her trip across the desert she was exceedingly eulogistic of the train men, who showed her every kindness possible," reported a Tucson newspaper shortly after her arrival in Arizona. "But for this it is quite evident, from what she said, that the silent steed and its lone rider would have been passengers on an incoming express." If, as some suspected, Annie had crossed the Southern California desert by rail, she wasn't letting on, saying only that the train crews eased her passage by offering milk and water to drink.

On June 14, accompanied by Art Bennett, editor of the *Yuma Times,* Annie reached Phoenix. "She has had an exciting time of it and has seen more than the average globe trotter," stated the *Arizona Republican.* "She was in China during the disturbance there and witnessed one of those bloodless battles in which she came nearer to being killed than anybody else except one man who really was killed. Miss Londonderry is an attractive and very bright young lady of twenty-five, though she doesn't look nearly so old."

Though Tucson, with a population of 5,100, was the capital of Arizona Territory in 1895, Phoenix, whose population barely topped 3,000, was already becoming the territory's political center of gravity. Electric streetcars plied the streets and new railroad links were being established. Just a few months earlier, the Santa Fe, Prescott and Phoenix Railroad ran its first train to the city, connecting Phoenix with northern Arizona and other parts of the west via Santa Fe. Yet despite its growth, Phoenix was, relatively speaking, a small and remote desert outpost, and the arrival of an around-the-world traveler, especially a woman on wheels, was a first-rate novelty.

As Annie explored the town in her cycling costume, she caused quite a commotion. Back east, her bloomers had raised some eyebrows, but in the sparsely settled west it was a real shock to some. It was here that an elderly woman coming out of a store "threw her hands up in speechless horror" upon spotting Annie in her bloomers and bemoaned the "depravity and boldness of the nineteenth century girl": " 'Wal if thar aint queer doin's now-a-days. I jest seen a woman wearin' men's pants.' The clerk explained that they were bloomers. 'Balloons, did you say! Wal if I ever ketch my darter wearin' balloons, I'll jest, I'll jest. . . .' " At least that's how the *Arizona Gazette* told it.

DURING ANNIE'S STAY in Phoenix, the Valley Cycle Club entertained her and the Sterling was put on display at Pinney & Robinson's, a bicycle dealership on North Second Street, to attract shoppers. An ad in the *Arizona Daily Gazette* trumpeted its appearance:

**ANNIE LONDONDERRY, THE LADY WHO IS RIDING AROUND THE WORLD ON A STERLING IS IN TOWN—HER WHEEL WILL BE ON EXHIBITION AT PINNEY & ROBINSON'S**

Annie also gave a "clever exhibition of fancy riding at the park" wrote an observer. "The way she can handle a wheel would make a male expert ashamed of himself."

After she left Phoenix, she spent the night of June 17 in Red Rock, about ninety miles south, and from there headed to Tucson. During this leg of her journey, a trick rider named Claude Leslie, of Los Angeles, joined her on the road. Trick riders were a popular entertainment during cycling's golden age, performing a variety of stunts on their bicycles.

So anticipated was Annie's arrival that by midafternoon a small crowd armed with a telescope had climbed a bell tower in the city to search the horizon for her. "Quite a little party went on the road to meet her, and there was considerable competition . . . as to who should meet her first," wrote the *Tucson Daily Citizen*. Three male cyclists named Hart, Heaton, and Sheldon got there first, riding twenty miles out to meet Annie, and the entourage picked up another twenty riders as they rode back toward the city. "All the Tucson riders unite in testifying to Miss Londonderry's ability as a rider," the *Tucson Daily Star* reported. But Annie was a little wobbly on her wheel for the ride into town. She had consumed a lot of water and, in the company of some two-dozen men, had no privacy. One of the riders remarked it was a good thing, though, for had she been in her best form they would have been unable to keep up with her.

Annie and her entourage arrived in Tucson at 5:30 P.M. She spent the night at the Orndorff Hotel as a guest of the local Sterling bicycle agent. While most guests who registered at the Orndorff that evening listed their city of residence, she registered with a flourish: "Annie Londonderry, Globe Girdler," read her entry. Leslie, too, registered at the Orndorff that evening.

Before retiring for the night, Annie, accompanied by Leslie, lectured at Tucson's opera house, honing her act and sharing stories. "Miss Londonderry, the lady of the bike, gave a talk last evening in the opera house, to a fair sized audience, on her experiences girdling the world around," stated the *Tucson Citizen*. Once again, Annie's ability to charm an audience was clear: She is "an interesting talker and very ladylike in her demeanor . . . she knew just what to talk about to be entertaining," said the *Daily Star.* Leslie demonstrated some "fancy riding" on the stage, but was "considerably hampered for want of room."

The following afternoon, Annie did a little sightseeing riding out by carriage to visit the San Xavier mission. She also spent the day debating how to proceed to Deming, New Mexico, some two hundred miles east: by bicycle or train. To cover her tracks, quite literally, she told the *Daily Star* that the wager terms included a five-hundred-mile allowance by rail. She was surely aware that time was becoming of the essence, for Chicago was still a long way off and she now had barely three months to get there to claim success.

Annie decided to start for Deming on her Sterling. She left Tucson, accompanied by several local wheelmen, including Bert Orndorff, on the morning of June 21. Temperatures during the day were in the mid nineties as the party passed through tiny Vail's Station.

Annie reached Wilcox, Arizona, on June 23. By the time she passed through Lordsburg, New Mexico, later that day, she was on a train. During her stopover in Lordsburg, she received a telegram from the *El Paso Daily Herald* with a series of questions she answered for an "interview" published the following day.

DH: What make of bicycle did you ride?
AL: A Sterling.
DH: On how many bicycles did you ride during your tour?
AL: One.
DH: The hardships you encountered?
AL: It would take hours to explain.
DH: The most serious difficulties you have overcome?
AL: Held up by highwaymen and shot at by Chinese.
DH: The toughest roads you have found?
AL: The Colorado desert.
DH: The most hospitable people on the route?
AL: Through France.
DH: Where have you received the meanest treatment?
AL: At Yuma, Arizona, after walking 61 miles in the desert was refused a drink of water.
DH: Where did you have the most serious break-downs?
AL: Through the desert country, only by punctures.

As the denizens of El Paso were reading her interview, Annie arrived by rail in Deming, eighty miles west of El Paso. It was June 25, exactly one year after her departure from Boston.

The *Deming Headlight* published that Annie had now earned $3,000 of the $5,000 she was required to earn under the terms of the wager and that such an amount had been "remitted to an eastern banking institution." (Again, as with accounts of her mileage, these figures are utterly inconsistent, and trying to reconcile them is impossible.) "The 'woman-hater' who wagered his $20,000 against her had better compromise or he must make a good show of losing his dinero," added the *Headlight,* confident that Annie would win the wager.

\*     \*     \*

No TOWN she had visited since Marseilles was to give her a warmer, more enthusiastic welcome than did El Paso. In fact, Annie's skills as a publicist served her well, for plans for her arrival in El Paso were already underway while she was still in Tucson. On the day she left the Arizona capital, the *El Paso Daily Herald* reported that she had departed that city and that "[t]he El Paso cyclists are preparing to give her a royal reception here, and Mr. Williams writes her today at Wilcox [Arizona] giving such information as he has at hand about the route and the reception she may expect here." The paper continued, "Preparations are now being made for a lecture on her trip. The cycling clubs [will] meet her out on the road and escort her to the city. Other entertainments may be prepared and an effort will also be made to get her to stay over here until the Fourth of July festivities." Clearly, Annie's arrival in El Paso was a civic event of major proportions and proof that she was now a true celebrity in her own country, or at least in Texas.

Later on the twenty-fifth, Annie arrived at the train depot in Strauss, just over the New Mexico border from El Paso. A party of cyclists met her there including a reporter for the *El Paso Daily Herald*. A wonderfully colorful account of the episode appeared in the paper the following day:

> Say reader, did you ever take a spin up the S.P. [Southern Pacific] road to Strauss? If you didn't, then you should try it. The trip as far as the smelter is delightful and the bike will carry you nicely, but after passing the bridge you will have to carry the bike. The railroad company makes the distance from El Paso to Strauss at 14 miles. Well, it may be fourteen miles if you ride in a Pullman, but it is certainly forty-one miles if you walk through sand and carry your bike, at least the writer thinks so and Jim Williams says so, and Jim don't talk about distances through his hat either. Miss Londonderry also agrees with Jim and she is a nice little lady from Boston who has been around the globe and knows something about distances—especially when it comes to desert country like that lying between the Rio Grande and Strauss. The scenery along the route is 'jist' beautiful, the sand dounces [dunes] rise to the hight [sic] of young mountains and there is noth-

ing else to be seen or heard in the land except the occasional hiss of the rattlesnake. . . .

Yesterday evening at 6 o'clock a telegram was received at the HERALD office saying that Miss Londonderry was at Strauss waiting for an escort into town. There was no time to hunt up an escort so the reporter notified Jim Williams and then mounted his bike and took the S.P. track to the smelter . . . Arriving at Strauss the reporter found that Jim Williams, Joe Mollinary, Randolph Terry and Herbert Bishop had passed him while at the smelter and had arrived at Strauss a few minutes in advance and were engaged in conversation with Miss Londonderry. Introduction followed and soon conversation about her trip around the globe became general. Afterwards a light lunch was spread and then all being tired out they retired for the night. Miss Londonderry being provided with a room and the balance finding peaceful slumber on the floor of the station house.

After an early start the party tramped back to Rogers station where coffee was served and several bicyclists were in waiting. Just this side of the bridge quite a number of bicyclists joined the party and in a few minutes they were rolling through the streets of El Paso and to the Vendome, where quarters had already been engaged, the party stopped and Miss Londonderry was shown to her room where her trunks and a large stack of letters awaited her. [Annie had trunks that she shipped ahead from point to point, a common practice for travelers of the era.]

In El Paso, a reporter for the *Herald,* possibly the same one who had ridden out to meet her, called on Annie at the Vendome and was obviously charmed. "She is a bright, vivacious woman, a good talker, and her all-round the world experiences will prove a Godsend to her for the 'rest of her born days,' " he wrote admiringly. "Miss Londonderry says that had she known really how to ride a wheel at the time of starting out, she never would have undertaken the tour."

Always eager to entertain and to appear larger than life, Annie told of a grueling ride across the "Hindustan Peninsular," a ride she described as "a terrible experience, especially because of insects. From Calcutta, Miss

Londonderry passed through Siberia and China, and saw the practical workings of the Russian system of treating political prisoners. She says the way the poor women were treated at the mines was simply horrible." Annie saw nothing of the sort, of course, but she never let the facts get in the way of a good story. She again related the story of the Yuma woman who refused her a drink. "The newspapers there got after the woman with hammer and tongs," reported the *Herald,* "which had some effect on her calcareous heart; she explained by saying she did not know who the rider was." Annie also said she had hopped a train the day before arriving in El Paso, only to be "put off . . . because she did not have eight cents to spare which would have made up the fare."

It was to the reporter from the *Herald* that Annie claimed the wager stipulated that she "should not contract matrimony" during her trip. Why did she say this? Perhaps she needed a gracious way to fend off the attentions of this very journalist without alerting anyone to the fact that she was a married woman, a fact that, even in wild El Paso, might have been looked upon with some scorn. "The necessity of this [condition of the wager] is patent, from the fact that she has received nearly 200 offers of marriage and written refusals to 147 of them . . . [A]ny horrid man who says she is not good looking ought to be taken out back of a cow shed and knocked in the head with an axe," wrote the reporter, obviously smitten. She may have appeared masculine to the French, but on the Western frontier men found Annie very attractive indeed. And though El Paso was surely no haven for a feminist, the feisty, independent frontier souls who came west to settle in places like El Paso had to admire Annie's free-spirited individuality and courage. In this respect, the lady from Boston was a lot like them.

Even the hotel extended a warm welcome to its famous guest. "The Vendome Hotel has made a special rate for the visitor which is allowable [under the terms of her wager], and efforts are being made to have her remain in town until after the fourth," reported the *Herald.* "As a New Hampshire granger would say, she is a woman of considerable many parts; in fact, all fired-up smart, and with her newspaper spirit and git up and git, she ought to greatly interest an audience."

Annie was, indeed, sure to find a receptive audience for her wild stories in a town as rough and ready as El Paso. In 1895, this was a raucous frontier town of about ten thousand, often called the "Sin City" because it was a magnet for outlaws, outcasts, and other desperados. Given its wild nature, a report that a special permit had to be coaxed from

El Paso's "horrified city fathers" to allow Annie to wear bloomers in public seems apocryphal. Its details lack the specificity to tell us whether she had returned to actual bloomers, or was instead wearing her male riding attire.

She was also the target of some good-natured fun as she arrived in El Paso. One prominent citizen, H. Godwin Mitchell, told her it was "against the laws of Texas for anyone to enter the state with a six shooter of less caliber than a 44" and that she "would be arrested if she entered the city limits in bloomer costume." It was as if Annie was just one of the guys.

No newspaper made more of a fuss over Annie during her entire trip than did the *El Paso Daily Herald*. Almost every day during her visit, small items about her doings were published and, on some days, additional lengthy features about her travels appeared, too. Annie, in turn, obliged the paper with marvelously detailed tall tales of tiger hunts in India and other adventures:

"She says the native princes prefer to hunt in the night time, which may be better understood when we consider the often fatal heat of the sun by day," reported the *Herald*. "In fact, she had to travel by night herself to escape the fierce solar rays. The hunting is on elephant back, while the natives 'shoo' up the tiger in his lair. Mister Tiger can make a break in but one direction, and as his cerulian optics are like balls of fire they make a daisy target from Winchesters from elephant back. Once in a while Mister Tiger is only wounded. Then he is just too mad for anything. He jumps right up on the elephant's prehensile ear, and starts to chewing leather in great shape. His remarks at the time are altogether too suggestive; so there is a grand rush to shoot and spear the amiable beast immediately if not sooner. The man who gets in the first effective shot 'captures the roast,' that is the tiger's lovely skin." Annie also told the *Herald* that Asia was filled with overly inquisitive natives who she had to fend off. "The plucky Bay state maiden had hard work keeping the gentle Asiatics from sticking their knives into her tires. They seemed just bent on doing this sort of thing; and she was just as bent on them not doing anything of the kind. So she wore her bike around her neck like an opera scarf when not riding it, and kept her hand close by her gun."

Annie regaled the newspaper with tales of bravery, primarily her own, at the Chinese front: "At Pen Yeng, Miss Londonderry on being released from capture started out in company with two war correspondents to get out of the country. They met several Chinese soldiers with spears who proposed to run in the whole outfit. The valiant war correspondents crawfished and weakened leaving it for Miss Londonderry to pull her gun and rattle the tar out of those Chinese soldiers." Such copy surely helped sell a lot of papers during her stay in the city, and as a result, it's no wonder Annie's lecture on the twenty-ninth was much anticipated; not only had she been around the world on a bicycle, she was practically a certified war hero.

During her stay in El Paso, however, the whispers that Annie was doing something less than riding around the world on a bicycle again caught up with her. A number of skeptics in town were expressing their doubts, too. Accusations flew that she was an outright fraud. The *El Paso Daily Times* rode to Annie's defense.

---

## MISS LONDONDERRY GENUINE—DOUBTING THOMASES CAN READ—CONFIRMATION COMES FROM BOSTON

The people of El Paso have been "taken in" so frequently that they have become skeptical of their own existence. A few weeks ago the *New York Herald* regaled them with a column write-up about the doings of "That Strange Young Man" who left El Paso fifteen months ago driving a burro and a white horse to make a tour of the world for a wager of $10,000. The people of El Paso knew that "The Strange Young Man" was a fake and as soon as many of them heard that a Miss Londonderry who started out from Boston a year ago to make a trip around the world on a bicycle for a wager of $30,000 was heading for El Paso on her return trip, quite a number of people in this city declined to believe she was genuine. When the plucky young lady arrived here, those who met and talked with her were satisfied she was no fake, but was a very bright, clever little woman. There were plenty, however, to look on her with suspicion and many of them wanted to know why the *Times* did not investigate her. And yesterday, when the *Lordsburg Liberal* arrived containing the following the Thomases won a number of converts:

"Miss Londonderry, the young lady from Boston, who claims to be making a trip around the world on a bicycle, arrived in town on a freight train from Wilcox Sunday night and left the next morning on the passenger train for Deming. The young lady may be going around the world on a wheel all right enough but most of her traveling in Arizona and New Mexico appears to be done on a car wheel instead of one of the pneumatic variety. Her bicycle was broken when she arrived here but she expected to get it repaired in Deming. She dropped her Los Angeles escort [Claude Leslie] somewhere in Arizona."

In order to let the people know positively whether Miss Londonderry was a genuine article or a fake, the *Times* sent the following to the *Boston Herald:*

"Miss Annie Londonderry is here. Claims she left Boston June 25th, 1894 to go around the world on a bicycle. Is she genuine?"

At 12:45 this morning the *Times* received the following reply:

"Annie Londonderry left Boston on such a trip. Cannot verify date." *The Herald.*

Miss Londonderry is the genuine article and there is no further occasion for doubting Thomases.

—*El Paso Daily Times,* June 29, 1895

Of course, the mere confirmation that Annie *left* Boston on such a trip didn't address the real question of how much of her trip she was making by bicycle. The *Herald* also discounted rumors that she was making the trip as a publicity scheme to promote the Sterling, but it was overly generous: "The impression is prevalent that Miss Londonderry is riding around the world as an advertisement for a certain bicycle. Such however is not the fact. The bicycle she rides she purchased with her own money and [she] is not advertising any special wheel." In any event, whatever doubts were floating around El Paso didn't put a damper on the festivities as the Fourth of July weekend approached, and Annie was at the center of it all. In one memorable instance, Will Rand, the star pitcher for the El Paso Browns baseball team, went about the town on his bicycle, dressed in bloomers, wearing "such a sweet and saint like smile that he was more than once taken for Miss Londonderry." One presumes this was meant as a compliment.

On Saturday evening, June 29, Annie gave her much-anticipated lecture at the McGinty Gardens, a building on a hilltop beyond the Southern Pacific train depot. It was here that she again lit up her lecture with the slides she had collected, and gave what might have been the best performance of her life, an act that was positively vaudevillian.

---

## MISS LONDONDERRY'S LECTURE

Our bicyclist visitor gave her lecture last Saturday night on the McGinty club grounds before an audience of about 100 people and was well received . . . The fair lecturer detailed some of her experiences . . . on reaching Chicago [she] had but three cents. She made the windy city, 1,235 miles, in six weeks [in fact, it took Annie about twice as long] . . . En route mademoiselle had to sleep in a barn, and fell through from the loft onto a horse's back. But in eighteen days [supposedly on the return from Chicago to New York] she traveled 1,030 miles and earned $835 in carrying advertisements.

When in France she was not allowed to talk French, according to the terms of her contract, which made it embarrassing for her, and landed in Paris with only seven cents in American money . . . so she earned $1,500 by carrying advertisements about town and by working in stores. Miss Londonderry was six days in riding to Marseilles [it was more like two weeks], during which time occurred the hold-up racket already detailed in the HERALD [a reference to the alleged hold-up north of Marseilles]. Ludicrous mistakes were made in trying to make people understand her necessities. Miss Londonderry tried by signs to ask for meat to eat, and a beefsteak was given her in a shoe. She wanted mushrooms and was given an umbrella. Then the cyclist tried to make a woman to understand that she wanted a place to sleep by lying down on the floor, whereupon the woman thinking it was a case of fainting threw a pitcher of water in her face. In Marseilles Miss Londonderry was treated royally so that in four days she earned $1,000. Thence she went to Egypt and Palestine, and thence to Singapore, Bombay and Calcutta. The Hindoos seemed afraid of the bicycle, thought it an evil spirit, so that the rider had to pay priests to pray for her in the temple, and a knowledge of this kept the natives at a more respectful distance. While in India, she visited a museum of freaks. She saw one man with a foot like a chicken, another with a leg shaped like that of an elephant, while there was one woman with a wen [a type of benign skin tumor] on her neck like a Saratoga trunk. Miss Londonderry was afraid that if she remained there longer she would see some such a sight as a man with an extra pair of legs dangling lightly from the sides of his neck, or some of the lovely creatures treated of in Gulliver's travels. So she beat a precipitous retreat.

Miss Londonderry went . . . to the battlefields of Wei Hai Wei where even little children were killed. She was favored with a guard by the French consul, but had the sleeve of her coat carried away by a bullet and was captured by the Chinese with two war correspondents and a doctor of divinity who were locked up in jail where neither food nor water was furnished. But for the snow water they would have died from thirst. The French consul finally sent forty gendarmes to release them . . . The lecturer said that the dead were unburied on the battle fields. The clergyman finally died from wounds he received and exhaustion from crossing a frozen river and breaking through the ice where the party came near drowning. The best they could do in the way of burial was to lay the poor man in a trench and cover him up with dead Chinese. In one shack where the party crawled in to sleep they had to brush aside the dead bodies to make a place to lie down on. . . .

[The lecture] concluded with the stereopticon exhibition with views taken by Miss Londonderry herself in Asia and elsewhere en route. The audience went away very much pleased.

—*El Paso Daily Herald,* July 2, 1895

The audience went away pleased, but did they believe half of what she said? It may not have mattered; a good evening's entertainment was had by all.

After more than a year on the road, she had reinvented herself so completely that she inhabited the character she had created with ease and comfort. One wonders whether she could even distinguish between Annie Londonderry and Annie Kopchovsky any more, or whether, indeed, she had by now shed her former identity completely.

Ironically, as Annie entertained the crowd at McGinty Gardens, another life-and-death drama—one indicative of the still wild nature of the West—was unfolding nearby at the El Paso city dump. John Wesley Hardin, one of the most infamous outlaws of the Old West, was one of El Paso's most prominent, and most feared, citizens. His outlaw days mostly behind him, Hardin was practicing law in El Paso when he fell in love with a woman by the name of Helen Buelah Mrose. As Annie lectured at the McGinty Gardens, four men—a local constable, John Selman, and three U.S. deputy marshals—all hired by Hardin, murdered Helen's husband, the desperado Martin Mrose. All the time, Hardin, with Helen at his side, sat in McGinty Gardens listening attentively to Annie's lecture.

Hardin was never arrested for the murder of Mrose, one of dozens in which he had been involved over the years, but he, too, came to a bad end just a few months later when Constable Selman killed him on August 19, 1895, in the Acme Saloon, perhaps over disparaging remarks Hardin made about Selman's son or because Hardin had failed to pay him for the murder of Mrose. In any event, while she was in El Paso for several days following her lecture, Annie likely heard about Mrose's murder, which was duly reported in the press. Whether she knew the infamous John Wesley Hardin was among her audience that night, is unknown.

Bizarrely, Annie's lecture apparently prompted Hardin to opine on the subject of the bicycle craze. The outlaw was almost always asked by the local newspapers for his comments on major civic events, but he was usually referred to only by such euphemisms as "a prominent citizen of El Paso" in the local newspapers, which treated him with kid gloves. "I am opposed to the bicycle, but I recognize the fact that opposition to the craze is very unpopular," a "well known citizen of El Paso" was reported to have told the *El Paso Daily Times* the day after Annie's lecture. "[T]he money that has been spent for and on bicycles during the last few months would pay for the schooling of every child in El Paso for three years." Hardin was, apparently, a killer with a social conscience.

\*   \*   \*

WHILE IN EL PASO, Annie also hosted groups of women at the Vendome for a series of lectures on physical development. "All those who have ridden with Miss Londonderry know of her strength and endurance and know that she is fully capable of giving ladies good advice on the subject," said the *Herald.* In fact, some of those who rode with her found the experience unforgettable. The day after her lecture, Annie was at the bicycle track where four young men took turns riding on the tandem behind her, but each vowed never do so again because, "the pace was too much for them."

Duly impressed, the local Cycle Track Association invited Annie to "make the pace" at one of the races to be held on the Fourth of July and announced that volunteers to "take the back seat" of the tandem pace bike were needed. "Those boys who are in the races will have to keep up good motion, if they want to keep tacked up to the hind end of that tandem," declared the *Herald.* One volunteer, Bart Allen, stepped forward but probably regretted it later. "The way Miss Londonderry pulled Bart Allen around the track on that tandem greatly amused the crowd," said the *Herald* the next day. "She pulled him along so fast that it was all he could do to keep his feet on the pedals."

Annie took advantage of her fame in El Paso by soliciting advertising to carry through the streets. The Cycle Track Association was one of her advertisers, and by the Fourth of July she had enough advertisements "to cover herself and her bike completely up." She cleared $52 in El Paso, $50 of which she sent back to Boston to be credited towards her earnings.

The *Herald* predicted a "tremendous welcome" when Annie returned to Boston. "Then Miss Londonderry can look over her freight train load of correspondence and select the fortunate man upon who she will see fit to bestow her fair hand. Then it will be oats, peas, beans and barley grows; and no more Colorado desert racket."

Annie left the embrace of El Paso on July 7 with $2 in her pocket and an escort of cyclists who were to accompany her "as far as their nerves will stand to ride." Her escorts took her as far as the Southern Pacific smelter—the same smelter at which she'd met her welcoming party some ten days earlier. From there, she headed north along the Santa Fe Railroad tracks alone.

# Chapter Eight

# A Whirl 'Round the World

MISS LONDONDERRY OF BOSTON HERE ON HER WAY HOME
VIA WHEEL—SHE WEARS BLOOMERS AND LIKES THEM—WAS
ON WEI-HEI-WEI BATTLEFIELD—WILL LECTURE TODAY

*Good health to all, good pleasure, good speed,
A favoring breeze—but not too high
For the homeward spin! Who rides may read
The open secret of earth and sky.*

—Anonymous, *Scribner's Magazine,* June 1895

On September 25, 1895, the bell on Annie's wager clock would toll. She left El Paso with just two and a half months to reach Chicago and claim success. The route ahead was still roughly 1,800 miles, some of it formidable country, but she was now homeward bound.

Just across the New Mexico line in the town of Anthony, Annie suffered another tire puncture. A repair kit was conveyed to her from El Paso the next morning and she "went on her way rejoicing." But the thirty-mile trip to Las Cruces was awful. She was caught in a "blinding rain" and spent the entire night exposed to the elements without shelter. Because washouts made many of the roads around Las Cruces impassable, Annie was compelled to remain in the city for several days longer than planned. She sold photographs of herself and gave a bicycle-riding exhibition to earn a little money, while also managing before heading north to ignite a controversy that raged for more than a month.

While in Las Cruces, the cyclist got into a highly publicized spat with a local newspaper editor, Allen Kelly, of the *Las Cruces Independent Democrat,* who denounced her as a fraud. When she reached Santa Fe and the town of Las Vegas, New Mexico, a couple of weeks later, Annie contended that Kelly "was on a whiz," or intoxicated, when she met him and that his real beef was "her refusal to go out buggy riding with him." Her grievance, she said, "was one that would properly come under the caption 'purely personal.' " As Annie made her way north through New Mexico and Colorado, four newspapers became caught up in a rhetorical melee about the whole affair.

"With the usual disregard for veracity, and the usual eagerness to fill up blank space, the *Independent Democrat* devotes nearly four columns to Miss Annie Londonderry, the lady cyclist who recently passed through Las Cruces," said the *Rio Grande Republican,* Kelly's crosstown rival. "While purporting to roast Miss Londonderry, the writer succeeds only in making a clown of himself. Such buffoonery is probably a relic of bear-training days, and it was thought those antics would please the readers of the *Democrat* . . . The people of our town, however, have become very tired of this kind of thing. When it is fiction they want, they know where to find something readable and less nauseating . . . While, not hoping for a reform in this line from our contemporary [Editor Kelly], we cannot but help but think how refreshing it would be to see at least an attempt made at something near the truth once in awhile."

A month after her departure, when she was already in Denver, Kelly was still feuding with Annie and trying to defend his reputation. "The alleged female person in nondescript apparel who went through here on a wheel some weeks ago claiming to have ridden around the world, did not succeed in fooling the editor of the *Las Cruces Independent Democrat* as easily as she did some others, and he exposed some of her extravagant pretensions," he wrote. "The libel is the assertion that we wanted the jade to go driving with us, but that is mitigated by the allegation that we were drunk at the time. Nobody in his sober senses would have sought the intimate society of the woman, and she appears to have realized that in order to give the appearance of probability to the one assertion it was necessary to prefix the other."

Kelly then demanded that two other newspapers, the *Las Vegas (N.M.) Optic* and the *Santa Fe New Mexican,* retract Annie's account of their encounter, which he deemed "a stupid slander." The *New Mexican* did run a letter from Kelly asking for "a correction," but only after letting loose with a barrage of personal insults by its staff. (Kelly seems to have been a regular punching bag for other editors around the state.)

"[Kelly] has been sloshing around in his editorial mudhole for over a year, butting his cranium against nearly everything and everybody in sight emitting copious quantities of splenetic nastiness," opined the *New Mexican*. Then, using words in Kelly's own letter calling on the newspaper to "be a little more careful in your personal allusions to me," the *New Mexican* urged the angry editor to be "a little more careful" himself, "whether dealing with his brethren of the press or with an unprotected female bicycle agent"—Annie.

The *Optic,* however, sought to placate Kelly and reiterated doubts about Annie's story, which it had published immediately after her departure from Las Vegas a couple of weeks earlier. Her declarations about Kelly, said the *Optic*, "had been spread all over town by Miss Londonderry and some of her new formed acquaintances. The *Optic* doubted its truth at the time, classing it with many of her traveler's yarns. Since then this paper has become assured of its falsity. Mr. Kelly, it has been learned, is not a whizzer in Miss Londonderry's sense of that term, nor does he invite strange women to take buggy rides with him. He was convinced of Miss Londonderry's unreliability, as were a large majority of those who came in contact with her, and with a fearlessness and a plainness of speech which has won him a distinguished position in New Mexico journalism, he told his convictions to the world. Miss Londonderry, unable to answer his charges, attempts to smirch his character."

Love her or hate her, Annie made great copy.

BETWEEN LAS CRUCES and Socorro, the Santa Fe tracks entered "ninety miles through the valley of death," the Jornada del Muerto, or "Journey of the Dead Man." This was the most rugged and desolate part of the famed Camino Real—the 1,800-mile highway established in the early 1600s between Mexico City and Santa Fe. The broad, flat valley had no water sources, no firewood, and no amenities for travelers. It baked in the summer sun and sizzled when massive summer thunderstorms punctuated by dazzling lightning strikes would suddenly dump several inches of water in violent downpours. Indeed, unusually heavy monsoonlike rains drenched the region in the summer of 1895, rains so heavy the main street of Silver City, a short distance north of Lordsburg and Deming, was washed away, leaving a massive ditch that remains today.

Exactly how Annie reached Socorro from Las Cruces isn't known, but it is plausible she rode most if not all of the distance, for it took her nearly a week to get there. She arrived in Socorro on Sunday, July 14, and left the same day by train, arriving in Albuquerque later that afternoon. There, she registered at the San Felipe Hotel as "Annie Londonderry, Round the World on a Wheel." The *Albuquerque Morning Democrat* was among those newspapers now focused on fixing Annie's precise mileage and reported that upon reaching that city she had traveled exactly 17,432 miles. Again, the numbers weren't consistent with previous reports, nor is it clear where the *Morning Democrat* obtained them, but it is probable that Annie provided the number, so precise that it had the ring of plausibility. Indeed, the figures were probably fairly accurate though she had not, of course, covered all those miles by bicycle.

Despite having taken the train from Socorro, Annie described the trip from El Paso as a harsh one: "I have gone hungry for days and slept out in graveyards, but that was nothing compared with my experience from El Paso here."

As early as March, when she arrived in San Francisco, Annie was in the home stretch; the closer she got to home, the more she was asked, and began to talk about, what she would do when her journey ended. "I started on account of a bet made between two sugar kings," she told a reporter from the *Morning Democrat* who met her at the hotel, "and if I make Boston by the stated time I get $30,000 and a name worth having. I intend writing a book and can easily place several editions. I started as a novice in every sense of the word. Even when on the road I had to borrow a chair to mount or get some good Samaritan to hold the machine." Annie never would write the book. She also repeated the story about hunting "the royal Bengal tiger in the jungles of India" and said the skin now adorned her mother's home in Boston, failing to mention that her mother had died several years earlier. "Since she has been on the road she has received upwards of 42,000 letters from admirers scattered all over the world," reported the *Morning Democrat*. "The heroine is just past 22 years and weighs at present 136 pounds. She is somewhat tanned from exposure but looks the picture of health."

"She is a charming, vivacious talker," wrote a reporter for the *Albuquerque Daily Citizen,* whose journalist also talked with Annie at her hotel. "The broad rim of a jaunty white straw hat trimmed with black ribbon bent and shook itself in response to her animated movements of the head when speaking. The right leg was thrown over the left, the hands crossed at the knee and from under the bottom of a plain, black skirt a shapely foot was visible. She carries a pistol on her body, and the quick penetrating flash of her dark eyes shows that she would not hesitate a moment to use it if necessary."

The *Raton Reporter,* a newspaper based some 220 miles north, reported that while in Albuquerque Annie earned $400, mostly from the sale of her photograph which she sold for 50 cents a piece. That Annie was only able to muster $52 in El Paso, where she had spent well over a week among people who embraced her enthusiastically, and $400 in Albuquerque, where she remained for a few days, again demonstrates how difficult it is to sort fact from fiction. Annie definitely did earn some coins when her Sterling was put on display in D. J. Abel's store window, however. "It looks a little worse for the wear," reported the *Daily Citizen,* "but is still in the ring. Like the rider it is thoroughly American . . . One half the so-called courageous sex of humanity would not attempt what this brave little Boston woman has accomplished."

On July 16, the eve of her departure, Annie was feted at a grand ball by the Albuquerque wheelmen. "[I]f no accident happens she will prove to the world woman's ability and woman's endurance," declared the *Morning Democrat.*

ANNIE'S NEXT destination was Santa Fe, some fifty-five miles to the northeast. She reached Cerillos on July 18 and arrived at the Claire Hotel in Santa Fe the following day, accompanied from nine miles out by members of the Capital City Cyclers Club. She lectured at the courthouse the next evening.

In Santa Fe, Annie again demonstrated her prowess as a cyclist. "Miss Londonderry . . . easily ran away from the [bicycle] club members in their dash over the city last evening," reported the *Santa Fe Daily New Mexican.* Her stay was brief. At six A.M. the next morning, she pedaled toward Las Vegas, New Mexico, and spent the night at Glorieta, a short distance east of the tiny town of Lamy.

Her trip into Las Vegas was a wet and unpleasant one. She was "a rather forlorn looking object when she dismounted in front of T. Brash's store yesterday afternoon," said the *Las Vegas Daily Optic.* When she wasn't walking, "the riding she did was on the railway bed, between the tracks, making her experience no little like that of the rider of an ox, who declared that he would rather have walked but for the grandeur of the thing."

"Miss Londonderry had on a slouched hat," the newspaper continued, "to which the rain had given all the slouch possible. The remainder of her attire consisted of a gray flannel jacket, without skirts, and large bloomer breeches of the same material. A skirt was wrapped around her shoulders for a shawl. Had she just been fished out of the Gallinas [River], she could not have been more damp, or a more perfect illustration of dampness."

Despite the miserable conditions in which she arrived, Annie still managed to be charming. Like any good showwoman, despite the difficulty of the ride or the harshness of the conditions, when there were people around to impress, Annie always put on a good show. "[A]ll the water in New Mexico showers could not dampen her pleasant manners, her sprightly expression, or the elastic ease with which she sprang into the saddle and started for the Plaza hotel," said the *Optic*.

LAS VEGAS WAS a bustling town of 2,300 souls, including prosperous Jewish immigrants from Germany. One such was Charles Ilfeld, who had come to New Mexico from Germany three decades before as a teenager, owned a prominent department store in town and engaged Annie as a "saleslady" to draw customers to a special weekend sale. Whether Annie revealed herself as a Jew to Ilfeld is unknown; there isn't a single reference to her Jewish heritage in the record of this incident and the name "Londonderry" certainly didn't betray it.

Annie lingered a few days in Las Vegas, earning some money for her work at Ilfeld's and basking in her celebrity. Her lecture, hosted by the Las Vegas Bicycle Club on July 26, was followed by a dance—admission was seventy-five cents—and a local music group, the Ramblers, played for her benefit. Annie was such a curiosity that a crowd of more than one hundred gathered at a local barbershop to watch her have her hair dressed. "Clearly," said the *Optic*, "she is a drawing card." And, just as clearly, in big towns and small, Annie's fame was now well established.

THOUGH SHE WAS welcomed warmly in Las Vegas, and the *Optic* painted a flattering portrait of her upon her arrival, calling her "sharp as a tack and as bright as a new silver dollar," the paper did an about face the day after she left town. The newspaper, now squarely in editor Alan Kelly's camp, alleged she was close to a fraud.

> Miss Annie Londonderry, jocularly referred to as Miss Boston-
> berry, who has been lionized in Las Vegas and at the hot

springs, for some days, took her departure eastward on her wheel yesterday morning, being accompanied up the road as far as Watrous by a number of local cyclists . . . The start was made from the city about 7 o'clock. Her first stop was made on Sixth Street, opposite the New England restaurant, where she breakfasted.

About 8 o'clock, accompanied by eleven local cyclists she started up the railroad track, on her way to the "Hub," where she expects to be the recipient of a few thousand dollars off the completion of her trip, and where the daring and bravery which she displayed on many occasions, as was related in her speeches, will be duly applauded . . .

Many have expressed doubts as to Miss Londonderry's having made a trip around the world at all, from the fact that nothing had been seen of her trip in the great dailies. [This was not true. Many major newspapers had reported on Annie's journey.] The *Optic* has been shown a copy of *The Bearings,* a weekly cycling periodical, published at Chicago, and very largely given to advertisements.

In the issue of May 10th, 1895 is a page given to Miss Londonderry and the wheel she rides, the opening sentence of which is: "Miss Londonderry, the first woman to ride around the world on a bicycle, is back: her mount was a gold and ivory Sterling." From that on, the account is part Londonderry and part Sterling . . .

A map of her route is published, showing the trip incomplete from San Francisco to Chicago. The letter press says, "she should stop at Havre, Marseilles, Colombo, Singapore, Hong Kong, Shanghai, Nagasaki, Kobe, and Yokohama, and then return to America." These are all seaports, and the map of the trip follows this description, showing her to have sailed from Boston to Hong Kong, with the insignificant wheeling across France from Havre to Marseilles. From Hong Kong she wheeled the short distance to Shanghai, sailed thence to Nagasaki, sailed from there to Port Arthur, wheeled around Corea, sailed to Japan, which she crossed, and thence sailed to San Francisco, lacking 700 or 800 miles of being in the neighborhood of Siberia . . .

The *Optic*'s conclusion of the whole matter is that she is a

plucky little woman making a trip to advertise the Sterling bicycle; that she has been around the world, wheeling but little
and riding a good deal on trains and ships; and that, like
many travelers, she has a vivid imagination, the incidents of
travel growing in number and startlingness the further she
gets from the scene of their supposed location.

The bicycle boys in particular, and the community in general, treated Miss Londonderry well, and the *Optic* is glad of
it; for, no doubt, when she comes to exercise her inventive genius about us, the recollection of her pleasant treatment will
cause the inventions to be of an agreeable character.

If Annie ever learned of this shot in the back, she never betrayed it,
but she would have been grateful for the attention. Controversy served
her purposes just as well as raves.

From Las Vegas, she traveled sixty-five miles north through Springer,
Maxwell City, and arrived in Raton, New Mexico, near the Colorado border, on Tuesday, July 30 at around four P.M., escorted by a group of local
cyclists who had ridden out to meet her. Annie checked in to the Gate
City Hotel and lectured at the opera house in Raton that evening, describing a trip "full of adventure and at times attended with danger," and later
gave a bicycle-riding exhibition.

"Her account of the Japan-China war was a wonderful revelation of
the cruelties that were practiced," reported the *Raton Range*. Annie, by
now, had also apparently become something of a military analyst. "She
stated that Japan won, not because her soldiers could fight, but for the
reason that the Chinese would not. The ordinary Chinese soldier carried
an umbrella and fan, and would surrender on the first opportunity that
presented itself." The cyclist also told her audience in Raton that her trip
through California was without incident, curiously leaving out the accident she suffered near Stockton, which she had earlier dramatized and
exaggerated in San Jose as a life-threatening catastrophe. There appears to
be no rhyme or reason to how she decided which stories to tell on any
given occasion.

ANNIE LEFT RATON at 8:00 A.M. on Wednesday, July 31, escorted by a Mr. D.
Leahy. It is only about twenty miles from there to Trinidad, Colorado,
which she reached about 1:30 P.M. with yet another delegation of cyclists

who had ridden ten miles to Morley, a tiny outpost just north of the New Mexico–Colorado state line, to meet her. To get to Morley, Annie crossed over the Raton Pass, which at 7,834 feet would have been a tough climb in thin air, though a toll road built in the mid-1860s facilitated the mountainous passage. The Santa Fe Railroad also ran through the pass. Did she cross the pass by train or bike? Although it's impossible to say for sure, the presence of escorts makes it likely that she made this climb on her Sterling.

Once at Trinidad, Annie was escorted through streets "thronged with people to see the plucky young lady" to the Columbian Hotel. "[E]laborate preparations" were underway by the local wheelmen for "a grand ball" to be given in her honor at the Jaffa Opera House, where Annie was to lecture the following night. The charge for admission was twenty-five cents for ladies and fifty cents for men.

Despite the warm welcome, doubts from the local press about Annie's journey followed her to Trinidad and increased after she left. On the same page that the *Trinidad Daily News* announced her arrival, it ran a separate item quoting the views of the *Las Vegas Daily Optic* that her undertaking was something much less than she claimed. On August 2, the day Annie departed to head for La Junta, the *Trinidad Daily News* reprinted an article about her that had appeared more than a year earlier, on July 3, 1894, in the *New York World*. When they read it, the residents of Trinidad learned for the first time that Annie was a married woman, that her real name was Kopchovsky, not Londonderry, and that she had three children at home in Boston. Many were likely shaking their heads in disbelief that the woman who had been in their midst was not at all who she appeared to be.

ON A DIRECT LINE, it is about seventy-five miles from Trinidad to Pueblo. But Annie traveled there via La Junta, almost twice as far. Why? The answer is quite simple: the Santa Fe tracks ran that way. Again, because no one else was present and she didn't say, it is impossible to know how she reached these points. The mere presence of the railway, however, doesn't necessarily mean she took the train. Following the tracks was one way to keep from getting lost in the vast expanses of the west. Annie took six days to reach Pueblo, spent one night there, then rode the forty-three miles to Colorado Springs on August 9. She was on hand the following morning at H. Weber's bicycle store, to draw customers.

On August 11, Annie made Palmer Lake, a small town along the Santa

Fe Railroad route about halfway between Colorado Springs and Denver, but not before a severe rainstorm had overtaken her. She arrived soaked, with a "broken machine," though the nature of its mechanical problem wasn't described. From there, she sent two telegrams to the Denver Wheel Club saying she would wait out the storm in Palmer Lake, and would reach Denver, some fifty miles north, the next day.

Annie did arrive in Denver on the morning of August 12, having covered the distance from Palmer Lake in four hours. Members of the club met her at Littleton. "Miss Londonderry when she was seen by a *News* representative last night was found to be a young lady who looked as if she might be an athlete, with coal black eyes, and a face tanned brown as a nut," reported the *Denver Daily News*. In Denver, Annie stayed at the Glenarm Hotel for nearly a week. Typically, when she lingered, it was to muster her energy and make plans for the trip ahead (as in San Francisco), because she was being celebrated (as in Marseilles and El Paso), or because there were good opportunities to earn a few dollars or soak in the glamour of a foreign capital (as in Paris). It appears she remained so long this time because she was ill. According to the *Omaha World Herald,* Annie had contracted pneumonia in Denver and was "confined to her bed for two weeks." But, eight days later, she headed for Cheyenne, yet again by means uncertain.

From there, according to the *Omaha World Leader,* Annie "followed the Union Pacific tracks to [Omaha]." She didn't exactly follow the Union Pacific tracks east as had been reported, however; she was on the train. According to the *Cheyenne Daily Sun-Leader* of August 20, "Miss Annie Londonderry, the lady cyclist who claims to have been around the world on a wheel, left the city before daylight this morning, taking the 2:30 train from here." After her departure from Cheyenne, there isn't a single report of Annie's whereabouts until her arrival in Columbus, Nebraska, nearly four hundred miles east, just two days later.

The day after she reached Columbus, Annie cycled to Fremont, forty-five miles further east, and spent the night at the New York Hotel. Said the *Fremont Daily Tribune:* "The wager made by two wealthy sugar merchants of Boston will be decided in a matter of days and the man who bet she could do it will be the winner, and so will she."

"The roads were very muddy yesterday and today and she was compelled to take the railroad tracks," reported the newspaper. "Under certain circumstances she is permitted to accept transportation but she has first to wire the circumstances to the parties who had wagered the money and get their permission." Annie had added yet another new provision to the purported wager, one apparently used to explain her passage across most of Nebraska by train. And, as usual, she attracted a crowd. The *Tribune* continued, "At the hotel this morning there were a large number of wheelmen present to talk with her. Her bicycle had on it 50 or 60 ribbons, badges of as many wheel clubs in different towns through which she passed and which she will retain as souvenirs."

Though the *Tribune* gave a thoroughly accurate list of the places she had actually been on her journey, Annie got a little more creative with the *South Sioux City (Nebraska) Star.* According to this paper, Annie had cycled in "France, Italy, Turkey, North Africa, Egypt, India, China and Japan. Her cyclometer registers 9,400 miles."

On August 24, in the company of several wheelmen from Fremont, Annie rode to Omaha and checked in to the Dellone Hotel.

## A WHIRL 'ROUND THE WORLD–MISS LONDONDERRY OF BOSTON HERE ON HER WAY HOME

Miss Londonderry arrived in Omaha yesterday afternoon with 9,400 miles of [her] journey completed and with nearly thirty days in which to finish the remainder of 500 miles . . .

To a reporter she said:

"I started to wear skirts and rode a drop frame, but I soon discarded the skirts and secured a diamond frame. I have been gone nearly fourteen months, have visited a dozen or more countries, been thrown into association with all classes and kinds of men, and have yet to receive an insult. I find it is not the bloomers, but the woman wearing them, that calls out the insults." . . .

Miss Londonderry weighed 105 pounds when she started from Boston, and upon reaching Chicago . . . she was reduced to eighty-five pounds. She tips the scales now at 140 pounds and her muscles, so she says, are like iron.

—*Omaha World Herald,* August 25, 1895

On the night of August 25, Annie gave another of her colorful lectures, adding some new twists and turns to her ever-evolving story.

---

## CHARMING LECTURE

---

The Omaha Wheel club was entertained yesterday in a novel manner, and in such an interesting manner that Omaha will not be surprised to see a dozen or more of young cyclists, fired with enthusiasm, starting out upon trips, with the intention of rivaling the adventures of the young lady who was the prominent feature of yesterday's entertainment . . . The entertainment was termed a lecture, but it did not follow the usual course of that sometimes wearisome class of entertainments. Miss Londonderry talked. And it was the kind of a talk in which her listeners were as much the founders of ideas as the speaker. She told tales of her adventures, not connected, but as drawn out by some question among her audience, so that the lecture had more the appearance and the interest of a personal conversation, and it proved highly delightful to the members of the club.

She told of her trip through India where she was compelled to wear over her bicycle costume the loose cloth in vogue in the country. In India, the best roads were through the cemeteries, the roads being miles in length, but it was a crime punishable by death or torture to ride through a cemetery, as one would cast a shadow on the grave of the dead. But Indian religion, like many others, was susceptible to a modification, and a ten rupee piece carried Miss Londonderry through several of the cemeteries.

In China, she describes the late war as not a fight, but a slaughter. For miles she rode through fields of dead . . . This was in the winter, so that putrifaction [sic] had not yet set in, but she says she cannot wonder that cholera holds sway in such a country. Even in times of piping peace the streets of Canton and other large cities swarm with vermin and filth . . .

In this country she has been compelled to do manual labor, such as sawing wood, milking cows or general farm
labor, while in foreign lands she was always afforded lighter
employment. . . .

—*Omaha World Herald,* August 26, 1895

By now Annie was a bona fide celebrity, and in Omaha local merchants were ready to capitalize on her presence and her ability to draw a
crowd. An advertisement in *The Omaha Evening Bee* of August 26 announced that "the greatest lady bicycle rider," her bicycle, and her "passports and credentials" would be on display at the Boston Store, a
department store in downtown Omaha. There, Annie would "give sensible wheel talk," and "sell handkerchiefs with her autograph on." To add
to the attraction, the store promised to give away a bicycle every evening
to a lucky customer. Annie spent a few more days in that city and, on the
evening of August 31, the night before her departure, the Omaha Wheelmen sponsored bicycle races for her benefit. As at previous stops, it was
not unusual for local wheelmen, to organize events, whether lectures,
balls or races, to raise money to help Annie continue on her way, testimony to both her fame and her ability to win people over with her wit
and enthusiasm.

BY THE NEXT DAY, September 1, Annie had passed through the small town
of Missouri Valley, Iowa, about twenty miles due north of Omaha, in an
uncharacteristically quiet way. Reported the *Missouri Valley Times,* "Miss
Annie Londonderry quietly wheeled into our city . . . from Omaha, and
were it not that her wheel had a large number of pieces of silk ribbon
hanging from one part of it, not one in twenty would have taken any special note of her incoming or outgoing from the Valley. Yet, the fact remains, she is a strangely unique, and, at present, noted character . . . She
looks fresh and healthy . . . She has never been ill on the road. She stayed
at the Cheney and started for Chicago this noon."

Annie's route toward Chicago through Iowa took her through Ames
and toward the town of Gladbrook in east-central Iowa, about halfway
between the two major railroad routes that ran east–west across Iowa: the

Chicago & North Western Railroad (C.&N.W.) and the Chicago Rock Island line. Now riding alone, she reached Marshalltown on September 3 and stayed at the Tremont Hotel.

Despite her quiet passage through Missouri Valley, Annie figured out what the people of Iowa wanted and, as she had with the French, gave them plenty of it. "The people of the peerless State of Iowa she had found to be the most hospitable of any during her journeyings," said the *Marshalltown Evening Times Republican,* noting that "[t]he cyclometer on her wheel registered 10.052 miles when she arrived in this city . . . To show her endurance and ability, she made the run from Ames to this city [about fifty miles] yesterday against the strong wind, leaving there at 8:15 A.M. and arriving here at 4:10."

In Marshalltown, Annie related an experience very similar to one with which she had regaled the French newspapers many months earlier, about nearly being run over by a train in New York State, only this time enhanced for local effect. "Last Sunday [September 1], while riding on the C.&N.W. right of way between Council Bluffs and Crescent, Miss Londonderry met with the closest call to death during the journey," wrote the *Times Republican.* "The fast mail suddenly came around a curve without whistling. There was no time to dismount, but with presence of mind she threw herself to one side, her wheel following, just in time to escape being struck. A farmer who was sitting on a fence nearby and with whom she had previously asked about the distance, was nearly scared to death, but managed to venture: 'Yer came near finishin' yer trip, didn't you?' " Was the story another of Annie's creative inventions? September 1 was the same day Annie had arrived in Missouri Valley, and the local paper there, a weekly, made no mention of the incident in its September 5 edition.

Shortly after leaving Marshalltown the next day, on a road near the towns of Tama and Gladbrook, Annie *did* suffer a serious accident that threatened to end her quest just as she was nearing the finish line. Speeding downhill, she fell and broke her wrist, though she later, not surprisingly, gave two different accounts of the accident. In Clinton, Iowa, a few days afterward she told the *Clinton Herald,* "Yes, my fall near Tama was a bad one and it is wonderful I was not more seriously injured. I was coming down a hill when my chain slipped off. A farmer was coming up the hill. I asked him to turn out a little so I could pass but his only answer was curses. I tried to stop my wheel by catching hold of the front wheel, but it struck a rut and I was thrown over the handlebars, my hand catching in the spokes and breaking my arm at the wrist. The pain was something terrible and after riding a couple of miles I got off and bound it up as best I could and rode on sixteen miles further until I reached Tama where I had it dressed." But, when she returned to New York a few weeks later, Annie said she had collided with "a drove of pigs" that was crossing the road as she sped downhill. That she broke her wrist is certain, however; she was still wearing the cast when seen by a *New York Times* reporter shortly after her return to the East Coast a few weeks later. However the accident occurred, Annie claimed in the *Cedar Rapids Evening Gazette:* "the farmer responsible for her injury did nothing to assist her and it is probable that the matter will be taken up by the L.A.W. Wheelmen in this city are highly indignant." In a moment of pique, she turned on the good people of the peerless state of Iowa for not making enough of a fuss over her injury. "If I had broken my arm in France, instead of out there in prosy old Iowa," a miffed Annie later said, "I would have been showered with money and attention."

Wrist now in a cast, Annie came to Cedar Rapids accompanied by Charlie Bell and Tom Bray and other riders who met her near the town of Fairfax, west of Cedar Rapids. "She was walking and had started from Belle Plaine at midnight Thursday [September 5]," said the *Gazette.* "She is at the Grand today and will leave the city with an escort some time tomorrow morning."

She rode out of Cedar Rapids on Sunday, September 8, spent the night in Lowden, and arrived in Clinton, on the Mississippi River, on the ninth. The *Clinton Herald* reported that Annie was required by the wager to travel 10,000 miles by wheel and noted that her cyclometer now read 10,200. This is peculiar because, in Omaha, two newspapers reported the cyclometer read 9,400 miles, and Omaha is less than 400 miles from Clinton. This discrepancy cannot be reconciled unless the cyclometer had been tampered with. With her arm in a cast, Annie surely did not ride 400 miles out of her way en route to Clinton. Perhaps "adjusting" the cyclometer was within her mechanical skills; it was not an easy task, but it certainly would not have been out of character. (In San Francisco, where the cyclometer reportedly read 7,280 miles, Annie had, in actuality, probably ridden a total of perhaps 3,000 miles, *including* 1,200 miles on her Columbia bicycle from Boston to Chicago.) To complicate matters even further, she later wrote that she had ridden precisely 9,604 miles by wheel on her journey. If the purported wager required her to ride at least 10,000 miles as many reports suggested, why would she sabotage that by saying she had covered 9,604 miles by wheel? Thus, in the end, she claimed to have ridden *fewer* miles than the cyclometer measured *before* she had even reached the end of the road in Chicago. It was pure Annie: neither the mileage on her cyclometer, the money she reportedly earned en route, or her stories added up, yet she seemed perfectly unperturbed about it.

"MISS LONDONDERRY . . . talked most entertainingly of her trip and her experiences, some of which are enough to make one's hair stand on end," declared the *Clinton Herald* of Annie's visit there. "She went first to Chicago and then started towards the rising sun. She reached Sagon, China, *[sic]* which is two degrees below the equator."

"And by the way," Annie said to the reporter, "that's the place you want to go to ride a wheel. You are not bothered with cold feet and you have no trouble in 'warming up' to get in condition to ride."

Of her broken wrist Annie said, "It has pained me a great deal ever since, but I shall be able to reach Chicago all right, and as I have only $100 to make until I have secured the required $5,000, I am not worrying in the least about not winning the wager. The doctors tell me I shall probably have to have my arm broken over after my arrival in Chicago, but I don't care for that so long as I arrive there before the time is up and succeed in winning the wager."

Though her critics were many, some were still swallowing her story hook, line and sinker, a testament to her charm, showmanship, and good luck. "It was never believed she would come anywhere near winning the wager," opined the *Herald,* "but she will and in so doing she will have accomplished a most wonderful feat and one which it is doubtful whether any other living person could . . . It is to be hoped that Miss Londonderry will some time write a book of her travels, for it would be one of the most interesting ever written."

On Tuesday, September 10, Annie left Clinton with two cyclists, Roy Upton and Clarence Rumble, for the final leg of her idiosyncratic and improbable journey. By the following morning they had passed through Rochelle, Illinois, nearly halfway to Chicago.

## HAS CIRCLED THE GLOBE—MISS LONDONDERRY PASSES THROUGH ROCHELLE WEDNESDAY MORNING

Miss Annie Londonderry . . . who has the proud distinction of being the only woman who has circled the globe on a wheel (that is the land portion thereof) passed through Rochelle Wednesday [September 11] forenoon, en route for Chicago, taking breakfast at Allen's restaurant . . . The wheel ridden by the young lady . . . is an ordinary stock wheel and has stood the journey remarkably well.

Miss Londonderry was well-equipped in point of education to make the trip, as she speaks six languages fluently. However, this, together with her wheel and a large share of American pluck constituted her only equipment . . . Miss Londonderry was dressed in knickerbockers and sweater, and carried a revolver, flask, and cup.

—*Rochelle Register,* September 13, 1895

As Annie's party closed in on Chicago on September 11, in Rochelle, about eighty miles to the west, the weather was oppressively hot. Temperatures at midday were in the mid nineties, the humidity soared, and the newspapers were reporting deaths in Chicago from heat prostration. Had it not been for a strong, steady southwest wind, the death toll may have been higher. Exactly where Annie spent the final night of her around-the-world journey wasn't reported, but it was somewhere east of Rochelle.

On September 12 at around one o'clock in the afternoon, she laid her wheel down at the Wellington Hotel in Chicago "with a thankful sigh. Mrs. Kapshowsky [sic] (her real name) . . . looked far from feeling well as she claimed to be. In fact she looked a sick woman. Her arm was broken and bound in a sling, and the last 300 miles were ridden with it in that condition," wrote the *American Wheelman.*

This rare reference to Annie by her real name seemed to bring down the curtain on her one-woman show. She was, once again, Annie Kopchovsky, the Jewish working mother of three who for the last fifteen months had played the flamboyant and provocative Annie Londonderry on the world stage.

Surprisingly, Annie's journey ended quietly. Neither the *Chicago Tribune* nor the *Chicago Daily News* appear to have so much as mentioned it (though the *Omaha World Herald* declared two days later, on page one, "Miss Londonderry Wins"); there was no parade (nor would there be one in New York or Boston); and no big-shot politicians were on hand to greet her. But she was given "a rousing reception by the wheelmen of the city under the auspices of the Sterling Cycle Club." Annie, Rumble, and Upton were also met in Chicago by representatives of the Sterling Cycle Works, "because of Miss Londonderry's fame, because of Roy's reputation for being the speediest local rider, and because of Mr. Rumble's success as a [Sterling] dealer," according to the *Clinton* (Iowa) *Semi-Weekly Age*. The *Age* also suggested that Annie did not raffle her Sterling, as she had contemplated to make up the balance of the $5,000. Rather, reported the newspaper, she was given a new wheel and $400 in exchange for the Sterling she was riding, which the company wanted for advertising purposes. That money purportedly put her over the top of the $5,000 she was required to earn under the terms of the wager.

BY SEPTEMBER 17, 1895, Annie was back east and her first stop was New Brunswick, New Jersey, to visit her younger sister Rosa. Although she had sold her Sterling in Chicago, she made one more dramatic entrance by wheel, perhaps the one she traded for the Sterling, "bowl[ing] down the long hill that leads to the Albany street bridge" before dismounting "in man fashion." Though she told a local newspaper she had two weeks to get to Boston to win the wager, the fifteen months would expire in just one.

When challenged that round the world walkers and cyclists "passed through New Brunswick on an average of three a day for the past six months," Annie "flared up, got very red in the face and denounced all the others as fakirs." She then produced an autograph book with signatures she had collected along her route as proof of her claim. She told of being held up on the California border by two thieves, "spoke fluently of sickening scenes on the battle fields of China," and admitted only to covering "over 4,000 miles by rail and water," technically correct but a vast understatement. In New York, she gave an interview to the *New York Recorder*: "With her left arm in a sling and her cheeks bronzed from exposure, Miss Annie Londonderry sat in the house of a friend at 208 East Broadway and chatted about her trip around the world on a bicycle. She is a remarkable young woman. This rash and foolhardy trip was, she says, the outcome of a discussion between Dr. Albert Reeder and John Dowe, a wealthy businessman."

"I met with a royal reception everywhere during my trip," Annie told the *Recorder,* "but I wouldn't take it again for $150,000. I have received the purse of $10,000 and never was $15,000 [the $10,000 purse plus the $5,000 earned en route] earned in so hard a manner. I go to Boston on Sunday and while there will arrange for the publication of my book. Then I will return here."

ON THE MORNING of September 24, fifteen months to the day after climbing aboard her Columbia bicycle in front of the State House, Annie arrived back home in Boston and was reunited with Max and their children. News that she had finished her trip was reported as far away as Milan and Honolulu. In Tama, Iowa, near the site where she had broken her wrist just a couple of weeks before, the *Tama Free Press* reported that Annie "[won] her race," despite the "considerable trouble and pain" of her injury. The *El Paso Daily Herald,* one of the cyclist's biggest boosters, reported the completion of her journey and noted, for the first time, and no doubt to the surprise of many in El Paso, that "Annie Londonderry is not her real name."

A few murmurs about Annie's authenticity continued to surface. In November 1895, H. D. McIlrath, the Chicago man who, with his wife, had set out in the spring to wheel around the world, and who sought for his wife the distinction of being the first woman to do so, commented on Annie to a Yokohama newspaper. Calling her "the globe-girdling sign board," McIlrath said that, while in Yokohama, Annie claimed to have appealed for help from the American consul general, a Colonel McIvor, and, having been turned down, had received aid from the French consul. Said McIlrath: "But as both gentlemen positively declare they never saw the lady I am inclined to believe [her] story is on a par with her visionary visits to Siberia prisons, Chinese and Japanese battles, etc." The McIlraths spent three years traveling the globe on their bicycles, returning home in 1898.

There is no record of Annie's reunion with Max, Mollie, Libbie, and Simon, all of whom must have changed considerably since she'd left. Libbie, who had turned four during her mother's absence, and Simon, who had turned three, were so young when Annie disappeared that they probably now had no memory of their mother. They may have wondered who the stranger was in their midst.

But for thousands of people she met along her route—Jessie Padman of South Bend; the Klinkenbergs of Kendallville, Indiana; C. J. Appel of Rochester, Mr. and Mrs. Victor Sloan of Paris; Mark Johnson of San Francisco; Art Bennett of Yuma; John Wesley Hardin of El Paso; Clarence Rumble and Roy Upton of Clinton, Iowa; and surely editor Allen Kelly of Las Cruces, to name but a few—and countless others who read about her and who were pulling for her—Annie's journey created memories of a smart, vivacious, and intensely charismatic woman of tremendous will, memories that no doubt lasted a lifetime as they did for Annie.

When the curtain came down on her traveling road show, she wasn't quite through with the limelight. Her trip had been one giant step on a path toward a life as an independent, freethinking woman, a woman who saw herself in every way as the equal of men. And just six weeks after it ended, she would prove it again.

# Chapter Nine

# Capture of a Very Novel "Wild Man"

### THE SUNDAY WORLD'S "NEW WOMAN" FINDS THE "FIEND" WHO HAS TERRORIZED WORCESTER COUNTY, MASS. SURPRISING DISCOVERIES WHICH BAFFLED FARMERS AND OFFICERS

On silent steed of steel she rides
Past nature's beauteous bowers;
Life's moments spent while thus she glides,
To her seem sweetest hours.

—M.S., *The American Jewess,* June 1896

On the night of October 26, 1895, six weeks after Annie put her bike down in Chicago, a stylish and enterprising young woman arrived in Boston by train from New York City, having been dispatched earlier in the day by her editors at the *New York Sunday World.* After arriving in Boston, the young woman went to Young's Hotel in the city's Back Bay section and registered as Nellie Bly. She was in Boston en route to the small town of Royalston, some seventy miles west, where, over the preceding weeks, a lanky young farmer named Charley Richardson had been the victim of a series of events so mysterious and so chilling that entire communities were held in fear.

It all began in late July 1895, when Richardson was riding in his farm wagon and a wheel fell off, throwing the farmer to the ground and injuring him. The wheel nuts had been removed, and Richardson later discovered them in his barn with a note warning him not to try and find out who had done the deed. Some days later, he found his rakes and pitchforks lashed to the high beams of his barn.

Perhaps it was all a practical joke. But with the approach of Halloween, as the night air in the hills around Royalston turned chill and darkness set in early, the harassment escalated. First, one of Richardson's sheep had its back broken. Then, on Monday, October 21, a heavy clock pendulum was thrown through his bedroom window, narrowly missing him as he slept. The next day, the farmer's cows disappeared from his pasture. His nerves frayed by the mysterious events of the previous days and weeks, he took a pistol and five cartridges and headed into the woods to search for his livestock. Noticing smoke in the distance, he walked slowly and cautiously toward the source, where he saw a man huddled by a fire in a small clearing.

Richardson's next step snapped a twig, and the man by the fire abruptly stood up and looked around. He was gaunt, about six feet tall, with a scraggly gray beard that stretched to his waist, sunken cheeks, and eyes that "blazed fiercely." Clothed in tatters, he looked more like a creature of the woods than a man.

Before Richardson could act, the "wild man," as he came to be known, drew a pistol and fired a shot that ripped through the farmer's coat near the hip. The wild man then fled into the woods, with Richardson in hot pursuit. The latter fired five times but missed. "I thought the man, by his appearance, must have been 70 or 75 years old," Richardson told the *Fitchburg Daily Sentinel.* "But when he began to run he went like a man of 21."

After the shooting, Richardson took his mother, who lived on the farm with him, to Athol for her safety. When he returned home about five P.M. with a friend, Leslie Woodbury, who had agreed to help search for the wild man, he went into the kitchen and lit the stove to make tea. The stove exploded, sending Richardson careering across the room. He was unharmed but soon discovered that not only had gunpowder been placed in his stove, but his pantry shelves had been emptied. The wild man had struck again. Later that same evening the young farmer was shot at again, this time during a corn-husking bee at his barn. The bullet passed through his hat, slightly burning his forehead, and shattered a windowpane. Several other people at the farm heard the shot fired that night, but none saw it. Richardson was sure the strange man he had chased through the woods was responsible for all the attacks.

As word of the violent events spread, panic gripped the residents of Royalston and neighboring Athol. On Thursday, October 24, a state detective identified only as Murray and the Athol deputy sheriff, Roswell L. Doane, a stocky, balding man with an impressive handlebar mustache, put together a posse of about two dozen well-armed men and led them into the woods to look for the wild man. The posse returned empty-handed after four hours—but in the meantime, the Richardson barn was set ablaze.


BY THIS TIME, news of the Massachusetts wild man had reached Boston and New York, where newspaper editors spied a story sure to find a wide audience. On October 24 and again on the twenty-fifth, the *Boston Daily Globe* carried stories describing the assaults against Richardson, the earlier one on the front page. The reporter, who had traveled to Royalston to investigate, suggested that a "little gray-bearded man" was the "probable miscreant" and reported the unsuccessful efforts to capture the "marauder."

In New York City, at the Park Row offices of the *New York World,* the crown jewel in Joseph Pulitzer's newspaper empire, two telegrams from Boston, both dated October 25, landed on the desk of Morrill Goddard, the *World's* Sunday editor. They outlined a story with all the elements of the sensational features that were a staple of the Pulitzer papers and their competitors. The first telegram read, "We have had two or three reports of the wild man's doing around Royalston, & farmers are surely in state of abject terror. From what I can learn, there is material for picturesque story. Have mailed clipping from local story of latest Escapade." The Western Union telegram was signed "Sanger."

Apparently concerned that Goddard might not have gotten the first telegram, or that it might not have conveyed enough urgency, Sanger sent a second telegram, this one via the Postal Telegraph Cable Company: "Athol Mass. Farmers are panic stricken over antics of supposed wild man. Men armed to the teeth whenever they leave home. Looks like good material for Sunday Special. Shall I go for it? This has no connection with Connecticut wild man. Sanger."

But Goddard did not tell Sanger "to go for it." Instead, on Saturday, October 26, the editor dispatched a young female reporter from New York, the one who, later that evening, registered at Young's as Nellie Bly. But the woman assigned to cover the story of the Massachusetts wild man was not Nellie Bly. She was, of course, Annie Kopchovsky.

As described in the nail-biting feature she wrote a week later for the *New York Sunday World* under the byline "The New Woman," Annie announced to Sheriff Doane that she had been sent by the paper "to capture the desperado" and convinced him to let her join a second posse that formed on Sunday, October 27 to track down the man who had been tormenting Charley Richardson.

Annie's dramatic piece about the capture of the wild man consumed almost a full page in the November 3, 1895, edition of the *World*. It included a sketch of an intrepid young woman armed with a pistol—and sporting dainty gloves—leading a large group of men wielding axes, pitchforks, and other weapons. She set the scene with flair: "One has a strange feeling in stepping into a town where all is mystery and excitement, where men are patrolling the streets armed to the teeth, and where women peer nervously at every passer-by. Where you hear frightful accounts of the murderous doings of a mysterious somebody."

Annie followed Sheriff Doane in a carriage as he set out to form his posse. "At every farmhouse farmers, all well armed, would join our party until a small army was traveling the narrow, winding, rocky road through a bleak barren country," she wrote. "Occasionally we passed a small church. But there were no divine services at them, even in Massachusetts. Everybody—pastors, deacons and brethren—was on the hunt." When they reached Royalston, everyone gathered around as Charley Richardson "carefully described his foe. At last all was ready for the hunt."

The group divided into squads. Fortuitously, though a dozen reporters were on hand, according to Annie, she was the only one who ended up in Charley Richardson's squad, and she engaged him in conversation along the way: "I sounded him on courage and found that he did not possess as much of the stuff as the knights of old. In fact, he was nothing but a timid boy."

When Annie quizzed Richardson about what books he liked to read, he replied that he was "fond of 'these wild Western stories where men shoot and raise Cain.' " She asked "if he had taken it into his mind to do wild things like the men in the books," and he said "sometimes he wanted to be a cowboy or a mountain hunter or a detective." Finally, Annie wondered aloud if he "was not tired of life on the farm." Richardson's response, that he "longed for life" in the West, "was about all I wanted," Annie declared. "I put two and two together, and with the facts I had put down out of the stories told me [about the wild man] I soon deduced the theory that Charles Richardson was the wild man who had been shooting at and attacking himself and appearing that he was frightened, and at the same time making idiots out of his neighbors."

Her theory was bolstered by some clever forensic work. Annie noted that the bullet holes in Richardson's coat and hat were made by a .22-cal-iber pistol. When Doane later showed her Richardson's pistol, it was a .22. She also noticed that the hole in Richardson's coat "ranged down-ward," though the farmer had said the bullet had come from below, and she spotted a powder burn on the coat, indicating a shot at very close range. "I asked the boy about this," wrote Annie.

" 'How far was the wild man from you when he fired?' I asked.

" 'About twenty paces.'

"This was a 'dead give away.' Anyone with any knowledge of gun or pistol shots knows that there could be no powder burn at that distance."

When Annie shared her theory with Sheriff Doane, he was inclined to agree, but, he said, he "would not dare tell the Royalston farmers our opinion: 'They would not believe us, and would most probably try to handle us roughly.' "

The next day Doane questioned Richardson at the district attorney's office in Worcester and, according to Annie, told the farmer that he sus-pected Richardson himself was the wild man. Per her account:

" 'How do you know?' asked the boy in a tremulous voice.

" 'Do you remember the young lady who was searching with us yes-terday?' asked the Sheriff. Charles did remember.

" 'Well, she is from New York, and is a mind-reader. She told us all.' "

Richardson then broke down and confessed, allowing Annie to brag, "I solved the mystery and found the Wild Man." Doane, she claimed, ac-knowledged his "grateful appreciation" in a letter to her: "Please accept my thanks for your valuable suggestions and services and your great courage. R. L. Doane, Deputy Sheriff." Annie had pulled the mask off the vicious wild man, revealing the scared young man underneath.

THE DENOUEMENT of the wild-man story was not reported in local news-papers quite the same way as it was in the *World*. One of them, the *Worcester West Chronicle* of Athol, questioned Richardson's guilt, opining, somewhat obtusely, that "the difficulty in [the] situation thus far, is be-cause the lack of other than circumstantial evidence. . . . The peace and safety of the community demanded a solution of the present mystery as far as possible by local investigation. With the broadest charity and the kindest sympathy, the public mind would rest more easily in a verdict of mental aberration, than to be confronted with the fact of the presence of a demon haunting our dwellings and crossing our pathway."

Most accepted that Richardson had invented the wild man himself, perhaps to scare his mother into selling the family farm so he could pursue his dream of life in the West. They balked, however, at making Annie the heroine of the story. For one thing, she had not been the first to suspect the young farmer. On October 25, two days before her arrival in Athol, a story in the *Fitchburg Daily Sentinel* had reported neighbors' suspicions that Richardson and the wild man were one and the same: "There are . . . Royalston people who take very little stock in these 'wild man' stories. It is said that Charley Richardson has for some time wanted to move away from his dismal home, but his mother has objected. . . . He has up to the present time been accepted as the soul of truthfulness. It would be a stranger mystery still if it were discovered that Charley had fired the shots himself, set fire to his own barn, blown up his own stove with powder, and all at the risk of his own life." After his identity was revealed, the *Athol Transcript* noted, "the 'Wild Man' turns out to be as has been suspected for two or three days past."

Annie's starring role in provoking the man's confession also strains credulity. Richardson admitted his guilt on the morning of October 28 to Detective Murray and Sheriff Doane after being questioned "sharply," according to the *Athol Transcript,* and the first local newspaper stories about the confession appeared the next day. It is possible that either Annie, Doane, Murray, or perhaps all of them working together had put the pieces together on the twenty-seventh. But if Annie's story in the *World* is to be taken at face value, she was either a very quick study, having just arrived on the scene, or local law enforcement was profoundly inept, or both.

The portrayal of a smart-as-a-whip city girl besting the local constabulary was bound to raise hackles in the hills of north-central Massachusetts. In the judgment of the *Fitchburg Daily Sentinel*, credit for solving the case was due "almost entirely" to Sheriff Doane, "who early formed the opinion that Richardson was playing upon the credulity of his friends and neighbors."

The *Athol Transcript* had harsher words for Annie and the *World,* charging Pulitzer's newspaper and its reporter with "fake reporting" in a story that appeared two days after Annie's feature (by the time she was in Royalston, of course, Annie was quite used to being the center of controversy with plenty of admirers and detractors):

The Royalston "wild man" case does not "down" at once. The sensationalists of the *New York World* have got hold of the

story and they are making the most of it that is possible. . . .
It claims that the "wild man" was in reality captured through
the efforts of the *World* Reporter, Nellie Bly, Jr., the sensation
writer of that newspaper and she publishes a card of thanks
purporting to come from Sheriff Doane, acknowledging his
great indebtedness to her for helping to solve the "mystery"
and this after the bottom had dropped out of the whole thing.
Mr. Doane informs us that he never wrote such a card, or endorsed her efficiency in the case. . . . The laugh seems to be
on Sheriff Doane for being published as endorsing this reporter's connection with the business, but we imagine there is
no little disgust at the unscrupulous attempt of a great newspaper to play upon the gullibility of its readers.

Annie's scrapbook does contain a receipt from Doane, but the word-
ing is much less effusive than the purported letter that she quoted in her
story. The receipt, written on a piece of notepaper from Young's Hotel, ac-
knowledges a payment of ten dollars to Sheriff Doane on October 27:
"Received of A. Londenery [sic] $10.00 for assisting in search of wild man
at Royalston Mass." (Apparently on the trip from Boston to Athol, Annie
had switched from her *World* alias, Nellie Bly Jr., the byline on the article
about her bike trip, to her cycling alias, Annie Londonderry.) The ten dollars could indicate payment for a scoop, but more likely she secured the
document as a way to confirm her role in the escapade. She had probably anticipated the very request that her editor Morrill Goddard at the
*World* made in a telegram addressed to "Mrs. Anna Kapchiwsky" in Athol
on October 28, which read in part, "can't you get some kind of letter of
thanks for your services signed by sheriff judge town officials or somebody." Annie's scrapbook containing documents related to the wild man
story has no notes from Doane other than the receipt.

But we shouldn't be too surprised to find Annie embellishing her role
for the sake of a good story. Like her namesake, Nellie Bly, she had already
demonstrated a "brazen capacity . . . to tell a white lie."

Although Annie's wild man story for the *World* may have stretched the
truth, it was typical of the sensational journalism of the day. Much like
her bicycle trip around the world, it was more farce than fraud, more mis-
chief than malice. And she concluded with a surprisingly forthright
avowal of how the newspapers benefited from the scandal: "Young
Richardson was released and allowed to go home, as he had really com-

mitted no crime. He had only frightened his poor old mother almost into fits, also his friends and neighbors for miles around, had given the local detectives and officers the hardest case they had ever tackled, and the Massachusetts papers the only occasion for months to bring out their big 'scare' headlines and the *Sunday World* an opportunity to show its usual expertise in exposing the whole business."

IF ANNIE SAW the article from the *Athol Transcript* labeling her a fraud, she probably would have been amused to see the fuss she had created at a time when the only two pieces she had written for the *World* were the account of her bicycle trip and an article on women farmers living in New York tenements that appeared under the byline "N.B. Jr." Annie had all of the characteristics the *World* would have coveted in any journalist, especially a woman journalist, of whom there were very few at the time. She was, as her bicycle trip demonstrated, fiercely independent, flamboyant, and a risk taker. She was also, by all accounts, a clever conversationalist, physically strong and courageous, bright, cunning, resourceful, and nothing if not persistent. She had *chutzpah,* "unmitigated gall," as she herself might have said.

Charley Richardson was never charged with a crime. He stayed on his farm, married in 1901, and fathered a daughter, Clara, born in 1905, and a son, Charles, born in 1908. He later served on the Royalston School Committee and the town finance committee, and died in 1942.

As for Annie, the wild man story marked the beginning of a brief career with the *World* and journalism became, for a time, another outlet for her showmanship, just as her cycling trip had been. Within a few months, however, she stopped writing altogether and the Massachusetts wild man soon became an obscure piece of local lore about mysterious doings in the haunted woods of north-central Massachusetts during Halloween week, 1895.

# Epilogue

In 1898, Susan B. Anthony wrote a letter to the editor of *Sidepaths*, a cycling magazine, in which she elaborated on her comment to Nellie Bly—the real one—two years earlier that "bicycling has done more to emancipate women than anything else in the world."

"The moment she takes her seat [a woman] knows she can't get into harm while she is on her bicycle, and away she goes, the picture of free, untrammeled womanhood," wrote Anthony. "The bicycle also teaches practical dress reform, gives women fresh air and exercise, and helps to make them equal with men in work and pleasure; and anything that does that has my good word. What is better yet, the bicycle preaches the necessity for woman suffrage. When bicyclists want a bit of special legislation, such as side-paths and laws to protect them, or to compel railroads to check bicycles as baggage, the women are likely to be made to see that their petitions would be more respected by the law-makers if they had votes, and the men that they are losing a source of strength because so many riders of the machine are women. From such small practical lessons a seed is sown that may ripen into the demand for full suffrage, by which alone women can ever make and control their own conditions in society and state."

Annie's fifteen-month, around-the-world odyssey in 1894–95 was an audacious and unprecedented one, and a colorful, if convoluted—indeed bizarre—chapter in cycling history. Truly, there is no way to measure the impact of her adventure on the larger struggle for women's equality—to know how many women it inspired or empowered. But Annie's journey epitomized perfectly the confluence of the woman's movement and the bicycle craze and is, therefore, a small, but revealing chapter in the story of women at the turn of the twentieth century.

Though some of her contemporaries were harsh in their judgments about what she was doing and how she was doing it—one Omaha wheelman said she was "one of the biggest frauds that ever passed through this city"—more than a century later, Annie seems more of a lovable rogue, a clever young woman who capitalized brilliantly on the major social forces of her day, than a charlatan. In the 1890s and early twentieth century, hundreds, if not thousands, of men and women were setting out to cross the country (or substantial parts of it), or to circle the world, by bicycle, on foot, or rolling along in barrels or pushing wagons. Though some rode, rolled and walked for pleasure, many, like Annie, also sought to cash in on the public's interest in bold, long-distance journeys. Indeed, the around-the-world traveler on a wager was such a fixture of the times that a play called *The Globe Trotter* opened the 1895 season at Boston's Hollis Street Theater on September 2, just ten days before Annie finished her journey in Chicago. The play, said the *Boston Globe*, "should meet with appreciation at the [H]ub which sent Paul Jones and Miss Londonderry on their journeys around the world. It presents the trials of one of these peripatetic tourists who started penniless from Boston to circumnavigate the globe and return with $5,000 in his pocket."

Annie was one of those cycling pioneers described by writer Irving A. Leonard: "Theirs were the glow and throb and the innocent ardor of the authentic adventurer, of the true traveler who subjects himself to the conditions of the strange places and languages through which he passes, unlike the tourist who merely transfers his accustomed style of life to a different setting. These pedaling wanderers were romantic heroes of the era wholly depending, as they did, upon their own physical resources during long stretches of time and space."

Indeed, around-the-world travelers of the 1890s provided a spectacle comparable to the contestants on today's reality TV shows, though their feats were not reported in real time. For people of that era, blow-by-blow accounts of the adventures of globetrotters such as Nellie Bly, Thomas Stevens, and Annie Londonderry was a form of entertainment (with money on the line often adding to the intrigue) that appealed then, as do such feats today, because the protagonists assumed risks most people did not, were willing to have their success or failure and their strengths and shortcomings made public, and because of the danger and suspense inherent in their perilous undertakings. Whether they followed such stories on television in the twenty-first century, or in the newspapers in the nine-teenth, people are, and were, captivated by the exploits of those who act on the dreams many have but few ever realize.

Annie was hardly the only globetrotter of her era who embellished her story, though no one raised the around-the-world-on-a-wager expedition to an art form as high as Annie did. Nor did any globetrotter of the era, except Nellie Bly, succeed in generating nearly as much publicity. Hardly a week went by when Annie wasn't in the press somewhere around the globe.

As with Annie, it was impossible to verify the claims of most of these travelers or to know when they hopped the train, hitched rides, or, in ex-treme cases, whether the person involved even existed. In the case of Margaret Valentine Le Long, for example, whose article about a bicycle ride from Chicago to San Francisco in 1896 appeared in the *San Francisco Chronicle* and later in *Outing Magazine,* some suspect the account was en-tirely fictional and that Le Long herself was a fiction, as well. Even renowned explorers such as John Wesley Powell, whose daring explo-ration of the Colorado River in the late 1860s charted one of the last great expanses of American wilderness, burnished his own legend in the ser-vice of what he saw as a noble cause—the sensible settlement of the American West and appreciation of the unique treasure that is the Grand Canyon.

At the beginning of her journey, the bicycle was little more than An-nie's ticket to freedom, fame, and fortune, and the opportunity to rein-vent herself and assume a new and glamorous identity. The United States was mired in a deep depression in the mid-1890s. That Annie succeeded in tough economic times bespeaks her remarkable ingenuity in achieving what was for most the difficult task of upward mobility, and she did it with her bicycle.

What Annie accomplished with her bicycle in 1894–95 was a tour de force of moxie, self-promotion, *and* athleticism. Though she was a skilled raconteur and gifted self-promoter with a penchant for embellishment and tall tales, she was also, as the evidence shows, an accomplished cy-clist who covered thousands of miles by bicycle during her journey. Hers was a remarkable achievement, all the more so because she was a female and she did it in the 1890s, as traveling around the world as she did was utterly unconventional for a woman of her day. The logistical hurdles were formidable as was the physical challenge. She rode through desert heat and winter cold, over rugged roads, and along lonely side paths at night. But she succeeded in her quest not because she could pedal, but because she was clever, brazen, and possessed of no end of grit and determination. Often alone, in an age when intercity telephone service was virtually nonexistent, Annie fended for herself for fifteen months on the road.

As with all popular phenomenona, the story of the long-distance traveler eventually grew stale. By 1901, those who imitated Annie in one form or another had become commonplace and a skeptical public grew wary of their claims. The *Washington Post,* had this to say about these wanderers:

> "Every once in a while," remarked The Man Who Declines to be Conned by the Dispatches, "we read in the telegraphic news about some fellow who is about to embark upon a bicycle tour of the world on a wager of $12,345.67, the conditions being that he shall start out without a soumarkee, and yet turn up at the end of two years, fat and sassy, with papers to prove that he has actually made the trip; or about some other chap, who on a wager of $19,236 has already started upon a walking tour of the globe, conditions the same, in so far as his setting off without money is concerned, only this one is to be allowed four years to fulfill the terms of his wager; or about still another peripatetic proposition who has undertaken to shove a wheelbarrow twice around the earth on a bet that he shall get away from the post without so much as the price of a package of punk tobacco in his homespuns, and return to the starting point within six years, four months, twenty-seven days, five hours and eighteen minutes. . . .
>
> "Now what I want to know, and what I want to know bad, is this: Who, and where are, and whyfore, the persons who put up these large wagers that these itinerant globe-trotters (on their own say-so) are essaying to yank down—also on their own statement of the case? What condition in life do these moneyed idiots hold? What possible good is it going to do for a man with many superfluous thousands to know that a bicycle sharp can wheel, or a strong-legged bilk can hoof, or an earth-roaming ex-gardener can wheel-barrow his way around the globe in a busted condition within a certain spec-

ified period of time? . . . Let me whisper something real confidentially in your ear, son: It hath been my opinion for quite a large assortment of years past that these coinless circumnavigators are nothing more nor less than ingenious hoboes, Wandering Willies With Graft, who frame their little spiels [about] world tours on wagers for the sake of the cordial mitts and the unhesitating hand-outs and the better facilities for pan-handling which they encounter in the many and sundry and divers towns and townships through which they pass. That's what I think. Far be it from me to indulge in sordid suspicion of my fellow man—but that's what I think."

Annie was emblematic of her times while also far ahead of them. She was the embodiment of the New Woman both on her bicycle and in her intrepid brand of journalism—indeed, she declared herself a New Woman in the very first line of her trip account for the *New York World*—and a harbinger of the equality women would achieve when they won the right to vote. She stepped far away from the traditional roles of the women of her times, blurred traditional gender roles by dressing as a man and riding a man's wheel, and pioneered sports-related marketing for women athletes. And what a sight she was to Victorian eyes! At a time when many considered it unbecoming for a woman to make a spectacle of herself, and reprehensible for a woman to leave her husband and children, especially for a frivolity like an around-the-world bicycle trip, Annie was utterly without qualms about—indeed, she was intent upon—making as big a spectacle of herself as she could. She didn't run away to join the circus; she *became* the circus.

Though not an active feminist or a suffragist, she was willing to act on her dreams in the face of what would have been, for most women, overwhelming social forces. For the vast majority of women of her day, what Annie did was simply inconceivable. In this regard she was a true feminist, willing to ride past the limitations that circumscribed the lives of women to seek fulfillment of her unconventional dreams. She was, in this sense, heroic, though she didn't always act heroically. Annie's decision to leave her family for fifteen months was a harsh one, and she dispatched her children as early as possible to boarding schools after her return. She clearly had little attachment to her children and little interest in being a mother in any meaningful sense. And she freely traded on the foibles and gullibility of others. More than a century later, one can both admire her temerity and see the humor in her escapades, but she wasn't above making fools of people in her pursuit of glory—editor Allen Kelly of the *Las Cruces Independent Democrat* and Sheriff Doane of Athol, Massachusetts, for example.

AFTER HER around-the-world journey, Annie moved her family to New York and had a brief stint as a feature writer for the *New York World*. Typically writing under the byline "The New Woman," some of her stories, like the wild-man story, were sensational accounts of derring-do. She spent a day with a self-proclaimed Messiah and his flock in New Jersey, and, posing as a lovelorn working girl, exposed the machinations of a New York City matchmaker. Not surprisingly, many of her stories were about women in their new roles. On assignment, she sorted mail on the New York mail train, once the exclusive province of men, and she wrote about a women-only stock exchange off Wall Street, among others.

Shortly after her trip was completed, Annie received at least three letters from the wife of Victor Sloan (her first name is not known), the Sterling bicycle agent with whom she had stayed in Paris. It is clear they grew very fond of her and the letters reflect the power she had to hold people in thrall. "Dear Miss Annie," begins a letter dated October 4, 1895, "We suppose you have not received our last letter, as we have not heard anything from you, but you are probably very busy by this time. What are you doing? Is your trip finished and how have you gone through? All this points [sic] would interest us so much. We hope you will kindly drop us a line down and we expect it will be from Boston, that means that you will be arrived; how happy it would make us." The letter continues: "you don't know how many times our thoughts were with you, it will be nearly a year that you have been in Paris, it seems now that time has gone so quick."

The letter also describes financial hardship. "Until now, our business is always at the same point, my dear husband is working very hard to make his Emery wheels [a brand of bicycle most likely], he has been disappointed many times . . . I hope, dear friend, the next time, we will write you, it will be good news. We are in good health & that's much for us, who have to work hard . . . Write us soon, dear, & let us know all about you. If you have the chance to come to Paris & if we have succeed [sic], what a good time we will pass together. Always yours truly, C. Sloan."

Annie replied to this because in a second letter dated November 5,

Mrs. Sloan begins by expressing great joy at hearing from her and the news that her trip has been successful. She thanks Annie for sending a copy of her article about her bicycle trip from the *New York World,* published just two weeks before. But then the letter turns plaintive. The Sloans had apparently been writing to her along her route after Paris, but had heard nothing from her. Whether Annie received the Sloans' letters en route or not, she excused her own lack of correspondence by claiming she hadn't been getting their mail.

"We learned that you have been successful & I must tell you, that we were a little surprised not to receive a little word from you," Mrs. Sloan continued, "but it explains us all now, if you have not received our mail, you thought we had forgotten you."

"You can't believe that since about two weeks, I was every night dreaming from you [sic], that you were coming to Paris and my husband, who says he never dreams, did to [sic], about 2 or 3 times this week. We hope you will come again soon, how happy we would be all together, you would interest us so much."

Clearly, the Sloans had fallen in love, but the sense that they are incomplete without her probably repelled Annie. And if the declarations of affection didn't cause Annie some discomfort, she went on to unburden herself about their business difficulties, telling Annie that they had been reduced to living "in a little room" near the office on the *Rue Sedaine.* "We are so happy together, but we have much trouble in business," Mrs. Sloan wrote, blaming their troubles on "that cursed money."

Annie, of course, had just won a $10,000 prize—at least the Sloans, familiar with her story, believed that to be the case. She may have thought they were hinting that they could use her financial help.

It appears Annie, despite the closeness implied in Mrs. Sloan's letters, never told the Sloans she was married, or indeed very much about herself, especially her lack of interest in parenting, for the November letter ends with this: "I expect you did find your little nephew in good health & that you were happy to see all your parents & friends again. I wish to have a little child, but until now there is nothing & we are sorry about it, but I hope also for this. Yours forever, C. Sloan."

At almost exactly the time the Sloans were complaining to her about their financial hardships and pleading for her affection and attention, Annie was being besieged by the needs, emotional and financial, of her younger sister, Rosa. On October 28, 1895, a little more than a month after her trip ended in Chicago, Rosa wrote Annie from her home in New

Jersey. Oddly, while Annie saved very little of her correspondence (or little of it was saved by her children), she saved this letter, one that hints at a very troubled family dynamic. Rosa was ill, for she tells Annie straight away that "the nurse went away." Then abruptly, and with anger at a slight, real or perceived, she, too, turns to the issue of money.

"I have that money already which you loaned me and thought I would write to you for the rest. I would not ask you for it if I had it, but as you promised to give it to me and did what you have done I thought I would write. I expected you over Sunday but you failed to come and would like to know the reason why. [sic] If you do not come yourself, send it."

Like the letters from the Sloans in Paris, Rosa's letter is self-pitying. "I must say that I am not feeling very well my leg is [so] sore that I can not stand on it long. [Rosa was a morbidly obese woman.] When night comes I can hardly walk on it," Rosa wrote. "I hope you will come at once. Come over. Be sure and come over." The letter is signed, somewhat incongruously, "Your loving sister Rosa."

On October 24, 1895, a few days before Rosa's letter to her, Annie had written a note, probably a draft of a telegram to Rosa's husband. "Dear Brother," said the message, "Telegram received. Over stacked with work. Get another woman in the house or else get a servant. Don't leave her alone. Answer at once."

Just back from fifteen months of unfettered freedom on the road, Annie was facing multiple demands, emotional and financial, from friends and family on both sides of the Atlantic and she once again had a husband and children who needed her attention, too.

It is, therefore, not surprising that Annie ended her communication with the Sloans. In a brief note dated February 28, 1896, Mrs. Sloan bemoans the lack of further word from Annie and seems almost desperate to keep the relationship going. But, this third letter also makes clear that the Sloans probably didn't even know Annie's real name, despite the intimate time they spent together. Annie saved this third letter *and* the envelope: it was addressed to "Miss Annie Londonderry." Annie knew how to draw people close, but she also knew how to keep her distance and leave them abruptly.

In 1897, almost two years to the day after the end of her bicycle trip, Annie and Max had a fourth child, Frieda. By 1900, however, Annie was living alone in a boarding house in Ukiah, California, and working as a saleslady. Why she went west and left her family yet again isn't known. Her three eldest children were off at boarding schools, and Frieda, only a toddler, was living with an unrelated family in Bristol, Maine. How long Annie was in Ukiah is also unknown. But shortly after 1900 she returned to Max once again in New York, where they built a small garment business, Kay & Company, adjacent to a home they purchased on East 214th Street in the Bronx. Annie employed about two dozen workers there. When that business was destroyed by fire in the 1920s, she used the insurance proceeds to start another business, Grace Strap & Novelty on 27th Street and Third Avenue in Manhattan, with a man named Feldman whom she met at a Horn and Hardart Automat in New York. (She was still very good at chatting up strangers.)

If Annie ever rode a bicycle again, it was purely incidental, but throughout her life she regaled friends and family with stories of her around-the-world bicycle trip and it remained a source of great pride for her. Annie and her husband remained together until Max's death in 1946, and Annie worked up until a few days before she died, of a stroke, on November 11, 1947.

In Annie's scrapbook is a torn piece of brown lined paper with a handwritten note from her to Arthur Brisbane, the legendary editor of the *New York World*. The note is undated and it is unclear whether the note relates to her bicycle trip or one of her other assignments for the *World*. Despite its few words, the note speaks volumes about Annie. Indeed, it is as if she wrote her own, very fitting epitaph on that piece of paper: "Mr. Brisbane, I am not afraid. I'll take the risk myself, Resp. Yours, Mrs. Kopchovsky."

# Afterword

I first learned about my great-grandaunt, Annie Cohen Kopchovsky, in the early 1990s from a complete stranger, a researcher named Michael Wells. I had never heard of her, or about her remarkable around-the-world journey, even though she was my great-grandfather's sister. Though she made headlines throughout the United States and Europe, appeared in advertisements for bicycles and spring water, and had been celebrated the world around, no one in my immediate family, and, as it turns out, almost no one in my extended family had ever heard of Annie, either. At some point many years ago, it's not clear when or why, the two branches of the family, Annie's, and my great-grandfather Bennett's, lost touch with one another.

In the late 1990s, I started cycling regularly, but had given little thought to Annie since first hearing about her several years before. Then, in 2003, Mr. Wells contacted me again to see if I had learned anything about Annie since we had last corresponded a decade before. I had not but my interest was piqued, in part because I was now cycling myself, and I decided to poke around a bit to see what I could learn. I knew from an old newspaper article Mr. Wells provided that Annie had started her odyssey at the Massachusetts State House, so I called the State House library to see if there was any record of the event there. I was surprised when librarian Eva Murphy told me without hesitation that she knew there was nothing at the State House because she had looked about two years before when a gentleman named Dennis McCown, from Austin, Texas, had inquired about Annie. I was astonished. Annie's story was obscure at best. Who else, I wondered, was on her trail? Ms. Murphy put me in touch with Dennis and he told me he had stumbled upon Annie while researching the murder of Martin Mrose in El Paso on the night of Annie's lecture there. Dennis told me that as John Wesley Hardin's men were dispatching Mrose at the El Paso city dump, Hardin, with Mrose's wife, Helen, by his side, was at Annie's lecture. The rest, as they say, is history.

That an ancestor of mine—my Jewish great-grandaunt from Boston—had crossed paths with such a notorious character of the Old West seemed utterly implausible, and I was hooked. I chased Annie through snow-covered cemeteries in icy rain, across cyberspace, and over miles and miles of microfilm of newspapers published from Chicago to Shanghai and dozens of cities in between. I phoned libraries, historical associations, funeral homes, academics, and newspapers all over the country. I located the descendants of people Annie had met during her travels and wrote them looking for long-lost remnants of her journey. And, after months of searching, I found her only direct, living descendant, her granddaughter, Mary, who had all of the artifacts that remain of Annie's journey (at least those I have been able to find), including her lantern-slide show. The slides are made of glass and, remarkably, they had survived shipment around the world in the 1890s and many moves in the years since.

During the chase, Annie's story became, in some respects, my story, too. As I struggled up the modest hills west of Boston on my superlight, carbon-fiber Trek bicycle, dressed in neon green breathable fabrics, cell phone in my saddle bag and a Gatorade in my bottle cage, I soon found myself thinking of Annie dressed in long skirts going over the Hudson Highlands on her forty-two-pound ladies' Columbia bicycle, or, later, in bloomers, crossing the Arizona desert on her men's Sterling, a hundred miles from nowhere with nothing but the hope of a passing freight in case of misfortune. She was, and is, my cycling muse. But that, alone, hardly explains the thousands of hours and the small fortune I've spent trying to recover this story of one Victorian woman's quest.

A few weeks after I started my research, I was diagnosed with thyroid cancer. I was nearing fifty, and although this disease is generally treatable, my deepening obsession with Annie and my cancer diagnosis were more closely linked than I understood at the time. As we face our own mortality we yearn, I think, to see ourselves as more than the sum of our years. If we look forward through the windshield, and have children or grandchildren, we gain a measure of reassurance in the knowledge that we will live on, in some way, through our children and their progeny. And if we look back, at our parents, grandparents, and other ancestors, we see the road in the rear-view mirror, too. Through family history we seek our connection to the past and the future and an appreciation of our place in the long human chain.

After my cancer surgery and treatment, the bicycle was my path back to health and a sense of well-being. During those days in the saddle, I felt as if my bike was tethered to Annie's; that *she* was pulling me up and over the hills west of Boston. She kept me company, provided inspiration, and occupied my imagination as the miles went by. Getting back on my bike as soon and as often as I could made me feel very much alive. That I was finding my solace, and my strength, on two wheels, as Annie had, connected me to her in ways that I could not have imagined before. I found myself sympathizing with her for taking control of her life, even though others, especially her children, paid a heavy price for her independence. In different ways, Annie and I each found freedom on two wheels and used the bicycle to exercise control over our own destinies. For both of us, the bicycle became an implement of power.

WHEN I FIRST began the search that eventually led to her granddaughter, Mary, I quickly learned that Annie was going to be an elusive quarry for an amateur historian such as myself. The official records—her marriage registration, the birth registrations for her children, and various census records—gave wildly conflicting information about two basic facts: Annie's place of birth and her age. She was either born in Russia, Poland, Massachusetts, New York, or Pennsylvania; and her age was all over the map, too. I was completely perplexed. Even if Annie's date and place of birth didn't promise to shed any light on her bicycle trip, trying to reconcile the conflicts and omissions provided valuable insight into Annie's character. It was clear that, when it came to giving information to various officials, she was hardly a slave to the truth, and I began to suspect that she was going to prove to be a rather roguish and impish personality (more than one person hearing this story has suggested she was pathological).

After seven months of searching, it was two small death notices in the *New York Times,* one for Max and another for Annie, that led me to the New Jersey cemetery where they are buried and, through the cemetery, to

Mary. (Coincidentally, the cemetery is just minutes from the house where I grew up and my paternal grandparents are buried there, as well. Annie is on my mother's side.) I didn't know if Mary was still alive when I learned her name (she was listed as the contact person in the cemetery records, but those records were thirteen years old) and I wasn't sure how she would respond to a letter from a complete stranger poking around in her grandmother's life. But I wrote, and feeling this was either going to be the end of the road or the beginning of a new one, I waited. Then, one evening, about ten days later, the phone rang.

"Peter," said a woman's voice, "this is your long-lost cousin, Mary." With those words my entire body quivered with emotion.

Mary told me that my interest in Annie, and in recovering her history, had lifted a burden. For decades Mary felt she was supposed *to do something* with Annie's legacy, but didn't know what. Now, I had come along out of the blue, a blood relation no less, to provide the solution. Mary wondered aloud whether our ancestors "up there" had colluded to bring us together. "If you write my grandmother's story," Mary said when we first spoke, "it will be the fulfillment of my dreams!" With those words, I was truly on a mission.

Mary was seventy-two when we first spoke in late October 2003, and she is Annie's *only* grandchild, the only child of Annie's youngest daughter, Frieda, and thus Annie's only living lineal, biological descendant. Mary knew Annie well. She was sixteen when her grandmother died on November 11, 1947, and during the final year and a half of Annie's life, after Max died, Annie and Mary shared a bedroom in the latter's home.

I asked Mary if she had the diary Annie reportedly kept. Alas, she did not, and its whereabouts, if indeed it ever existed, remain a mystery. Mary has her doubts. "If my grandmother kept a diary," she told me, "she almost surely would have shown it to me." Annie spoke often and with pride about her bicycle trip to friends and family throughout her long life, and Mary believes she would have brandished the diary if she had kept one, though it could have been lost or destroyed at some point.

"She loved the drama of telling a story," Mary explained, "more than she did the living of ordinary life, and when she spoke of her bicycle trip it was if she was again very far from her later life as a business woman and a Jewish housewife. Even in business she thrived on the drama and the manipulation, being somewhat less moved by the results. Even the idea of motherhood, at least in the early years, probably outweighed the actual living out of the experience of being a mother."

"And," in a comment that seemed especially apropos, Mary said, "my grandmother had to be moving all the time. She was very persuasive, too. She could tell a story and you would just believe. If she wanted to sell you the Brooklyn Bridge, you would buy it."

When Mary and I first met in early November 2003, shortly after that first telephone conversation, I asked her about the two simple facts that had so bedeviled my early research, Annie's date and place of birth. It didn't surprise Mary in the least that her grandmother might have been the source for much of the conflicting information, for Annie, she suggested, had a casual relationship with the truth and was an inveterate storyteller.

One family story Mary related was especially strange and fueled my growing suspicion that the ghost I was chasing was a wily and imaginative one, and that the story of her bicycle trip would not be a straightforward one.

Annie had always spoken of a twin brother, Jake, who had died when she was young. And Mary's mother, Frieda, no doubt repeating a story told to her by Annie, had said that Jake had frozen to death on Boston Common as a young man, after a fight with his father. The suggestion was that Jake had gotten drunk after the fight and passed out in the cold. Annie did, in fact, have a brother Jacob; he was the *younger* brother who died of a lung infection at age seventeen in May 1894, just before she left on her bike trip. But a twin who froze to death on Boston Common?

First, Jacob was born at least five or six years *after* Annie. They weren't twins. Second, Jacob died on May 12, 1894, and while snow has been known to cover the tulips in Boston in spring, it would have been quite a feat to freeze to death in May. Finally, Annie and Jacob's father, my great-great grandfather Levi, died in 1887, seven years *before* Jacob's birth. Jacob didn't die after a fight with his father. The whole story struck me as an especially peculiar family legend to pass down, particularly because it clearly wasn't true. Annie really knew how to spin a yarn, that much was becoming clear, and I now had a clear sense of what an outrageous character she was.

After showing me articles Annie had written for the *New York World,* including her story about the wild man, Mary and I leafed through a scrapbook, fragile with age, in which Annie kept various mementos of her bicycle trip, and several family photograph albums. I asked Mary why Max agreed to his wife's leaving. She replied that he was a passive man and adored the ground Annie walked (or rode) on. Though Annie told the *World* in July 1894 she would not have taken the trip without her husband's consent, Max had little choice; she called the shots. "She was pretty good at disappearing," said Mary. But, Mary also described her grandparents as having a very caring relationship, one devoid of acrimony. However, whenever Annie talked about her bike trip later in her life, as she often did, it was never in front of Max and he never, ever discussed it.

As I dug deeper into Annie's life, I was especially curious to know about her eldest daughter, Mollie, who had been five when her mother had disappeared from her life for fifteen months. Mollie was not mentioned as a survivor, as her siblings were, in Annie and Max's death notices, nor was she buried in the family plot in New Jersey where her parents and siblings are buried. I was sure, based on this information, that Mollie predeceased them. When I asked about Mollie, Mary, to my surprise, looked shaken and wept softly. The story she was about to tell me left me practically speechless.

As noted earlier, when Annie returned home from her bicycle trip, she was no more enamored of motherhood and domestic life than when she had left. As soon as her children were old enough, five or six years old, she and her Orthodox Jewish husband sent them to boarding schools—*Catholic* boarding schools! Though Annie kept a kosher home, she was not as devout as Max and was even, perhaps, agnostic, but she had a strong cultural identity as a Jew. Nevertheless, they first sent Mollie and Libbie to a French-speaking school run by the Dominican Sisters in Lewiston, Maine. Simon, Jr. was dispatched to a Catholic school in Arthabaskaville, Quebec. Annie visited them infrequently. Eventually, however, all the girls, Mollie, Libbie, and Mary's mother, Frieda, attended Mount Saint Mary's in Newburgh, New York, ostensibly so they would be closer to home.

Why Catholic schools? As my own Jewish mother might say, "Don't ask." It was, no matter how you look at it, a bizarre decision, though Mary suggested Annie believed the children would receive a superior education and be well cared for there.

All of Annie's children had suffered profoundly, "been damaged," in Mary's words, by their mother's inability or lack of interest in mothering them, as evidenced by both her bicycle trip, during which she left them for fifteen months, and her dispatching them to boarding schools when they were very young. Mary told me my letter had unleashed a flood of conflicting emotions because the ripple effects of Annie's choice to leave her young children to bicycle the world—and of subsequent decisions borne of the same fierce independence—are still felt today. Mary believes that many of the emotional struggles Annie's children faced in their lives, and that she faced in hers, can be traced to her grandmother's virtual abandonment of her children when they were very young. Annie's son, Simon, was deeply embittered, never married despite several engagements, and always lived in a perfectly neat, rented room. He spent most of his life in a rage, mostly directed at the Catholic Church. Libbie had an unsuccessful marriage and another romance that ended tragically. Frieda, Mary's mother, constructed a fantasy in which no better parents than Annie and Max had ever walked the earth, a fantasy she held tightly into old age. But no one responded to Annie's mothering—and to being sent away to Catholic boarding school—more dramatically than had Mollie.

Mollie attended Catholic schools until she was in her late teens. In 1911, in her early twenties, in a startling though perhaps not surprising act of rebellion, she converted. But Mollie didn't simply convert to Catholicism, she became a nun and was, forever after, known as Sister Marie Thaddea of Sion. Mary asked me to refer to her as Sister Thaddea wherever possible in this book.

The violent impact of Sister Thaddea's conversion on her family is clear from a profoundly bitter letter I obtained from the archive of the Nostra Signora di Sion at the Vatican in Rome. Written to Sister Thaddea on November 14, 1912, by her brother Simon, then twenty, it is a blistering indictment of her conversion. "Had you pierced my heart with a murderous bullet, or with the glistening blade, I shouldn't have felt the pang of pain any stronger," he wrote. His life, he said, had been forever ruined by the "curse" Sister Thaddea (whom he referred to throughout as Mollie) had inflicted on the family. He foresaw a life of degradation in carrying the burden of Sister Thaddea's "secret" to the grave. And he despaired for his parents, Annie and Max. "With pain and sorrow I watch my . . . harried young mother strive to keep up a home under almost, in fact under impossibly removable obstacles. With a pain of intenseness I see her daily, go to work. God! It's terrible, it's frightful. Insanity is a joy compared to this. Can't you realize the extent of your damage, my dear sister."

The letter continues: "Your father is no longer gray, he is 'white.' Your mother and mine is no longer gray. She is 'white.' . . . You are driving inch

by inch, a mother to her grave. Do I speak truthfully? Positively. And a father also. Mollie, I predict you will be a murderess in a very short time.
Did God command us to kill or did He say? 'Thou shalt not kill.' "

It is clear from Simon's letter that Annie had regaled her children with
stories (again with a grandiose twist) about her bicycle journey as they
were growing up. Simon saw her as a heroine and took a sarcastic tone
with Sister Thaddea for not recognizing it: "You forget who your mother
is; the world famous globe girdler has no charm for you, has she: a
woman who was good enough to interview every living ruler and sover-
eign in the world. God, how can you remain away as you do?"

The letter also suggests Simon suffered some form of abuse during his
years in Catholic school, explaining perhaps why his letter is so filled
with rage. "Mollie, I spent eight years of my life amongst those people
who claim to be good by closing themselves up, when their leader told
them to go out into the world and preach 'good' and 'virtue' . . . I know
their innermost secrets, and some day the world will be startled; both
sexes I make no exceptions. The armies of the nations will rise against
them. Do you want to be of them?" Indeed, Simon appears to have fore-
seen today's clergy sex-abuse scandal.

His pleas that Sister Thaddea reverse course were to no avail. She
eventually found her way to Saskatchewan, where she lived most of her
life in Prince Albert, and later in Saskatoon, teaching school and living in
a convent. When Sister Thaddea's letters arrived home, Annie and Max
would recite Hebrew prayers and burn the letters. As far as they were
concerned, their daughter was dead. They never saw or spoke with her
again, and to ensure the Catholic Church wouldn't receive any of her
money, Annie disinherited her eldest daughter.

"After Mollie's defection, so to speak, the only god that my grandmother knew would have been a god she feared," Mary told me. "I never
had a sense that my grandmother relied on any kind of god, or that she
even believed, but she had a great fear. I remember that whenever my
grandfather took me as a little girl to shul, my grandmother would cry.
Now I realize she was crying for Mollie."

One can imagine it wasn't easy for Sister Thaddea, left motherless for
fifteen months only to be dispatched to a Catholic boarding school at a
tender age shortly after her mother's return. Indeed, her obituary in a
Saskatoon newspaper reads, in part: "Why an American girl of 21 years
started a new life under a new religion on the cold Canadian prairies will
never be told. Mother Superior Noreen . . . a pupil and beloved compan-

ion of Sister Marie [Thaddea] said: 'Her decision to come west was made a great many years ago, but a few old wounds might be opened and a few feelings hurt if too much probing were done. . . . A sister and niece [Mary] still live in New York.' "

Perhaps it was the shame they felt about Sister Thaddea that kept Annie and Max from sustaining contact with their relations in Boston, my branch of the family, and the secret of their eldest daughter was very tightly held, at least from Mary, for decades. Mary didn't even learn of her aunt's existence until 1961, when Mary was thirty and Sister Thaddea was in her seventies. A family friend let the secret slip.

Though Annie and Max never saw or spoke with Sister Thaddea again, and Annie had disinherited her, they gave tacit approval of her sibling's ongoing contact with her. In 1961, Sister Thaddea traveled to Montreal for a conference. It was Mary's thirtieth birthday and her mother, Frieda, telephoned her aunt there. Mary heard her mother say, "Hello, Mollie. It's Frieda. Yes, I know it's Mary's birthday and I'm going to let you talk to her." She then handed the phone to a stunned Mary. "Her voice was my grandmother's voice," Mary told me, "and I started to cry." Indeed, in recounting this episode Mary began to cry quietly again.

As it turns out, a secret had been kept from Sister Thaddea, too. When Mary was born, her aunt had begun sending her birthday presents, but those presents were intercepted by Mary's parents. When Mary turned nine, Sister Thaddea learned for the first time that her niece did not know she existed.

Mary showed me photographs of Sister Thaddea in her nun's habit. She also shared with me long, beautiful letters written in a neat hand that she and her mother received at the time of her aunt's death in 1961, letters from Mother Edeltrude, the Reverend Mother at St. Mary's Convent in Saskatoon. Sister Thaddea sounded not unlike Annie from Mother Edeltrude's description. "You just can't imagine how we miss her," Mother Edeltrude wrote, "she was so outlandish in her ideas at times . . . She was a great entertainer." The same could have been said of Annie, of course.

Shortly after I met Mary in November 2003, I contacted St. Mary's Church in Saskatoon and was put in touch with Sister Catherine Seeman, who had known Sister Thaddea. She wrote me from "a house for our aged Sisters," as she described it, and told me she first met Sister Thaddea while living in Prince Albert Convent from 1944 to 1947. Sister Catherine told me of "House Journals" that were kept at St. Mary's Convent, and she offered to go back and transcribe portions that pertained to Sister

Thaddea. The journal entries begin in 1913 and continue, with great poignancy, right up to the last days of Sister Thaddea's life in November 1961. The journals are mostly the daily comings and goings of the Sisters. But, the entry for November 17, 1961, was somber: "M. Thaddea was anointed as a precaution."

For me, the most poignant entries were dated August 31 and September 23, 1961, the latter just two months before Sister Thaddea's death. "Rev. Mother received a night letter from Sr. Thaddea who is visiting Montreal telling of a phone call from New York when not only her sister Frieda and her husband spoke to her but also Mary, her niece, who had just learned of the existence of her aunt," read the first. "This was looked upon as a miracle." The entry for September 23 is equally moving: "All rejoice with M. Thaddea who received a letter (the first) from her niece Mary." Sister Thaddea died two months later, on November 27, having found in the Church the love and acceptance that had eluded her in childhood.

Until I read these transcripts to Mary, she knew nothing about how the joy of her "meeting" her aunt had been recorded a continent away in the House Journal of a small convent on the Canadian prairie. Mary's letter was surely a comfort to Sister Thaddea in the last weeks before her death. Another circle, and a wound that opened on June 25, 1894, when Annie took off on her bicycle, had been closed.

WHENEVER I RIDE my bike, and often when I am not, my thoughts drift to Annie, to the remarkable life she led, and to the family—my family—that she sometimes left behind. I marvel that fate somehow brought Annie and me together and gave me the privilege of telling her story, a story virtually lost over the generations, not only to history but within my family, too. Before taking my own journey with her I had no idea it was possible to become so involved in the life of a person I'd never met, a person who had died six years before I was born. I have to admit that I love her, like one loves a slightly off-kilter old aunt, even though my focus has been on her life when she was just in her early twenties. She's like a relative who dropped in for a visit and ended up staying, but it is a most welcome stay.

The process of resurrecting Annie's story was endlessly fascinating because every tiny shard of evidence had to be held up and examined to see where else it might lead. It was, in essence, one long scavenger hunt and it was really great fun to pursue Annie across time and space. It was also, at times, very emotional. Some discoveries were more illuminating than others, of course, and finding Mary after months of genealogical detective work was the most exciting of them all. Second only to finding Mary was the discovery, in her basement, of Annie's original slide show. In fact, Mary didn't even know it was in her basement. She thought the slides had been discarded years ago. But her husband, Paul, remembered, and when he came upstairs with two dusty boxes of lantern slides, slides I had read about in the old newspaper accounts, I was absolutely astonished. Piece by piece, bit by bit, Annie's legacy was reappearing, literally, from under the dust of history. For me, as a writer, her story has been the story of a lifetime—hers *and* mine.

Over the past four years, no matter how much I learned about Annie, and no matter how much material I unearthed, I was and remain frustrated that there is so much I don't know and that cannot be known because so much has been lost to time—a diary (maybe), letters (surely), and the memories of those who knew her but who are now long passed. But I always believed that Annie's story needed to be told using whatever remnants of her life I could find, not only because it illuminates the larger story of women at the turn of the twentieth century—but because it's such a hoot! What I wouldn't give to have just one evening to talk to Annie, to ask her my questions, and to listen to her tell tales of her much heralded spin around the world more than one hundred years ago.

# Appendix

On October 20, 1895, Annie's first-person account of her journey appeared in the *Sunday World* of New York. The article was a full six columns wide on the front page of the *World's* special Sunday features section, and was accompanied by two large sketches, one drawn directly from a photograph Annie had taken at Root Studios in Chicago (see the photo insert).

It is possible that Annie's professional relationship with the *World* was forged as early as July 1894, when she spent nearly a month in New York City after leaving Boston. Although it is never mentioned in any other newspaper accounts of her trip, the editorial lead to Annie's account in the *World* claimed that on her journey she carried only a skirt, a pistol, and "a document of credentials from the *Sunday World.*"

If it ever existed, Annie didn't save this document, or it was lost or destroyed. But, it is odd that she never mentioned her association with the *World,* if there was one, to any reporters.

Parts of Annie's account in the *World* are downright implausible and others demonstrably false. Much is simply unverifiable at this remove. Some of the factual errors are inconsequential—for example, she gives the date of her departure from Boston as June 26, 1894—others are more significant. For example, Annie claims to have made the return trip from Chicago to New York in eighteen days. Since she left Chicago on October 14 that would have put her in New York City on November 2. Yet, on November 2, the *Buffalo Express* reported that she had just left

Buffalo for Rochester the previous day. Other parts of her story are utterly fantastical, especially her brief account of her imprisonment in China.

Parts of Annie's account read as a sort of feminist manifesto, but one that reflects the feminism of the 1890s, not of today. While she declares herself the equal of men in her very first sentence, she goes on to assure "her sisters" that the wearing of bloomers, which many saw as unfeminine, would not undermine their prospects for marriage.

Also interesting is what Annie leaves out of this account. She never explains why she rode west to Chicago, only to return to New York and make her way around the world in an easterly direction. Nor does she provide a timeline, perhaps because that would have allowed readers to readily draw the conclusion that she made most of the trip from France to San Francisco by steamer.

Nevertheless, her story, like Annie herself, is colorful and filled with drama. While the fact-checking left something to be desired, and such an article would never appear in a reputable newspaper today without a more rigorous vetting, it is quite typical of the sensationalism that characterized journalism at the turn of the twentieth century. Indeed, the newspapers of the 1890s were perfectly suited to Annie's purposes. As the first woman to attempt to circle the world by bicycle, she was certainly a legitimate news story by any standard, and the media seized on it. But with her gift for hyperbole and drama, she fed the need that all journalists and editors had for attention-grabbing copy. Fortunately for her, Annie didn't have to worry about creating a completely consistent narrative as she traveled. In those times, not only was it extremely difficult for a reporter in El Paso, for example, to check news accounts published in previous months in Syracuse, Cleveland, or Chicago, but the premium wasn't on getting the story "right"; it was on getting a sensational story that would sell tomorrow's newspapers. Thus, Annie could claim, at various times and depending on the circumstances, to have been a Harvard medical student, a lawyer, an orphan, a wealthy heiress, an accountant, or the founder of a newspaper she sold for a large sum before leaving on her journey, none of which was true, but all of which made her irresistibly good copy.

What follows is the only account of the journey by Annie's hand, and it makes for highly entertaining reading. Portions have been quoted elsewhere in this book, but this is Annie's account in its entirety.

# The World

*New York, Sunday, October 20, 1895—Copyrighted by the Press Publishing Co., 1895.*

### Around the World on a Bicycle

*Nellie Bly, Junior, Makes the Most Extraordinary Journey Ever Undertaken by a Woman*
*Shot by Chinese Soldiers and Thrown into a Military Prison by the Japs*
*A Remarkable Diary of Fifteen Months in All Parts of the World in her Bloomers*

---

*A young woman of most astonishing courage and determination has just completed a tour around the world on a bicycle. She went all alone and she brings back a practical experience of fifteen months in bloomers. In crossing China and Japan she was shot in the arm by a Chinese bullet on the battle-field of Gasan. Then she was captured by the astonished soldiers and locked up for a time. This young woman carried a skirt wound around the cross-bar of her bicycle and a pistol in the hip pocket of her bloomers, and that was about all except a document of credentials from the Sunday World. Her trip also decided a wager made that no woman could accomplish such a feat. In many respects this unparalleled journey by wheel is more remarkable than Nellie Bly's record breaking trip around the world in 1890.*

I am a journalist and a "new woman"—if that term means that I believe I can do anything any man can do. Nellie Bly, the readers of the Sunday World all know, went around the world in seventy-two days and beat the record. But she had the comforts of steamships and parlor cars.

I have been around the world on a bicycle and I think that beats the record of any feminine undertaking to date.

The first idea of this trip came into my head when I heard

in June a year ago of a wager that had been made that no woman could traverse the globe on a wheel. I accepted the burdensome end of the wager and determined to win it. The Sunday World, as usual, was interested in the project.

I knew nothing whatever about a bicycle. I had never ridden one, and there I had agreed to ride one around the world. Of course, the first thing to do was to get a bicycle and learn to ride. Two lessons sufficed for the learning and then I announced my readiness to start.

## Conditions of the Trip

These are the conditions under which the trip was taken: I was to start from Boston, Mass., with nothing but one suit and my bicycle; was allowed five cents per diem for expenses; was permitted to earn money to defray my expenses in any honorable way other than by my profession as a journalist; was obliged to speak only the English language; was obliged to earn $5,000 over and above my expenses; was obliged to register at certain specified points, and secure the vouchers of the various American consuls that I had reached these various stages in my journey.

Well, of course, the only thing I could do as a starter in Boston was to transform myself into an advertising medium; received $100 from one firm and smaller sums from others, and in a few hours I was enabled to equip myself properly and present myself in front of the State House for the start. Lieut.-Gov. Wolcott made a little speech and wished me success and then I was off. This was June 26, 1894.

I found it altogether different riding on the uneven road than in the academy, and my progress was at first slow and painful. I reached Providence in due time, but it was not a record-breaking ride. After a good rest I made myself known and was engaged as a clerk in a drugstore for a day. I received $5 for my work. From Providence I came to New York. I remained here three weeks. It was necessary for me to earn enough money here to defray me expenses across the ocean. Again I became an advertising medium, and received $600 for carrying four ribbons for as many firms.

One of several formal portraits taken of Annie on June 25, 1894, the day she officially began her trip. Note the white ribbon, the symbol of the Women's Christian Temperance Union, on her right lapel and the advertising placard for Londonderry water attached to the skirt guard on the rear wheel. This may be the first image ever made of a woman engaged in sports-related marketing.

A formal portrait of Annie, most likely taken in autumn 1894, when she first reached Chicago. Selling her photograph and her autograph were just two of many ways the resourceful Annie earned money as she traveled.

The Bicycle ridden by Miss Annie Londonderry.

A nnie began her trip, attired in skirts, on a 42-pound drop-frame (women's) Columbia bicycle ill-suited for long distances. When she reached Chicago in September 1894, the Sterling Cycle Works offered her a men's bike weighing 21 pounds. The Sterling, like the Columbia, had a single gear and no free-wheel mechanism, which meant that if the wheels were spinning, so were the pedals. Unlike the Columbia, the Sterling had no brake. The device on the front wheel is a cyclometer, an odometer for bicycles. The American flag wrapped around the frame was a gift of an American diplomat in Paris. This photograph was taken in San Francisco in early spring 1895.

The images in the lantern slides Annie collected and used to illustrate her lectures were often exquisite. That these fragile slides survived multiple shipments by land and sea during the course of Annie's trip is remarkable. That they were found intact more than one hundred years later is equally remarkable. Many of the lantern slides Annie collected to illustrate her lectures were of exotics, sure to be of interest to curious small-town Americans.

By the time Annie reached California in early spring 1895, she was a woman transformed. She began the trip in the long skirts and high-collared blouses typical of Victorian dress. In Chicago, in autumn 1894, she switched to bloomers because she could no longer ride in skirts with a men's bike. Here she is seen in a men's riding suit. Even for a "new woman" of the 1890s, this gender-bending attire was quite radical.

Annie was also a consummate promoter and inveterate storyteller. She staged this photograph near San Francisco in spring 1895 and used it to illustrate lectures she gave across the American west to earn money. With her keen sense of how to appeal to an audience, her lectures were filled with fantastic tales of danger and high adventure.

This advertisement for the Londonderry Lithia Springs Water Company appeared in the *Rocky Mountain News* of Denver on August 12, 1895. The company, based in Nashua, New Hampshire, paid Annie to hang the advertising placard on her bike and to assume the name Londonderry. This is another early example of women's sports-related marketing, testimony to Annie's ingenuity and acumen in promoting herself.

Annie, as depicted in an illustration published with the first-person account of her trip in the *New York World* on October 20, 1895, under the byline "Nelly Bly, Jr." The real "Nelly Bly," Elizabeth Jane Cochran, was the best-known journalist of her day, a pioneer of undercover investigative reporting. But Bly was also a world-famous globetrotter. In 1889, as a publicity stunt for the *World*, she had broken the *fictional* record for circling the globe "set" by Phileas Fogg in Jules Verne's *Around the World in Eighty Days*. Bly made the trip in just over 72 days and returned to New York an international celebrity.

At right, Charley Richardson, the Massachusetts "Wild Man," about the time of the Royalston attacks. *(Photo courtesy Jim Richardson)*

Below, Annie leads the search for the Massachusetts "Wild Man."

W JRLD: SUNDAY, NOVEMBER 3, 1895.

SEARCHING THE WOODS FOR THE "WILD MAN."

Though she left her husband, Max, and three small children for fifteen months to go cycling around the world, the marriage survived until Max's death in 1946. Annie died the following year. The above photograph was taken in the 1940s.

At right, Annie's daughter Libbie with Sister Thaddea.

## Roughing It

That money I sent to the man who had been agreed upon as the holder of whatever money I should be able to earn. After picking up what money I could in New York I went to Chicago via Michigan. I had some very funny experiences en route. It was my first attempt at "roughing it," and I'm afraid I was a sorry specimen of a tramp. I had to sleep out of doors, under haycocks, in barns—anywhere, in fact, where I could find shelter. I could not beg, but the people en route were very kind, as a rule, and I did not suffer except from the unaccustomed strain of riding the wheel.

Nine weeks from the time I left Boston I rode into Chicago with three cents in my pocket. I had worn a short riding skirt thus far but in Chicago I swallowed my pride and donned bloomers. I quickly saw that this despised garment was the only practical thing to wear, and I will say right here that those bloomers won for me everywhere the respect and consideration which a woman has the right to expect. After the novelty had worn off I felt a certain degree of independence which I had never before experienced.

## A Word for Bloomers

I firmly believe that if I had worn skirts I should not have been able to make the trip. It must not be thought that I lost the attention which is supposed to be associated with feminine apparel. I was everywhere treated with courtesy, and for the benefit of my sisters who hesitate about donning bloomers I will confess that I received no less than two hundred proposals of marriage. I will not attempt to guess how many were worthy of serious consideration. Many favored too strongly of dime museums, and as I had no desire to pose as a freak I paid no attention to them. I mention this to prove that bloomers are no handicap to matrimonial aspirations.

In Chicago I exchanged my forty-five pound wheel for one weighing only twenty pounds. Again I decorated myself with advertising ribbons in exchange for $185 in cash and started back to New York. I found this return trip much pleasanter than the first one. The bicycle clubs en route gave me an opportunity to earn money, and when I reached New York again, in eighteen days after leaving Chicago, I had enough money to pay my passage to Havre.

I sailed on La Touraine. I made myself known to the passengers and earned 150 francs lecturing. This was stolen from me the first day of my arrival in Havre. I was in a predicament for I was not permitted to speak in French and I found it difficult to make myself understood in English. The American Consul printed a large placard which explained in French the object of my visit and asking for an opportunity to earn some money.

## Earning Money Rapidly

The French people were very quick to catch the spirit of the occasion and I was overwhelmed with offers of one kind and another. I distributed dodgers [small handbills], gave exhibitions of riding, sold my photograph and served as clerk in different stores. In this way I collected $1,500 in five days. The Viscount de Mahia paid me $100 for a photograph. I visited different cities in France before reaching Paris. There I received a handsome silk American flag from the American Consul. He told me to keep that flag prominently displayed wherever I went and that it would always protect me. You may rest assured that I followed his instructions.

I lectured at the Crystal Palace and took in $1,000. I gave an exhibition ride and received a medal and a diamond pin. I must say that the French are the most patriotic people I met in my journey around the world. I have to laugh when I think of myself standing before a big hall full of people jabbering away in English which not one in a hundred could understand. Every few minutes I would shout "Vive la France!" Then how they did cheer! It was positively inspiring. I found out what they liked and gave them plenty of it. The American or English people, if there were any present, must have thought I was a candidate for a lunatic asylum. But the Frenchmen enjoyed the "Vive la France" part of my lecture, and they were the ones I was trying hardest to please. I was able to forward $1,500 from Paris.

I was quite the rage there as an advertising medium. I remained there two weeks and then started for Marseilles.

## Attacked by Highwaymen

One night I had an encounter with highwaymen near Lacone [Laçon, about 30 miles north of Marseilles]. I think they were waiting for me, for they knew I had been earning money in Paris. There were three men in the party, and all wore masks. They sprang at me from behind a clump of trees, and one of them grabbed my bicycle wheel, throwing me heavily. I carried a revolver in my pocket within easy reach, and when I stood up I had that revolver against the head of the man nearest me. He backed off but another seized me from behind and disarmed me. They rifled my pockets and found just three francs. They were magnanimous enough to return that money to me. My shoulder had been badly wrenched by my fall, and my ankle was sprained, but I was able to continue my journey.

Several wheelmen of the Lacone Club rode out to meet me, and when they understood the cause of my injuries they would not let me travel alone while I remained on French soil.

Great preparations had been made for my reception in Marseilles, but I cut a sorry-looking figure when I reached the city. My ankle was so badly swollen that I could not use it, so I was forced to ride into the city with my injured foot in bandages hanging over the handle-bar and pedaling with the other. I was escorted to the hotel by a long procession of cyclists, and the streets were lined with people who were anxious to see the American lady who was riding around the world on a bicycle. My Stars and Stripes were hung from a staff attached to my handle-bar, and it was heartily cheered.

## Hunting Big Game

In five days at Marseilles I earned enough money to pay my passage on a steamer to Alexandria. I visited Jerusalem, Port Said, Aden, Bombay, Calcutta, Ceylon and Singapore. In

India I fell in with a party of ten, consisting of Prince Leland of Germany, and his guests. They were on a tiger hunt and rode elephants. I accepted their invitation to join the hunt, and saw a tiger shot. Prince Leland made me a present of the skin. All through that region I aroused the greatest curiosity of the natives, but the missionaries were not very cordial. They did not approve of women riding bicycles. I earned only $200 from the time I left Paris until I reached China.

I registered at all the places stipulated in the agreement, and when I reached Shanghai I heard of the danger of traveling through that country. I had unwittingly approached the very seat of hostilities. I was warned to get out of the country as quickly as possible, but my American spirit was up, and I was determined to see the fun. I knew that here was a glorious opportunity for me to collect material that would yield a good financial return when I reached my own country, for that was my only hope of raising the stipulated $5,000.

So I determined to go to the front, and I went. I knew that I could fill any hall in the United States with the announcement that I was an eye-witness of battles in China. The result proved that I was right, for I easily completed the amount as soon as I reached this country.

## At the Great Massacre

From Shanghai I went to Nagasaki and met two war correspondents bound for the front. I received passports from the Japanese Government and accompanied them. We landed near Port Arthur with the second Japanese Army. Wei-heiwei was their objective point. We followed. I shall never forget the horrible scenes I witnessed at Port Arthur. We arrived there after the butchery, but the dead remained unburied. I saw the bodies of women nailed to the houses, the bodies of little children torn limb from limb. Everywhere there was evidence of the most horrible butchery and mutilation of the dead. At Wei-heiwei the slaughter had been worse than at Port Arthur. When we passed through Chefoo the streets were filled with the dead.

I was an eye-witness of the battle of Gasan. It was the first

I had seen, and I don't want to see another. The fighting continued from 9 o'clock in the morning until 4 o'clock in the afternoon. The Chinese had laid some mines for the destruction of the Japanese Army, and then by some mistake the Chinese Army occupied that identical position. The stupid men in charge of the mines exploded them at that moment and caused a frightful slaughter of their own people. Fifteen hundred Chinamen were killed and only twenty-two Japanese. Great chasms fifty feet in depth were formed by the explosion. They proved to be burial places for the dead. It was a horrible experience.

## Shot in the Arm

I crossed the Pontoon River accompanied by a Japanese guide and a British missionary named F. A. Moffatt. The river was frozen over, but when near the shore the ice broke and we all fell in. While in that predicament a party of Chinamen appeared on the opposite bank and fired at us, killing the Japanese guide, and wounding both Mr. Moffatt and myself. I was shot in the shoulder. Both of us reached the shore alive, but Mr. Moffatt died from the effects of his wound a few days later.

That same day we were captured by the Japanese and were thrown into a cell, and left without food for three days. Mr. Moffatt would have lived if he could have received proper medical attention. The cell was merely a hut with lattice-work sides. There was no protection from the bitter cold and I suffered keenly. While thus imprisoned a Japanese soldier dragged a Chinese prisoner up to my cell and killed him before my eyes, drinking his blood while the muscles were yet quivering.

I appealed to the American Consul, but he paid no attention to my call. Then I requested the French official to secure my release, and he sent a troop of forty soldiers. I was released in a hurry. Before leaving for Japan I took a run up to Siberia, and saw the prisoners working in the mines. I saw one string of forty prisoners arrive. They had walked 1,400 Russian miles.

## Again in America

When I reached Yokohama I needed just 86 yen to secure my passage across the Pacific. The American Consul refused to interest himself in my trip. He said: "You've been receiving so much attention from the French that you'd better let them see you through." I took him at his word and appealed to the French Consul. He introduced me to friends, who gave me the chance to earn 250 yen.

I sailed for San Francisco on the steamer Belgic, arriving there March 23˙ of the present year, forty-eight days ahead of schedule. I was glad enough to get away from the land of rats and rice and into a country where one could get a decent bed. The furnace beds of Corea are peculiar institutions. A fire is built underneath and the occupant is obliged to keep turning in order to avoid roasting to death. One side will freeze while the other is being roasted.

Well, when I reached San Francisco I felt as if my journey was ended. I never made a greater mistake in my life. The hardest part of the entire trip was through Southern California and the desert in Arizona. At Stockton I was nearly killed by a runaway, and was laid up five weeks. My experience in China had undermined my nervous system, and I collapsed under what would have been a trifle at another time. The enforced rest did me a lot of good, though. Otherwise I would not have been able to have made my way through the desert. I succeeded in acquiring the trick of jumping my wheel from railroad tie to railroad tie, a really not difficult thing to learn, and I traveled along the railroad quite comfortably.

## The Worst Part of the Trip

I had a journey of 165 miles through the sand. Engineer Zeigler, of the through express, stopped when he saw me and offered me a ride, but I explained why I could not accept his offer. He gave me some iced milk. At Yuma, Ari., a woman refused to give me a drink of water. It was the first act of inhospitality I had experienced and in my own country, too. Her excuse later, when questioned by the local newspaper men was: "I didn't know her. I thought she was a tramp."

At another place I was given some stale bread and then forced to saw wood in payment. I explained that I had never before tackled a woodpile and told her of my journey. I had to chop wood, nevertheless.

In another place I could find no shelter and spent the night in a graveyard. I slept comfortably with a grave for my pillow and was awakened by a shrill voice exclaiming: "Hi, there! Get off my old man's grave!" Inasmuch as the command was backed by an uplifted broom, I obeyed in a hurry.

## Finished on Time

An amateur photographer "caught" us just as the old lady caught me. In all the different countries I visited the only affront I received was from my own sex. I was treated with uniform courtesy by the men.

Well, I reached Chicago safely on Thursday, Sept. 12, fourteen days ahead of the time allowed by the agreement. This completed my journey, for I had already touched Chicago and I had thus completed the girdle around the world. The gentleman who had won the wager presented me with the stake—$10,000—and in addition I had the $5,318.75 which I had earned. My expenses for the entire time had been $1,200. I rode 9,604 miles on the wheel, and the ocean travel and walking in addition made a grand total of 26,000 miles travesed in the fourteen and one-half months.

—NELLIE BLY, JR.

# A Note on Sources

∞

In reconstructing Annie's story, I faced an obstacle familiar to others who have undertaken similar endeavors: primary sources that have gone missing over the years. Family members don't always preserve the artifacts of the lives of ordinary people, even of those who do extraordinary things. They may not recognize that the artifacts are worth saving. The stories of women in particular, especially those who lived their lives more than a century ago, may be especially underappreciated by family members. Anger, resentment, or even shame may lead to the destruction of documents, diaries, and memoirs. It is clear that Annie's journey had some serious adverse consequences on members of her immediate family, but why more remnants of her journey did not survive is impossible to know. Annie's first business, in the Bronx, was destroyed by fire and it is possible she kept her personal papers there. In cases like hers, we are left to pull together a picture with whatever bits and pieces of her life can be gathered.

Linda Lawrence Hunt, the author of *Bold Spirit: Helga Estby's Forgotten Walk Across Victorian America,* calls this the "rag-rug" approach to history. It is akin to making a quilt from the remnants of cast-off bits of fabric. This is not to say that I didn't uncover a lot of material, especially newspaper accounts. Indeed, I was able to find hundreds of newspaper accounts from the United States, Europe, and even Vietnam, Singapore, and other places that provide a colorful picture of the entire arc of Annie's journey.

Despite what I *do* know, my knowledge of Annie is necessarily incom-

plete. For example, other than what she shared with newspaper reporters—and she was quite a talker—we don't have the benefit of her
day-to-day observations of her circumstances or access to her inner
thoughts about, say, leaving her children or the import of her own journey. We don't know how her family fared back in Boston during her absence. But without the "rag-rug" approach to the stories of women such
as Annie, many valuable stories that illuminate important parts of our
history will forever be left untold. Indeed, as Ellen Smith, curator of the
American Jewish Historical Society, told me, "if we only told the stories of
women who left diaries and letters behind, we wouldn't have women's
history."

There is, of course, no way to know the boundaries of one's own ig-
norance. No matter how much material I have unearthed, I have no way
of knowing what else might be out there. Annie crossed paths with thousands of people during her journey. How many of them kept a photograph, or recorded a memory in a diary, now gathering dust in a Paris
attic, a Yokohama library, or a Yuma, Arizona, ranch house? Whose descendants might have a letter penned by Annie more than a hundred
years ago, postmarked Marseilles, Saigon, or Trinidad, Colorado?

Despite my efforts to learn everything I could about Annie's around-
the-world tour, it is possible evidence will later come to light that will
prove some of my assumptions and conclusions to be off the mark. But I
don't think they will detract from Annie's singular accomplishment nor
dim this remarkable chapter in her life.

# Bibliography

Bryson, Conrey. *Down Went McGinty: El Paso in the Wonderful Nineties*. El Paso: Texas Western Press, 1977.

Collins, Gail. *America's Women: 400 Years of Dolls, Drudges, Helpmates and Heroines*. New York: William Morrow, 2003.

Dodge, Pryor. *The Bicycle*. Paris-New York: Flammarion, 1996.

Gibb, Evelyn McDaniel. *Two Wheels North: Bicycling the West Coast in 1909*. Cornwallis, OR: Oregon State University Press, 2000.

Goddard, Stephen B. *Colonel Albert Pope and His American Dream Machines: The Life and Times of a Bicycle Tycoon Turned Automotive Pioneer*. Jefferson, NC, and London: McFarland & Company, Inc., 2000.

Gordon, Sarah A. " 'Any Desired Length': Negotiating Gender Through Sports Clothing, 1870–1925," in *Beauty and Business: Commerce, Gender, and Culture in Modern America,* edited by Philip Scranton. New York and London: Routledge, 2001, 24–51.

Herlihy, David V. *Bicycle: The History*. New Haven: Yale University Press, 2004.

Jamieson, Duncan R. *On Your Left: A History of Bicycle Journeying*. Unpublished manuscript.

Leete, Harley M., ed. *The Best of Bicycling!* New York: Pocket Books, 1970.

Leonard, Irving A. *When Bikehood was in Flower: Sketches of Early Cycling*. Tucson: Seven Palms Press, 1983.

Loher, George T. *The Wonderful Ride: Being the True Journal of Mr. George T. Loher who in 1895 Cycled from Coast to Coast on his Yellow Fellow Wheel*. San Francisco: Harper & Row, 1978.

King, Gilbert. *The Bicycle: Boneshakers, Highwheelers, and Other Celebrated Cycles*. Philadelphia-London: Courage Books, 2002.

Kinsman, Brian. *Around the World Awheel: The Adventures of Karl M. Creelman*. Hantsport, Nova Scotia: Lancelot Press, 1993.

Kroeger, Brooke. *Nellie Bly: Daredevil, Reporter, Feminist*. New York: Times Books, 1994.

Middleton, Dorothy. *Victorian Lady Travelers*. New York: Dutton, 1982 (first American paperback edition).

Petty, Ross D. "Women and the Wheel: How the Bicycle Led from Social Control to Social Freedom." *Cycle History: Proceedings of the 7th International Cycle History Conference,* Rob van der Plas, ed., San Francisco: Van der Plas Publishing, 1997, 112–133.

Pridmore, Jay, and Jim Hurd. *The American Bicycle*. Osceola, WI: Motorbooks International, 1995.

Sarna, Jonathan D., and Ellen Smith, eds., *The Jews of Boston*. Boston: The Combined Jewish Philanthropies, 1995.

Schriber, Mary Suzanne, ed. *Telling Travels: Selected Writings by Nineteenth-Century American Women Abroad*. DeKalb: Northern Illinois Press, 1995.

Sherr, Lynn. *Failure Is Impossible: Susan B. Anthony in Her Own Words*. New York: Times Books, 1995.

Sims, Sally. "The Bicycle, the Bloomer and Dress Reform in the 1890s," in *Dress and Popular Culture,* edited by Patricia A. Cunningham and Susan Voso Lab. Bowling Green, OH: Bowling Green State University Popular Press, 1991, 125–45.

———. "The Bicycle, The Bloomer, and The 'New Woman': Images of the American Woman Awheel, 1890–1899." Unpublished masters thesis (George Washington University, 1975).

Smith, Robert A., *A Social History of the Bicycle,* New York: McGraw Hill, 1972.

Starrs, James E., ed. *The Literary Cyclist: Great Bicycling Scenes in Literature*. New York: Breakaway Books, 1997.

Stevens, Thomas. *Around the World on a Bicycle*. Mechanicsburg, PA: Stackpole Books 2001. Originally published in two vols.: 1887; 1888.

Tye, Larry. *Home Lands: Portraits of the New Jewish Diaspora*. New York: Henry Holt & Company, 2001.

Verne, Jules. *Around the World in Eighty Days*. New York: Modern Library Classics, 1993. Originally published in 1872.

Ward, Geoffrey C., and Burns, Ken. *Not for Ourselves Alone: The Story of*

*Elizabeth Cady Stanton and Susan B. Anthony.* New York: Alfred A. Knopf, 1999.

Willard, Frances E. *A Wheel Within a Wheel: A Woman's Quest for Freedom,* Bedford, MA: Applewood Books, 1997. Originally published in 1895.

## News Articles About Annie's Around-the-World Ride

Note: Gathering this collection of contemporaneous newspaper and journal accounts of Annie's journey required reliance on many different people and methods. In some cases, I was assisted by librarians in distant cities or hired local researchers. Copies were not always entirely legible, depending on the quality of the microfilm or the microfilm reader and printer, and page numbers were not always noted. Many articles from the French press, and a few from U.S. newspapers, were in a scrapbook Annie kept and, in most cases, she did not note the name of the newspaper, the date, the page number, or even the city of publication, though that was often discernible from the text itself. In a few cases, I was able to locate other copies of these stories and to source them completely. An asterisk indicates articles in Annie's scrapbook that could not be further identified. In writing this book I also relied on countless newspaper articles that had nothing to do with Annie directly. For example, old newspapers provided valuable information about local weather, about cycling in the 1890s, and about international events that were relevant to Annie's journey, primarily the Sino-Japanese War of 1895. The articles listed here are only those that relate specifically to Annie. Where other articles are specifically quoted or referenced in the text, they appear in the endnotes.

"A Woman to Rival Paul Jones," *New York Times,* February 25, 1894, 12.

"New Feature in Globe Trotting," *Washington Post,* February 25, 1894, 1.

Item, *Boston Evening Transcript,* June 25, 1894, 1.

"Emulating 'Paul Jones,'" *Boston Evening Transcript,* June 25, 1894, 8.

"Going Woman," *Boston Post,* June 26, 1894.

"Will Journey on a Wheel," *Boston Journal,* June 26, 1894.

"Female Paul Jones on a Wheel," *Boston Daily Globe,* June 26, 1894, 2.

"Mrs. Kapchowsky Has a Big Contract," *Chicago Daily Inter Ocean,* June 26, 1894, 1.

Item, *Chicago Tribune,* June 26, 1894, 1.

Item, *Oswego (NY) Daily Times,* June 28, 1894, 3.

"A Female Globe Pedaller," *Poughkeepsie (NY) Weekly Enterprise,* June 8, 1894, 1.

Item, *Pittsburgh Press,* July 2, 1894.

"Wheeling 'Round the World," *New York World,* July 3, 1894.

"Wheel Around the World," *New York Herald,* July 3, 1894.

"Wheeling 'Round the World," *Washington Post,* July 15, 1894, 7.

Item, *Freeborn County (Albert Lea, MN) Standard,* July 18, 1894, 2.

"Wheeling 'Round the World," *Cambridge (OH) Jeffersonian,* July 19, 1894.

"Boston's Globe Trotter," *Atlanta Constitution,* July 19, 1894, 5.

Item, *New York Daily Tribune,* July 27, 1894.

"Mlle. Londonderry Coming to Albany," *Albany Times-Union,* July 27, 1894, 1.

"Off on a Long Journey," *New York Times,* July 29, 1894, 3.

"Around the World on a Bicycle," *Brooklyn Daily Eagle,* July 29, 1894, 3.

"Miss Londonderry Heard from Again," *Boston Daily Globe,* July 29, 1894, 7.

Item, *New York Herald,* July 29, 1894, 11.

"Will Circle the Globe," *Elyria (OH) Republican,* August 2, 1894, 8.

"Mlle. Londonderry Starts," *The Referee,* August 3, 1894.

"Another 'Round the World," *Bicycling World,* August 3, 1894, 326.

"Around the World," *Hagerstown (MD) Herald & Torch Light,* August 23, 1894.

"Around the World via Brocton," *Brocton (NY) Grape Belt,* August 31, 1894, 1.

"To Encircle the Globe," *Westfield (NY) Republican,* September 5, 1894, 1.

"Around the World on a Wheel," *Chicago Daily Inter Ocean,* September 25, 1894.

"Annie Londonderry's Long Ride," *Chicago Daily Tribune,* September 25, 1894, 11.

Item, *Cycling Life,* September 27, 1894, 9.

Item in "Among the Wheelmen," *New York Times,* October 11, 1894, 6.

"Londonderry, Globe-Girdler," *Cycling Life,* October 11, 1894, 19. (Same image in *L.A.W. Bulletin* on the same date.)

"Miss Londonderry Ready to Start," *The Bearings,* October 12, 1894.

"Miss Londonderry Away Again," *The Referee,* October 12, 1894.

Item, *Chicago Daily Tribune,* October 14, 1894, 6.

"Plucky Miss Londonderry," *Chicago Sunday Inter Ocean,* October 14, 1894.

"Miss Londonderry to Start Again," *Chicago Sunday Herald,* October 14, 1894, 8.

"Miss Londonderry Departs," *Chicago Daily Inter Ocean,* October 15, 1894.

"A Brave Woman," *South Bend (IN) Daily Times,* October 15, 1894.

Item, *Elkhart (IN) Daily Review,* October 17, 1894, 3.

Item, *South Bend (IN) Daily Times,* October 17, 1894.

"Around the World," *Elkhart (IN) Daily Truth,* October 17, 1894.

Item, *Pittsburgh Press,* October 18, 1894.

Item, *Cycling Life,* October 18, 1894, 9.

"An Earth Navigator," *Kendallville (IN) Weekly News,* October 18, 1894.

"A Couple of Transcontinentalists," *Goshen (IN) Daily News,* October 18, 1894, 1.

"She Rides in Bloomers," *Oakland (CA) Daily Evening Tribune,* October 18, 1894.

Item, *Mishawaka (IN) Enterprise,* October 19, 1894.

"A Woman of Accomplishments," *Los Angeles Times,* October 19, 1894, 1.

Item, *Fort Wayne (IN) News,* October 20, 1894.

"A Woman with Nerve," *Sandusky (OH) Register,* October 22, 1894.

"Item, *Newark (OH) Daily Advocate,* October 22, 1894.

"Round the World on a Wheel," *Boston Herald,* October 22, 1894, 10.

"Miss Londonderry's 'Cycle Ride," *Syracuse Post,* October 22, 1894, 6.

"The Female Globe Girdler," *Middletown (NY) Daily Argus,* October 22, 1894, 7.

"On a Long Journey," *Toledo Commercial,* October 22, 1894.

"Even with Her Schedule," *Boston Daily Globe,* October 22, 1894, 1.

"Three Cents and a Bicycle," *Philadelphia Inquirer,* October 22, 1894, 6.

Item, *Tacoma Daily News,* October 22, 1894, 4.

"Miss Londonderry's Trip," *Dallas Morning News,* October 22, 1894, 7.

"Touring on Three Cents," *Salt Lake Tribune,* October 22, 1894, 2.

"Turning the World on 3 Cents," *Ogden (UT) Standard Examiner,* October 22, 1894, 1.

"Daring Woman Cyclist," *Buffalo Evening News,* October 23, 1894, 1.

"Annie Londonderry in Norwalk," *Sandusky (OH) Register,* October 24, 1894, 1.

Item, *Goshen (IN) Democrat,* October 24, 1894, 3.

"Around the World on a Wheel," *Davenport (IA) Weekly,* October 24, 1894, 3.

Item, *Ligonier (IN) Leader,* October 25, 1894, 5.

Item, *Ligonier (IN) Banner,* October 25, 1894, 5.

Item, *Elyria (OH) Republican,* October 25, 1894, 1.

Item, *Cycling Life,* October 25, 1894, 9.

"Around the World in Bloomers," *Freemont (OH) Democratic Messenger,* October 25, 1894, 5.

Item, *Butler (IN) Record,* October 26, 1894, 5.

"Long Bicycle Rides," *Freemont (OH) Journal,* October 26, 1894.

"Bicycling," *Cleveland Plain Dealer,* October 26, 1894.

"Around the World," *Cleveland Leader,* October 26, 1894, 7.

Item, *Chicago Tribune,* October 26, 1894, 11.

"Chat About the Pedal Pushers," *Philadelphia Inquirer,* October 28, 1894, 24.

"Cycling Up to Date," *Syracuse Post,* October 30, 1894.

"Cycling Up to Date," *Syracuse Standard,* October 30, 1894, 8.

"Around the World in Eight Months," *Erie (PA) Morning Dispatch,* October 31, 1894, p. 2.

Item, *Syracuse Courier,* October 31, 1894.

"Ramblers' Halloween Party," *Buffalo Express,* October 31, 1894.

"Miss Annie Londonderry," *Les Journal de Vélocipédistes,* November 1894.

"Miss Londonderry's Ride," *Buffalo Commercial,* November 1, 1894.

"A Globe Trotter," *Elyria (OH) Republican,* November 1, 1894, 7.

"Rambler's Social Season," *Buffalo Commercial,* November 1, 1894.

"Round the World," *Buffalo Express,* November 1, 1894.

"Social Cyclers," *Buffalo Express,* November 1, 1894.

"Miss Londonderry," *Buffalo Courier,* November 1, 1894.

Item, *The American Farmer,* November 1, 1894, 63.

"Miss Londonderry in Cleveland," *The Bearings,* November 2, 1894.

"Miss Londonderry Continues," *Buffalo Express,* November 2, 1894.

"Miss Londonderry," *Syracuse Post,* November 2, 1894, 6.

Item, *Syracuse Courier,* November 2, 1894, 2.

"Will Soon Reach Syracuse," *Syracuse Daily Journal,* November 2, 1894, 6.

"Around the World," *Rochester Post-Express,* November 2, 1894.

"Another Dead Broke Rider," *Rochester Democrat and Chronicle,* November 2, 1894.

Item, *Syracuse Courier,* November 3, 1894.

Item, *Syracuse Daily Journal,* November 3, 1894.

"Miss Londonderry Coming," *Syracuse Post,* November 3, 1894.

"Starts Tomorrow," date and source unknown (probably Rochester).*

"Likes Bloomers," *Rochester Herald,* November 3, 1894.

"Globe Circling Cyclers," *Rochester Herald,* November 4, 1894 (reference to Annie in first paragraph but not by name).

"The Woman Globe Girdler," *Syracuse Standard,* November 4, 1894, 6.

"Miss Annie Londonderry Coming," *Syracuse Herald,* November 4, 1894, 3.

"Miss Londonderry Here," *Syracuse Herald,* November 5, 1894, 5.

"Bad, Bad Roads," *Syracuse Daily Journal,* November 5, 1894, 5.

"A Young Woman on a Wheel," *Geneva (NY) Advertiser,* November 6, 1894, 2.

Item, *Geneva (NY) Advertiser,* November 6, 1894, 3.

"Mlle. Londonderry En Route," *Syracuse Daily Standard,* November 6, 1894, 8.

"Is it a Girl?" *Syracuse Courier,* November 6, 1894.

"A Daring Young Woman," *Syracuse Post,* November 6, 1894.

"On Her Way Round the World," *Wheeling (WV) Register,* November 6, 1894, 1.

"Working Eastward," *Lowell (MA) Daily Sun,* November 6, 1894, 1.

"A Brave Woman," date and source unknown.*

"Plucky Lady Rider," date and source unknown (Cleveland).*

"Miss Londonderry's Novel Adventure," date and source unknown.*

Item, *Cycling Life,* November 8, 1894, 9.

"Off on Her Wheel Again," *Syracuse Post,* November 8, 1894.

"A Fair Traveller," *The American Athlete,* November 9, 1894, 385.

"A Plucky Wheelwoman," *Illustrated Buffalo Express,* November 11, 1894, 8.

"A 'Dead Broke' Girl," *Utica Sunday Journal,* November 11, 1894, 1.

"Where is Cyclist Lenz?" *Utica Sunday Journal,* November 11, 1894, 1.

"Miss Londonderry the Cyclist," *Utica Sunday Tribune,* November 11, 1894.

Item, *Salt Lake Tribune,* November 11, 1894, 9.

Item, *Los Angeles Times,* November 12, 1894, 8.

"Miss Londonderry in Town," *Utica Daily Press,* November 12, 1894.

Item, *Utica Observer,* November 12, 1894.

"Anna Londonderry in Utica," *Utica Morning Herald,* November 12, 1894.

Item, *Syracuse Courier,* November 13, 1894, 2.

Item, *Canajoharie (NY) Courier,* November 13, 1894.

"A Riding Advertisement," *Cycling Life,* November 15, 1894, 12.

Item, *Syracuse Courier,* November 15, 1894, 2.

Item, *Nairn's News of the Wheel* (London), November 28, 1894, 27.

Item, *Cycling Life,* November 29, 1894, 8.

"Passengers on La Touraine," *Journal de Havre,* December 2–3, 1894, 3.

Items (2), *Le Vélo,* December 4, 1894, 2.

Item, *La Libre Parole* (Paris), December 5, 1894.

"Le Tour du Monde d'une Américaine Sans Argent," *Le Figaro* (Paris), December 7, 1894.

Item, *Echo de Paris,* December 8, 1894.

Item, *Le Charivari* (Paris), December 8, 1894, 2.

Item, *Paris-Sport,* December 8, 1894, 4.

"Annie Londonderry," *National Police Gazette,* December 8, 1894, 13.

"Miss Londonderry," *New York Herald* (Paris Edition), December 8, 1894, 3.

"Poor Miss Londonderry!" *New York Herald* (Paris Edition), December 9, 1894, 3.

"An American Lady on Tramp," *Galignani Messenger* (Paris), December 10, 1894.

"Le Tour du Monde d'une Parisienne sans Argent," *Le Journal* (Paris), December 10, 1894. (Cartoon spoof.)

"Le Tour du Monde en Bicyclette," *Le Jour* (Paris), December 14, 1894.

"Fantaise Américaine," *La France* (Paris), December 18, 1894, 3.

Item, *Nairn's News of the Wheel* (London), December 19, 1894, 62.

Item, *L'Autorité* (Paris), December 19, 1894.

Item, *L'Autorité* (Paris), December 20, 1894. 4.

"Whitworth," *Le Vélo* (Paris), December 21, 1894.

"Daily Gossip," *Le Vélo* (Paris), December 21, 1894.

Item, *Journal de Débats* (Paris), December 22, 1894, 3.

Item, *Le Vélo* (Paris), December 22, 1894.

Item, *New York Times,* December 23, 1894.

Item, *La France* (Paris), December 23, 1894.

Item, *Echo de Paris,* December 23, 1894.

Item, *Le Vélo* (Paris), December 24, 1894.

Item, *Syracuse Standard,* December 25, 1894.

Item, *Le Vélo* (Paris), December 25, 1894, 2.

Item, *Le Charivari* (Paris), December 26, 1894.

"Le Tour du Monde: Avec 5 Centimes!" *Le Figaro* (Paris), December 27, 1894.

Item, *Patrie* (Paris), December 27, 1894.

Item, *Le Voleur Illustré,* December 27, 1894, 802.

"Le tour du monde en vélocipéde," *La Bicyclette* (Paris), December 28, 1894, 4129.

"Le Tour du Monde avec Cinc Centimes," *Le Vélo* (Paris), December 28, 1894, 2.

Item, *Le Petit Parisien,* December 29, 1894.

"En route pour Marseille," *Le Vélo* (Paris), December 29, 1894.

"Le Tour du Monde avec 5 Centimes," *Lyon-Vélo,* December 29, 1894, 3.

Item, *Echo de Paris,* December 29, 1894.

"En Route pour Marseilles," *Le Vélo* (Paris), December 29, 1894.

Item, *Journal de Débats* (Paris), December 29, 1894, 4.

Item, *Le Vélo* (Paris), December 30, 1894, 3.

Item, *New York Herald* (Paris Edition), December 30, 1894, 3.

Item, *Le Figaro* (Paris), December 30, 1894.

Item, *La France* (Paris), December 30, 1894.

Item, *Nation* (Paris), December 30, 1894, 3.

Item, *Nouvelliste de Seine et Marne,* December 30, 1894, 3.

"Miss Londonderry," *Le Quotidien Illustre,* December 31, 1894, 6.

Item, *Revue Mensuelle du Touring Club de France,* January, 1895.

"Sur la route de Chine," *Le Vélo* (Paris), January 1, 1895, 1.

Item, *Le Quotidien Illustre,* January 2, 1895, 7.

Item, *Le Voleur Illustré,* January 2, 1895, 2.

Item, *Cycling Life,* January 3, 1895.

"Sur la Route de Chine," *Le Vélo* (Paris), January 3, 1895.

"Le Tour du Monde avec 5 Centimes," *Le Véloce-Sport* (Bordeaux), January 3, 1895, p. 18.

"Vélocipédie," *Le Nouvelliste* (Melun), January 3, 1895, 3.

"Le Voyage de Miss Londonderry," *Le Jour* (Paris), January 4, 1895.

Item, *L'Abeille de Fontainebleau,* January 4, 1895, 1.

"Sur la route de Chine," *Le Vélo* (Paris), January 4, 1895.

"Miss Londonderry," *La Bicyclette,* January 4, 1895, 4156.

"Le Tour du Monde à Bicyclette," *La Revue Vélocipédique,* January 4, 1895, 8–9.

"Miss Londonderry," *Boston Daily Globe,* January 5, 1895.

"Voyage à Travers Le Monde en Bicyclette," *La Parole de Nemours,* January 5, 1895, 1.

"Le Tour du Monde à Bicyclette," *Le Cosnois* (Cosne-Cours-sur-Loire), January 5, 1895, 2.

"Miss Annie Londonderry," *Salut Public* (Lyon), January 5, 1895.

"Le Tour du Monde en Bicyclette," *L'Express,* (Lyon), January 5, 1895, 3.

"Miss Annie Londonderry," *Lyon Républican,* January 5, 1895.

Item, *L'Abeille de Fontainebleau,* January 5, 1895.

"A bicyclette autor du Monde: Miss Londonderry," *A Travers le Monde,* 39. Paris: Hachette, 1895. (This article was located in the 1895 edition of a book published annually from 1895 to 1914 by the Parisian publisher Hachette. These books were compilations of articles; this one originally appeared in a journal titled *Le Tour du Monde* on January 5, 1895.)

"Un Voyage autour du Monde," *Le Petit Provençal* (Marseilles), January 6, 1895, 2.

"Sur la Route de Chine," *La Vélo* (Paris), January 7, 1895.

"Une Intrépide Cycliste," *Messager de Valence,* January 7–8, 1895, 2.

"Le Tour du Monde à Bicyclette," *Journal de Valence,* January 7–8, 1895, 2.

"Sur la Route de Chine," *Le Vélo* (Paris), January 8, 1895, 1.

"The Girdler," *Syracuse Courier,* January 8, 1895, 2.

Item, *Nairn's News of the Wheel* (London), January 9, 1895, 105.

"Sport Vélocipédique: Miss Londonderry," *Messager de Valence,* January 9, 1895.

"Le Tour du Monde à Bicyclette: Miss Londonderry à Valence," *Journal de Valence,* January 9, 1895.

"Sport Vélocipédique," *Le Semaine Mondaire* (Avignon), January 9, 1895, 1.

Item, *Mistral* (Avignon), January 9, 1895, 3.

"Pedale," *Messager de Valence,* January 10, 1895, 2.

"Miss Londonderry," *Journal de Valence,* January 10, 1895, 2.

Item, *Messager de Valence,* January 11, 1895, 2.

"Miss Londonderry," *La Bicyclette,* January 11, 1895, 4190.

"Miss Londonderry," *Lyon-Vélo,* January 12, 1895, 2.

Item, *Journal de Montélimar,* January 12, 1895, 1.

"De Valence à Orange avec Miss Londonderry," *Messager de Valence,* January 12, 1895, 3.

"Arrivée de Miss Londonderry," *Le Petit Provençal,* January 12, 1895, 2.

"Sur la Route de Chine," *Le Vélo* (Paris), January 13, 1895, 1.

"Miss Londonderry," *Le Petit Provencal,* January 13, 1895, 2.

"Voyage autour du Monde," *L'Echo du Jour* (Avignon), January 13, 1895, 2.

"Miss Londonderry," *Le Petit Provençal,* January 13, 1895.

"Causerie," *Le Progres Illustré* (Lyon), January 13, 1895.

Item, *Courier du Midi* (Avignon), January 13, 1895.

"Intrépidité fin de-siècle," *La Croix de la Drome,* January 13, 1895.

Item, *Le Radical* (Marseilles), January 13, 1895, 2.

"Miss Londonderry," *Soleil du Midi* (Marseilles), January 13, 1895.

"Chronique Lyonnaise," *La Revue Vélocipédique,* January 14, 1895, 33.

"Miss Londonderry," *Le Petit Provençal,* January 14, 1895.

"Miss Londonderry," *Le Radical* (Marseilles), January 14, 1895, 2.

"Miss Londonderry," *Le Petit Provençal,* January 14, 1895, 2.

"Le Tour du Monde d'une Américane," *Soleil du Midi* (Marseilles), January 14, 1895.

Item, *Pittsburgh Chronicle-Telegraph,* January 14, 1895.

"Sur la Route de Chine," *Le Vélo* (Paris), January 15, 1895.

"Miss Londonderry," *Journal de Marseilles,* January 15, 1895, 5.

"Les globe-trotters," *Journal de Marseilles,* January 15, 1895, 5.

"Arrivée de Miss Londonderry," *Journal de Marseilles,* January 15, 1895.

"Sport Vélocipédique," *Le Semaine Mondaine* (Avignon), January 16, 1895, 2.

"Les Aventures de Miss Londonderry," *Le Petit Marseillais,* January 16, 1895.

"Miss Londonderry, *Messager de Valence,* January 16, 1895, 3.

"Echos Vélocipédique," *Mistral* (Avignon), January 16, 1895.

"Le Tour du Monde à Bicyclette," *Le Jour* (Paris), January 16, 1895.

"Miss Londonderry," *Soleil du Midi* (Marseilles), January 16, 1895.

Item, *Le Quotidien Illustre,* January 17, 1895.

"Le Tour du Monde avec 5 Centimes," *Le Véloce-Sport,* January 17, 1895, 36.

Item, *Le Petit Provençal,* January 17, 1895, 3.

Item, *Cycling Life,* January 17, 1895.

"Les Glob' Trotters," *La Bicyclette,* January 18, 1895, 4221.

Item, *Le Petit Provençal,* January 18, 1895, 2–3.

"Miss Londonderry," *Le Radical* (Marseilles), January 18, 1895, 3.

Item, *Le Petit Provençal,* January 19, 1895, 2.

Item, *Le Quotidien Illustre,* January 19, 1895.

Item, *Lyon-Vélo,* January 19, 1895, 3.

"Miss Londonderry," *Le Petit Provençal,* January 19, 1895.

"Miss Londonderry," *Journal de Montélimar,* January 19, 1895, 2.

Item, *La Sartan* (Marseilles), January 19, 1895, 1.

"Le Tour du Monde de Deux Journalists," *L'Echo du Jour* (Avignon), January 20, 1895, 2.

"Départ du Courier de Chine," *Semaphore* (Marseilles), January 20–21, 1895, 1.

"Miss Londonderry," *Le Petit Provençal,* January 20, 1895.

"Le Depart de miss Londonderry," *Le Petit Provençal,* January 20, 1895, 2.

"Le Depart de miss Londonderry," *Le Petit Provençal,* January 21, 1895, 2.

Item, *Nairn's News of the Wheel* (London), January 23, 1895, 123.

Item, *Cycling Life,* January 24, 1895.

"Miss Londonderry," *Le Véloce-Sport,* January 24, 1895, 17.

"Notes de la Semaine: Miss Londonderry," *La Bicyclette,* January 25, 1895, 4249–50.

"Miss Londonderry," *Le Cosnois* (Cosne-Cours-sur-Loire), January 26, 1895, 2–3.

"Sur la Route du . . . Japon," *Le Vélo* (Paris), January 26, 1895, 1.

"A Lady Cyclist," *Egyptian Gazette,* January 26, 1895.

Item, *New York Clipper,* February 2, 1895, 771.

"Miss Annie Londonderry," *Le Cycle,* February 3, 1895. (Image and caption.)

"Miss Londonderry," *La Revue Vélocipédique,* February 4, 1895, 96.

Item, *Illustrated Buffalo Express,* February 3, 1895, 7.

"Autour de Monde," *Le Cycle,* February 10, 1895.

"Miss Annie Londonderry," date and source unknown.*

"Miss Londonderry," *Le Petit Provençal,* date unknown.*

"Miss Londonderry," *Le Petite Provençal,* date unknown.*

"Daily Gossip, " *Le Petit Provençal,* date unknown.*

"Miss Londonderry Distributrice de Prospectus," *Le Petit Provençal,* date unknown.*

"24,000 kilomètres avec un Soul," date and source unknown.*

"Une Bicycliste qui Fait le Tour du Monde," date and source unknown.*

"Le Sport: Le Tour du Monde à Bicyclette," *Le Progrés,* date unknown.

"Le Depart de Miss Londonderry," date and source unknown.*

"L'arrivée à Paris de miss Londondery [sic]: Une visite de l'intrépide voyageuse," date and source unknown.*

"An Unusual Scene in the Fort," *Ceylon Examiner,* February 7, 1895, 3.

Item, *Illustrated Buffalo Express,* January 27, 1895, 7.

"An Up-to-Date Lady-Cyclist," *Overland Ceylon Observer,* February 8, 1895.

Item, *New York Times,* February 10, 1895.

"A Woman on Wheels," *Straits Times* (Singapore), February 14, 1895.

"The New Woman in Singapore," *Singapore Free Press,* February 14, 1895.

"Une Célébrité va Encore Nous Arriver, Aprés-Demain par le Sydney: C'est Miss Londonderry," *Progrés de Saigon,* February 14, 1895.

"Chez Miss Londonderry," *Progrès de Saigon*, February 14, 1895.

Item, *Le Courrier de Saigon*, February 18, 1895.

Item in "Critique Théâtrale" column, *Le Courrier de Saigon*, February 18, 1895.

"Miss Londonderry," *Le Courrier de Saigon*, February 20, 1895.

"Le Tour du Monde avec 5 Centimes," *L'Indépendance Tonkinoise* (Hanoi), February 20, 1895, 1.

Item, *Hong Kong Daily Press*, February 22, 1895.

"Around the World Without a Cent," *Celestial Empire* (Shanghai), March 1, 1895, 293.

"Around the World for a Wager," *Japan Weekly Mail*, March 9, 1895.

"Shipping News," *Japan Weekly Mail*, March 9, 1895.

"Passengers, Arrived," *Japan Weekly Mail*, March 9, 1895.

Item, *La Bicyclette*, March 15, 1895, 4468.

"Annie Has a Start," *The Referee*, March 22, 1895, 1.

"The New Woman on a Tour," *San Francisco Examiner*, March 24, 1895.

"She Rides a Wheel," *San Francisco Chronicle*, March 24, 1895.

"Made Her Way on a Wheel," *San Francisco Call*, March 24, 1895.

Item, *Cycling Life*, March 28, 1895, 20.

Item, *Le Petit Parisien*, March 29, 1895.

Item, *Salt Lake Tribune*, March 29, 1895, 2.

"Got as Far as Shanghai," *Boston Daily Globe*, March 30, 1895.

"Miss Londonderry Found Again," *Radfahr-Chronik* (Munich), April 3, 1895, 1027.

"Miss Londonderry," *La Bicyclette*, April 5, 1895, 4572.

"Annie on Her Way Home," *The Referee*, April 5, 1895, 2.

"Annie Londonderry in America," *The Bearings*, April 5, 1895.

Item, *Sandusky (OH) Register*, April 8, 1895, 1.

"A Circular Spin," *Oakland Tribune*, April 10, 1895.

"Bicyclists Hurt," *Stockton Evening Mail*, April 11, 1895, 1.

Item, *Cycling Life*, April 11, 1895, 13.

"A Wonderful Woman's Pluck," *Stockton Daily Independent*, April 11, 1895, 3.

"Will Arrive Today," *Stockton Daily Independent*, April 11, 1895, 3.

"A Wheelwoman Arrived," *Stockton Evening Record*, April 11, 1895, 1.

"Injured Near Stockton," *San Francisco Morning Call*, April 12, 1895, 12.

"Miss Londonderry's Lecture," *Stockton Daily Independent*, April 12, 1895, 3.

"Lady Bicyclist Injured," *Fresno Weekly Republican*, April 12, 1895, 1.

"Accident to a Woman World Girdler," *Trenton (NJ) Times,* April 12, 1895.

"Annie Londonderry Hurt," *Salt Lake Tribune,* April 12, 1895, 2.

"The Great Meet," *San Jose Mercury News,* April 12, 1895, 4.

"It Rounds the Form Well," *Stockton Evening Mail,* April 13, 1895, 1.

Item, *Decatur (IL) Daily Republican,* April 13, 1895.

"New Woman on a Tour," *Chicago Daily Tribune,* April 13, 1895, 16.

"Wheeling Around the World," *Chicago Saturday Blade,* April 13, 1895, 5.

Item, *Tacoma Daily News,* April 13, 1895, 11.

"A Girl Globe Trotter," *Washington Post,* April 14, 1895.

"The Adventures of a Woman on Wheels," *English Sport & Amateur Wheelman,* April 17, 1895, 167.

Item, *San Jose Mercury News,* April 19, 1895, 4.

"Around the World," *San Jose Mercury,* April 19, 1895.

"Around the World," Annie Londonderry Arrives in San Jose," *San Jose Weekly Mercury,* April 20, 1895, 5.

"On a Wheel," *San Jose Daily Herald,* April 19, 1895, 8.

Item, *Radfahr-Chronik* (Munich), April 27, 1895, 1201.

Item, *Placerville (CA) Mountain Democrat,* April 27, 1895.

Item, *Omaha World Herald,* April 28, 1895, 20.

Item, *Sandusky (OH) Register,* April 29, 1895, 8.

Item, *Chicago Daily Tribune,* April 30, 1895, 11.

Item, *Morgan Hill (CA) Sun,* May 2, 1895.

"A Lady Cyclist," *Salinas Weekly Index,* May 2, 1895.

"A Fair Globe Girdler," *Olean (NY) Democrat,* May 3, 1895.

Item, *Paso Robles Record,* May 4, 1895.

Advertisement for Sterling Bicycles titled "Annie Is Back," *The Bearings,* May 10, 1895.

"Annie Is Back Again," *The Referee,* May 10, 1895, 27.

Item, *Santa Maria Times,* May 11, 1895.

"Around the World," *Santa Barbara Independent,* May 14, 1895, 1.

"The Races," *Santa Barbara Independent,* May 14, 1895.

"The Plucky Girl Who Is Cycling the Globe," *Los Angeles Times,* May 15, 1895, 11.

Item, *Oswego (NY) Daily Times,* May 16, 1895, 3.

Item, *Santa Maria Times,* May 18, 1895.

"Globe Girdling by Rail," *Watertown (NY) Daily Times,* May 18, 1895, 10.

"A Globe Wheeler," *Los Angeles Times,* May 19, 1895, 10.

"A Cycling Tour," *Mansfield (OH) News,* May 19, 1895.

"A Plucky Wheelwoman," *Auburn (NY) Bulletin,* May 20, 1895, 3.

"Globe Girdling by Rail," *Boonville (NY) Herald,* May 22, 1895, 8.

"The Globe Wheeler," *Los Angeles Times,* May 24, 1895, 7.

Item, *Santa Maria Times,* May 25, 1895.

Item, *Los Angeles Times,* May 27, 1895.

Item, *Los Angeles Times,* May 29, 1895, 7.

Item, *Cycling Life,* May 30, 1895, 8.

"A Girl Girdling the Globe," *San Bernardino Daily Sun,* May 30, 1895.

Item, *Los Angeles Times,* May 31, 1895, 11.

"The Globe Girdler," *Riverside Daily Press,* May 31, 1895.

Item, *Los Angeles Times,* June 1, 1895, 11.

"Winder's Wendings," *Illustrated Buffalo Express,* June 2, 1895, 11.

Item, *Los Angeles Times,* June 3, 1895, 9.

"Annie Londonderry," *Radfahr-Chronik* (Munich), June 5, 1895, 1511.

Item, *Arizona Republican,* June 13, 1895, 5.

Item, *Tucson Daily Star,* June 13, 1895.

Advertisement for Sterling Dealer Pinney & Robinson announcing personal appearance by Annie Londonderry, *Arizona Daily Gazette,* June 15, 1895, 5.

"A Woman on Wheels," *Arizona Republican,* June 15, 1895.

Item, *El Paso Daily Herald,* June 15, 1895, 1.

Items (2), *Arizona Daily Gazette,* June 16, 1895.

Item, *Tucson Daily Citizen,* June 18, 1895.

Item, *Tucson Daily Star,* June 18, 1895.

Item, *El Paso Daily Herald,* June 18, 1895, 1.

"Long Bicycle Riding," *Los Angeles Times,* June 19, 1895, 7.

"Indio," *Los Angeles Times,* June 19, 1895, 11.

Item, *Tucson Daily Citizen,* June 19, 1895.

Item, *Tucson Daily Citizen,* June 20, 1895.

Items (2), *Tucson Daily Star,* June 20, 1895.

"Miss Londonderry Arrives," *Arizona Star,* June 20, 1895, 4.

Item, *Arizona Star,* June 20, 1895.

Item, *Weekly Phoenix Herald,* June 20, 1895.

Item, *Los Angeles Times,* June 21, 1895, 9.

Item, *Tucson Daily Citizen,* June 21, 1895.

Item, *Tucson Daily Star,* June 21, 1895, 4.

"Tour on a Bike," *El Paso Daily Herald,* June 21, 1895, 1.

Item, *Tucson Daily Star,* June 22, 1895, 4.

Items (2), *El Paso Daily Herald,* June 24, 1895.

Item, *Los Angeles Times,* June 24, 1895, 3.

"Miss Londonderry Interviewed," *El Paso Daily Herald,* June 25, 1895, 1.

Item, *El Paso Daily Herald,* June 25, 1895.

"A Tramp to Strauss," *El Paso Daily Herald,* June 26, 1895, 1.

"Miss Londonderry This Morning," *El Paso Daily Times,* June 26, 1895.

Item, *Weekly Phoenix Herald,* June 27, 1895.

Items (4), *El Paso Daily Herald,* June 27, 1895, 1.

"Miss Londonderry," *El Paso Daily Herald,* June 27, 1895.

"Declined Many Offers of Marriage," *Frederick (MD) News,* June 27, 1895, 1.

"Woman Bicycling Around the World," *Warren (PA) Evening Democrat,* June 27, 1895, 1.

"Progress of a Fair Globe Wheeler," *Davenport (IA) Leader,* June 27, 1895, 1.

Item, *Lordsburg (NM) Western Liberal,* June 28, 1895, 2.

Item, *El Paso Daily Times,* June 28, 1895, 4.

"The New Woman," *Deming (NM) Headlight,* June 28, 1895.

"Miss Londonderry Genuine," *El Paso Daily Times,* June 29, 1895, 2.

Item, *El Paso Daily Times,* June 30, 1895, 5.

"Miss Londonderry's Lecture," *El Paso Daily Herald,* July 2, 1895.

Items (7), *El Paso Daily Herald,* July 2, 1895.

Item, Unidentified, El Paso.

Item, *Los Angeles Times,* July 5, 1895, 6.

"Declined 150 Offers of Marriage," *Renwick (IA) Times,* July 5, 1895.

Items (2), *El Paso Daily Herald,* July 5, 1895.

Item, *El Paso Daily Herald,* July 6, 1895.

"Lady Cyclist on Her Way Here," *Albuquerque Morning Democrat,* July 6, 1895.

Item, *Las Vegas (NM) Daily Optic,* July 6, 1895, 1.

"Miss Annie Londonderry," *Penny Illustrated Paper* (U.K.), July 6, 1895, 19.

Item, *El Paso Daily Herald,* July 8, 1895, 1.

"She Is Coming!" *Albuquerque Daily Citizen,* July 11, 1895.

Item, *Santa Fe Daily New Mexican,* July 11, 1895, 2.

"Annie Londonderry's Trip," *Salt Lake Tribune,* July 11, 1895, 3.

"She's Winning the Wager," *Las Cruces (NM) Rio Grande Republican,* July 15, 1895, 1.

"She Arrives!" *Albuquerque Daily Citizen,* July 15, 1895.

"Miss Londonderry Here," *Albuquerque Morning Democrat,* July 16, 1895.

"The Female Biker," *Santa Fe Daily New Mexican,* July 16, 1895, 4.

Item, *Santa Fe Daily New Mexican,* July 18, 1895, 4.

"The Female Biker," *Santa Fe Daily New Mexican,* July 19, 1895, 4.

"One of the Many," *Las Cruces (NM) Rio Grande Republican,* July 19, 1895, 1.

Item, *Socorro (NM) Chieftain,* July 19, 1895, 1.

Item, *Las Vegas (NM) Daily Optic,* July 19, 1895, 4.

Item, *Las Vegas (NM) Daily Optic,* July 20, 1895, 4.

Item, *Santa Fe Daily New Mexican,* July 20, 1895, 4.

Item, *Las Vegas (NM) Daily Optic,* July 22, 1895, 4.

Item, *Lincoln (NE) Evening News,* July 22, 1895.

Item, *Las Vegas (NM) Daily Optic,* July 23, 1895, 4.

"She Cycles into the City," *Las Vegas (NM) Daily Optic,* July 24, 1895, 4.

Items (3), *Las Vegas (NM) Daily Optic,* July 24, 1895, 4.

Item, *Marion (OH) Daily Star,* July 24, 1895, 7.

Item, *Las Vegas (NM) Daily Optic,* July 25, 1895, 4.

Item, *Las Vegas (NM) Daily Optic,* July 26, 1895, 4.

"Clearly She Draws," *Santa Fe Daily New Mexican,* July 27, 1895, 4.

"Will Pass Through Trinidad," *Trinidad (CO) Daily News,* July 27, 1895.

Item, *Raton (NM) Reporter,* July 27, 1895.

"She Gone From Us," *Daily Optic,* July 29, 1895, 4.

Item, *Raton (NM) Reporter,* July 30, 1895.

Item, *Trinidad (CO) Daily News,* July 30, 1895.

Items (2), *Trinidad (CO) Daily News,* July 31, 1895.

"Woman Globe Bicycler," *Eddy (NM) Weekly,* August 1, 1895, 5.

"Miss Anna Londonderry," *Raton (NM) Range,* August 1, 1895.

"Miss Anna Londonderry," *Raton (NM) Reporter,* August 1, 1895, 2.

"Miss Londonderry," *Raton (NM) Reporter,* August 1, 1895, 3.

"Arrives at Trinidad," *Rocky Mountain News,* August 1, 1895.

Item, *Trinidad (CO) Daily News,* August 1, 1895.

"Miss Londonderry," *Trinidad (CO) Weekly Advertiser,* August 1, 1895, 1.

Item, *Arizona Republican,* August 1, 1895, 5.

Item, *Santa Fe Daily New Mexican,* August 1, 1895, 2.

Item, *Santa Fe Daily New Mexican,* August 2, 1895, 1.

Item, *Trinidad (CO) Daily News,* August 2, 1895.

"Wheeling 'Round the World," *Trinidad (CO) Daily News,* August 2, 1895.

Item, *Santa Fe Daily New Mexican,* August 5, 1895, 4.

"Editor Kelly's Complaint," *Santa Fe Daily New Mexican,* August 5, 1895, 2.

Item, *Las Cruces (NM) Rio Grande Republican,* August 6, 1895, 1.

Item, *Castle Rock (CO) Journal,* August 7, 1895, 2.

"The Current Cases," *Las Cruces (NM) Rio Grande Republican,* August 9, 1895, 1.

Item, *La Junta (CO) Semi-Weekly Tribune,* August 10, 1895.

"Courageous Woman Cyclist," *Colorado Springs Gazette,* August 10, 1895.

"Annie Londonderry To-Day," *Rocky Mountain News,* August 12, 1895, 3.

Advertisement for Londonderry Lithia Spring Water Company: "Miss Londonderry in Denver," *Rocky Mountain News,* August 12, 1895, 3.

"Around the World on a Wager," *Rocky Mountain News,* August 13, 1895.

"Editor Kelly Makes His Point," *Las Cruces (NM) Independent Democrat,* August 14, 1895.

"Two Journalistic Types," *Las Cruces (NM) Independent Democrat,* August 14, 1895.

Item, *Las Cruces (NM) Independent Democrat,* August 14, 1895.

Item, *El Paso Daily Herald,* August 16, 1895.

Item, *Cheyenne Daily Sun Leader,* August 20, 1895.

Item, *Boston Globe,* August 20, 1895, 4.

Item, *Nevada (IA) Representative,* August 21, 1895.

Item, *Las Cruces (NM) Rio Grande Republican,* August 23, 1895, 1.

"A Bicycle Globe Trotter," *Fremont (NE) Daily Tribune,* August 24, 1895, 1.

"A Whirl 'Round the World," *Omaha World Herald,* August 25, 1895, 5.

"Tells Large Stories," *South Sioux City (NE) Star,* August 25, 1895, 3.

"A Charming Lecture," *Omaha World Herald,* August 26, 1895, 8.

"A Benefit for Miss Londonderry," *Omaha World Herald,* August 26, 1895, 2.

Advertisement for Boston Store, Omaha: "Greatest Lady Bicycle Rider," *Omaha Evening Bee,* August 26, 1895, 8.

"For Her Benefit," *Omaha World Herald,* August 28, 1895, 2.

Item, *Columbus (NE) Journal,* August 28, 1895, 3.

Item, *Omaha World Herald,* August 31, 1895, 1.

"Plays and Players," *Boston Globe,* September 1, 1895, 17.

Item, *Davenport (IA) Daily Leader,* September 3, 1895, 6.

"Circling the Globe," *Marshalltown (IA) Evening Times Republican,* September 4, 1895.

"Around the World," *Missouri Valley (IA) Times,* September 5, 1895.

Item, *Deming (NM) Headlight,* September 6, 1895.

"In the City," *Cedar Rapids Evening Gazette,* September 7, 1895.

" 'Round the World," *Clinton (IA) Herald,* September 10, 1895.

"Miss Londonderry on Her Wheel," *Dallas Morning News,* September 10, 1895, 2.

"Another Round-the-World Wager," *Fort Wayne (IN) News,* September 10, 1895.

"She is Nearly Home," *Brooklyn Daily Eagle,* September 10, 1895, 5.

"On Her Way Home," *Wheeling (WV) Register,* September 10, 1895, 1.

"Miss Londonderry Heard From," *Santa Fe Daily New Mexican,* September 11, 1895, 1.

Item, *Decatur (IL) Republican,* September 12, 1895.

"Her Task Is Finished," *Chicago Times Herald,* September 13, 1895.

"Has Circled the Globe," *Rochelle (IL) Register,* September 13, 1895, 1.

"Circled the Globe on a Bicycle," *New York Herald,* September 13, 1895, 12.

"Miss Londonderry Wins," *Omaha World Herald,* September 14, 1895, 1.

Sketch, *Chicago Sunday Times Herald,* September 15, 1895.

"A Woman Globe-Trotter," *Chicago Saturday Blade,* September 21, 1895, 5.

"Bikeology: Messrs. Upton and Rumble with Miss Londonderry," *Clinton (IA) Semi-Weekly Age,* September 17, 1895.

"A Globe Rider," *Rochester (NY) Democrat and Chronicle,* September 18, 1895, 1.

"Miss Londonderry Coming Back," *New York Times,* September 19, 1895, 6.

"A Woman's Long Ride," *Auburn (NY) Bulletin,* September 19, 1895, 3.

Item, *The American Wheelman,* September 19, 1895, 23.

Item, *Tama (IA) Free Press,* September 19, 1895, 5.

"Londonderry is Back," *The Bearings,* September 19, 1895.

"A World Girdler," *American Cycling,* September 20, 1895.

"Female World Girdler," *Fort Wayne (IN) Times-Post,* September 20, 1895, 1.

"Londonderry Has Returned," *Syracuse Standard,* September 22, 1895.

Item, *Pittsburgh Press,* September 23, 1895.

"Won a $10,000 Purse: A Woman Girdles the Globe on Her Wheel," *Oswego (NY) Daily Palladium,* September 24, 1895.

"Has Ridden Around the World," *Brooklyn Eagle,* September 24, 1895, 5.

"Won a $10,000 Purse: A Woman Girdles the Globe on Her Wheel," *Newark (OH) Daily Advocate,* September 25, 1895, 5.

"Miss Londonderry's Trip Ended," *New York Times,* September 25, 1895, 6.

Item, *Arizona Republican,* September 25, 1895, 5.

"Feat of a Bloomer Girl," *San Francisco Call,* September 26, 1895, 2.

"Around the World on a Bicycle," *Elyria (OH) Lorian County Reporter,* September 28, 1895, 2.

"Won a $10,000 Purse: A Woman Girdles the Globe on Her Wheel," *New York Recorder,* September 29, 1895.

"Won a $10,000 Purse: A Woman Girdles the Globe on a Wheel," *Marion (OH) Daily Star,* September 30, 1895.

"Woman 'Globe Trotter,' " *Davenport (IA) Daily Leader,* October 1, 1895.

"Woman 'Globe Trotter,' " *Davenport (IA) Weekly Leader,* October 2, 1895, 2.

Items (2) *El Paso Daily Herald,* October 2, 1895, 1.

"Miss Annie Londonderry," *The Wheeler* (Bolton, Lancashire, UK), October 9, 1895, 448.

"Miss Annie Londonderry's Tour of the World," *Hawaiian Gazette,* October 18, 1895.

"Around the World on a Bicycle," *New York Sunday World,* October 20, 1895, 29.

"Won a $10,000 Purse: A Woman Girdles the Globe on a Wheel," *Warren (PA) Evening Democrat,* October 22, 1895.

"Il Viaggio di Miss Londonderry," *Il Ciclista* (Milan), October 31, 1895.

"Miss Annie Londonderry," *La Bicicletta* (Milan), November 3, 1895.

"Around the World on Wheels for the Inter Ocean," *Chicago Sunday Inter Ocean,* December 29, 1895, 16.

Item, *Watertown (NY) Daily Times,* September 15, 1896.

"Around the World on a Wheel," *Delphos (OH) Daily Herald,* October 26, 1897.

"Around the World on a Wheel," *Cato (NY) Citizen,* November 13, 1897.

Item, *Omaha World Herald,* November 14, 1897, 24.

# *Notes*

༄

## Prologue

2 **"elite of the French nation"** Unidentified Marseilles newspaper clipping in scrapbook owned by Annie Londonderry's granddaughter, Mary Goldiner, hereinafter referred to as "Goldiner Scrapbook." Locating hundreds of contemporaneous newspaper and journal accounts of Annie's journey required reliance on many different people and methods. In some cases, I relied on local librarians or hired local researchers both in the U.S. and abroad. Copies were not always entirely legible, depending on the quality of microfilm, and page numbers were not always noted or available. Many articles from the French press, and a few from U.S. newspapers, were located in the Goldiner Scrapbook. In most cases Miss Londonderry did not note the name of the newspaper, the date, page number, or the city of publication, though the city of publication was often discernible from the text itself. In a few cases, I was able to locate other copies of these stories and to source them completely. Where I have page numbers I have cited them, but it would be a Herculean task to recover every one.

**"captured the hearts"** "Les Aventures de Miss Londonderry," *Le Petit Marsaillais,* 16 January 1895.

3 **"inventive genius"** "She's Gone From Us," *Las Vegas (NM) Daily Optic,* 29 July 1895, 4.

## Chapter One: Going Woman

5 **"Going Woman"** (chapter title) *Boston Post,* 26 June 1894. Kapchowsky is a misspelling.

6 **"the event lost something"** "Emulating 'Paul Jones,' " *Boston Evening Transcript,* 25 June 1894, 8.

**"Her face was unmistakably Polish"** "Going Woman," *Boston Post,* 26 June 1894.

**"a State dignitary"** "Emulating 'Paul Jones,' " *Boston Evening Transcript,* 25 June 1894, 8.

**"the same chances as men"** The short piece of dialogue and descriptions that follow has been reconstructed from "Emulating 'Paul Jones,' " *Boston Evening Transcript,* 25 June 1894, 8; "Will Journey on a Wheel," *Boston Journal,* 26 June 1894; "Going Woman," *Boston Post,* 26 June 1894; "Female Paul Jones on a Wheel," *Boston Daily Globe,* 26 June 1894, 2.

7 **"the advertising man"** "Mrs. Kapchowsky [sic] Has a Big Contract," *Chicago Daily Inter Ocean,* 26 June 1894, 1.

**"didn't come up to say goodbye"** "Going Woman," *Boston Post,* 26 June 1894.

**Bennett may have thought** Annie's younger sister, Rosa, was also present at the State House according to the *Boston Post.*

**"like a kite"** "Emulating 'Paul Jones,' " *Boston Evening Transcript,* 25 June 1894, 8.

**"one of the most novel wagers"** " 'Round the World," *Clinton* (IA) *Herald,* 10 September 1895.

**$20,000 to $10,000** The terms of the wager were described repeatedly in newspaper accounts of Annie's journey, though not always with consistency. While most reports said the bet was $20,000 to $10,000 that Annie would not succeed, some news accounts reported the wager to be $10,000 a side (see, e.g., "Wheeling Around the World," *Cambridge* (OH) *Jeffersonian,* 19 July 1894, and "Will Soon Reach Syracuse," *Syracuse Daily Journal,* 2 November 1894, 6); or simply $10,000 (see, e.g., "Around the World on a Wheel,"

*Chicago Daily Inter Ocean,* 25 September 1894); or some simply $30,000 (see, e.g., "Mlle. Londonderry en Route," *Syracuse Standard,* 6 November 1894, 8). One French cycling journal put the wager at $10,000 "against" $5,000 ("Miss Londonderry," *La Bicyclette,* 25 January 1895, 4249.) Regardless, a lot of money was at stake. Some newspapers reported Annie was required to ride a minimum of 15,000 miles on her bicycle (see, e.g., "Round the World," *Buffalo Express,* 1 November 1894); a few newspapers said the minimum was 10,000 miles (see, e.g., 'She Is Nearly Home," *Brooklyn Daily Eagle,* 10 September 1895, 5.). One newspaper reported Annie had to cover a minimum of "15,000 miles on foot or on a bicycle (see "An American Lady on Tramp," *Galignani Messenger* [Paris], 10 December 1894.) Most never mentioned a minimum. Some reports suggested Annie was allowed 500 miles by train across the American desert (see, e.g., "She Arrives!" *Albuquerque Daily Citizen,* 15 July 1895, and Item, *Tucson Daily Star,* 21 June 1895); another that train travel was prohibited "where the earth's surface is to be traversed" ("A Girl Girdling the Globe," *San Bernardino Daily Sun,* 30 May 1895), and yet another that she could travel 2,200 miles by train *or* boat (see, "Miss Londonderry in Town," *Utica Daily Press,* 12 November 1894, and Item, *Canajoharie (NY) Courier,* 13 November 1894). The last seems preposterous since short of riding over the North Pole Annie would have to cover more than 2,200 miles by sea unless she had figured out how to ride a bicycle on water (something she just might have claimed to have done). The *San Bernardino Daily Sun* reported that the wager permitted Annie no train travel "where the earth's surface is to be traversed," and on water Annie was required to book "the highest priced cabin passage." Also there were to be "[n]o lodging houses, or cheap hotels or staying with friends, but the best hotel in the town, and no accepting free entertainment at the hand of big hearted landlords." While on land, said the *Daily Sun,* Annie was required "every day" to "report . . . and send her net receipts, after deducting expenses, to Boston, certified by some club man, or hotel keeper, or banker, and then start for the next place empty handed. Therefore, at every new town she arrives dead broke and must earn enough money at least to pay her expenses. If she can't make terms with the best hotel and can't earn enough money to pay board and lodging, she sleeps out of doors. Frequently, I have been obliged to do this," Annie told the *Daily Sun.* ("A Girl Girdling the Globe," 30

May 1895). One French newspaper reported that the wager required Annie to make the journey in one outfit. ("Le Tour du Monde à Bicyclette," *Journal de Valence,* 7–8 January 1895, 2.) Many French newspapers and cycling journals reported that Annie had 16 months to make the circuit (see. e.g., "Le Tour du Monde avec 5 Centimes," *Le Véloce-Sport,* 3 January 1895, 18, and Item, *L'Abeille de Fontainebleau,* 4 January 1895, 1.) A Colorado newspaper reported that Annie could "carry no more than five cents from any one town or city, but what money she earns must be forwarded to a Boston paper." ("Miss Londonderry," *Trinidad [CO] Weekly Advertiser,* 1 August 1895, 1.)

8 **the formidable sum** There is no simple way to determine the current value of an 1895 dollar. Some calculations suggest that $1 in 1895 would be $15 dollars today. But other calculations suggest a dollar in 1895 would be worth $80 or more today. For perspective, the average annual salary for a working American in 1895 was about $1,000. $5,000 was a daunting sum, and the wager stakes were quite substantial, to say the least.

**If she succeeded** See, e.g., "Miss Londonderry," *Buffalo Courier,* 1 November 1894.

**Talking to reporters** "Around the World on a Bicycle," *New York Sunday World,* 20 October 1895, 29. See also, "Around the World," *San Jose Daily Mercury,* 19 April 1895, and "A Lady Cyclist," *Salinas Weekly Index,* 2 May 1895.

**earning money as a journalist** "Around the World on a Bicycle," *New York Sunday World,* 20 October 1895, 29.

**"must dispatch a postal card"** Item, *New York Daily Tribune,* 27 July 1894.

**prohibited her from contracting matrimony** "A Tramp to Strauss," *El Paso Daily Herald,* 26 June 1895, 1.

9 **the West End** I am grateful to Ellen Smith of Brandeis University for sharing her knowledge of the history of Boston's West End with me. This description of life in the West End is also drawn from Jonathan D. Sarna and Ellen Smith, eds., *The Jews of Boston* (Combined Jewish Philanthropies of Greater Boston, 1995), 71–90.

"**Anybody who knows Boston**" Mary Antin, *The Promised Land* (Penguin, 1997), 145–146.

10 "**No one in the tenements**" Gail Collins, *America's Women: 400 Years of Dolls, Drudges, Helpmates, and Heroines* (William Morrow, 2003), 264.

11 "**what America was all about**" Jonathan Sarna, *American Judaism: A History* (Yale University Press, 2004), 158.

12 **when she was just sixteen** The precise date of Annie's birth is uncertain. The weight of the evidence suggests she was born in 1870 or 1871.

"**a baby under my apron**" This according to Annie's granddaughter, Mary Levy Goldiner. (Interview with Mary Levy Goldiner, 6 November 2003.) Late in her life Annie did on occasion acknowledge some guilt about how her children had grown up, but never any regret about her bicycle trip.

14 "**a heaven-born talent**" "Boston's Globe Trotter," *Atlanta Constitution,* 19 July 1894, 5.

"**by selling candy**" "Wheel Around the World," *New York Herald,* 3 July 1894.

"**I have studied medicine**" "Wheel Around the World," *New York Herald,* 3 July 1894. Annie's claim to have studied medicine, a claim she would repeat at various points on her journey, was dubious.

15 "**a man named Kapchowsky**" This is one of the last references I could find to Annie by either her maiden or married name for most of the duration of her trip. The last reference to her by a name other than Londonderry was a reprint of this article that appeared in the *Hagerstown (MD) Herald and Torch Light* on 23 August 1894 and in the *Trinidad (CO) Daily News* more than a year later on 2 August 1895. After the trip, she was again identified as Mrs. Kapshowsky [*sic*] in the September 19, 1895, edition of *The American Wheelman.*

"**the world will see**" "Wheel Around the World," *New York Herald,* 3 July 1894.

16 **the first truly global news story** Simon Winchester, *Krakatoa: The Day the World Exploded: August 27, 1883* (HarperCollins, 2003), 194.

**excavation of a canal**   David McCullough, *The Path Between the Seas: The Creation of the Panama Canal 1870–1914* (Simon & Schuster, 1977).

**Thomas Stevens**   Stevens wrote an exhaustive account of his trip, recently republished in 2001. Thomas Stevens, *Around the World on a Bicycle,* (Stackpole Books, 2001).

**a hero's welcome**   See. e.g., Brooke Kroeger, *Nellie Bly: Daredevil, Reporter, Feminist* (Time Books, 1994). 139–84.

17 **the cycling craze**   The cycling craze and the woman's movement, two of the most powerful social trends of the 1890s, are discussed in more detail in chapter 2.

**"on to Honolulu"**   "Wheel Around the World," *New York Herald,* 3 July 1894.

**208 East Broadway**   This address pops up in news stories and on correspondence just after the end of her trip, too, for she stayed with the same friends when she returned to New York in September 1895. Efforts to identify the residents at that address through the 1900 and 1910 censuses were of no avail, however.

**"I must have something different"**   "Wheel Around the World," *New York Herald,* 3 July 1894.

**"dark blue Henrietta cloth"**   "Boston's Globe Trotter," *Atlanta Constitution,* 19 July 1894, 5. Henrietta cloth is a fine, wide wooled fabric often used for women's dresses.

**"In her opinion"**   "Wheel Around the World," *New York Herald,* 3 July 1894.

18 **"Not a breath of cool air"**   "It Was Only a 'Scorcher,' " *New York Daily Tribune,* 29 July 1894.

**"many of them street Arabs"**   "Around the World on a Bicycle," *Brooklyn Daily Eagle,* 29 July 1894, 3.

**"Nellie Bly hat"**   "Mlle. Londonderry Starts," *The Referee,* 3 August 1894, 1.

**"a deafening shout"**   "Around the World on a Bicycle," *Brooklyn*

*Daily Eagle,* 29 July 1894. 3. *The Referee,* a cycle trade journal, re-ported Annie's departure somewhat differently. "Six hoodlums yelled 'hurrah' and then promptly forgot all about her." "Mlle. Londonderry Starts," *The Referee,* 3 August 1894, 1.

**"will never finish the trip"** "Off On a Long Journey," *New York Times,* 29 July 1894, 3. The day after Annie left New York City was even hotter: the temperature reached 104 degrees, and ten people died of heat-related causes, according to the *New York Herald* of 30 July 1894 ("Ten Died of Heat").

**crossed the Harlem River** The Washington Bridge is not to be con-fused with the George Washington Bridge (GWB) that spans the Hudson between Manhattan and New Jersey. The GWB didn't exist in 1894.

19 **rode into Albany** The L.A.W. route from New York to Chicago is not the most direct route. On a direct line it would be shorter to travel across New Jersey and the breadth of Pennsylvania. But this would be a rugged trip over hilly terrain. By following the Erie Canal across New York State, cyclists enjoyed a relatively flat ride on the well-worn Erie Canal Tow Paths.

20 **"three square meals a day"** "A Fair Traveler," *The American Athlete,* 9 November 1894, 385.

**George T. Loher** Loher's journal was published as *The Wonderful Ride: Being the True Journal of Mr. George T. Loher who in 1895 Cycled from Coast to Coast on his Yellow Fellow Wheel* (Harper & Row, 1978).

21 **possessed with abundant muscle** Brocton *(NY) Grape Belt,* 31 Au-gust, 1894, 1.

**a Harvard student** *Westfield* (NY) *Republican,* 5 September 1894, 1.

**"is in the city"** "Around the World on a Wheel," *Chicago Daily In-ter Ocean,* 25 September 1894.

22 **"kicking her heavy cycle"** "A Globe Girdler," *Rochester Union,* date unknown, clip in Goldiner Scrapbook.

## Chapter Two: Female Paul Jones on a Wheel

23 **"Female Paul Jones"** *Boston Daily Globe,* 26 June 1894, 2.

24 **his plan was a "fake"** "Paul Jones Taken to Jail," *Boston Daily Globe,* 25 February 1894, 7.

**a small headline** "A Woman to Rival Paul Jones," *New York Times,* 25 February 1894, 12. Note that this story doesn't speak of a trip around the world *by* bicycle, only that the traveler will "travel *through* cities on a bicycle." (emphasis added) A similar story appeared in the *Washington Post* the same day: "New Feature in Globe Trotting," *Washington Post,* 25 February 1894, 1.

**"Emulating 'Paul Jones' "** "Emulating 'Paul Jones,' " *Boston Evening Transcript,* 25 June 1894, 8.

**"Female Paul Jones"** "Female Paul Jones on a Wheel," *Boston Daily Globe,* 26 June 1894, 2.

**"backed by rich merchants"** "Going Woman," *Boston Post,* 26 June 1894.

**John Dowe** "Round the World," *Clinton (IA) Herald,* 10 September 1895; "Won a $10,000 Purse," *Oswego (NY) Daily Palladium,* 24 September 1895. This last article also appeared, verbatim, in at least two other newspapers "Won a $10,000 Purse," *New York Recorder,* 29 September 1895, and "Won a $10,000 Purse," *Marion (OH) Daily Star,* 30 September 1895.

**"two wealthy clubmen"** See, e.g., "The New Woman on a Tour," *San Francisco Examiner,* 24 March 1895, 8.

**"two rich men"** "Wheel Around the World," *New York Herald,* 3 July 1894.

**"Stock Exchange Men"** "Annie Londonderry's Long Ride," *Chicago Daily Tribune,* 25 September 1894, 11.

**"Sugar-men of the Hub"** "Round the World," *Buffalo Express,* 1 November 1894. The Hub is Boston's egocentric nickname, as in "hub of the Universe."

**Albert Reeder** Reeder was in his early forties at the time of Annie's trip. He died tragically, some sixteen years later, by his own hand on Christmas Day 1910, at age fifty-eight. He did himself in by inhaling illuminating gas. In one of those ironic twists that cannot help but make you shake your head and wonder, the doctor who signed Reeder's death certificate was Timothy Leary, MD. Harvard Professor Timothy Leary—who would earn fame in the 1960s and '70s for his advocacy of the ingestion of other substances, namely LSD—was the grandson of a Massachusetts physician by the same name. But *that* Dr. Timothy Leary hailed from Springfield, not Boston, and he is probably not the same Timothy Leary who signed Reeder's death certificate. There were other doctors in Boston named Timothy Leary at the time so it was more likely one of the Boston physicians.

25 **"There are those who say"** "Going Woman," *Boston Post,* 26 June 1894.

**"an advertising scheme"** "Will Journey on a Wheel," *Boston Journal,* 26 June 1894. The subhead on this article also cast some doubt on what Annie was up to. It read, "Mrs. Annie Kapchowsky [sic] Starts from the State House on an Alleged Trip Around the World."

**a leading industrialist** See, e.g., Stephen B. Goddard, *Colonel Albert Pope and His American Dream Machines* (McFarland & Co., 2000).

**Alonzo D. Peck** I am grateful to Pope historian Bruce Epperson for much of my information on Pope and Pope Manufacturing. We spoke at the International Cycling History Conference held in Davis, California, in September 2005.

26 **an advertising solicitor** On June 25, 1894, the *Boston Evening Transcript* reported that Annie "has been an advertising solicitor for local papers for several years." Many newspapers also reported that she had been a journalist or a newspaperwoman, and some, the *Syracuse Daily Journal,* for example, were even more specific. The *Journal* reported on November 5, 1894, that Annie had been "a dramatic writer and telegraph editor on the *Boston Advertiser.*" This cannot be verified, however; and if she did work for the *Advertiser,* it is odd that the paper didn't cover her June 25, 1894, departure from Boston.

**"The Great Bicycle Exhibition"** The exhibition was described in "The Big Bicycle Show at the Garden," *New York Sunday World,* 19 January 1896, 19.

27 **"a general intoxication"** Irving A. Leonard, *When Bikehood was in Flower* (Seven Palms Press, 1983).

**"more to emancipate women"** "Champion of Her Sex," *New York Sunday World*, 2 February 1896, 10.

**the size of the front wheel** In some cases, the larger wheel was the rear wheel.

28 **"It knows no class distinction"** "A Blessing for Women," *The Bearings*, 5 September 1895.

29 **"their relationship with their garments"** Sarah Gordon, in *Beauty and Business: Commerce, Gender, and Culture in Modern America*, Philip Scranton, editor (Routledge, 2001), 25.

**"Miss Londonderry expressed the opinion"** "A Whirl 'Round the World," *Omaha World Herald*, 25 August 1895, 5.

**"depravity and boldness"** Item, *Arizona Daily Gazette*, 16 June 1895.

30 **"provided a space"** Sarah Gordon, 26.

**"future ill health"** "Taking Chances," *Iowa State Register*, 28 August 1895.

**"When woman wants to learn anything"** "Woman and Her Bicycle," *Chicago Daily News*, 17 October 1894, 8.

31 **"Why, pray tell me"** Quoted in Lynn Sherr, *Failure Is Impossible: Susan B. Anthony in Her Own Words* (Times Books, 1995), 196.

**"the first new woman"** "The First New Woman," *The Washington Post*, 11 August 1895, 20.

**"every reef and sail"** "Mrs. Stanton Likes Bloomers," *Rocky Mountain News*, 11 August 1895.

**"an abomination"** "Bloomers Abhorred," *Iowa State Register*, 7 September 1895.

**"all honorable means"** "They Don't Like Bloomers," *Chicago Sunday Times-Herald*, 8 September 1895.

32 **"The New Woman of Ancient Egypt"** *Omaha World-Herald*, 25 August 1895.

"**Her bloomers were too loose**" *San Francisco Chronicle,* 1 April 1895.

"**a freedom machine**" Robert A. Smith, *A Social History of the Bicycle* (McGraw Hill, 1972), 76.

**Frances Willard's 1895 book**" Frances Willard, *A Wheel Within a Wheel: A Woman's Quest for Freedom* (Applewood Books, 1997). Willard's essay was originally published in 1895 as "How I Learned to Ride the Bicycle."

"**The occasional denunciation**" "Woman and the Bicycle," *Scribners,* June 1895, 702–703.

33 **the number of Female cyclists** Petty, Ross, "Women and the Wheel: How the Bicycle Led from Social Control to Social Freedom," published in the Proceedings of the Seventh International Cycling History Conference (van der Plas Publishing, 1997).

**hardly the only woman** The brief descriptions of women bicycle tourists are derived from Duncan Jamieson, *On Your Left: A History of Bicycle Touring,* unpublished manuscript.

34 "**gone wheel mad**" "Woman Awheel," *Boston Daily Globe,* 19 April 1896, 36.

**many famous women**" Russell cut quite a figure riding through New York's Central Park on a bicycle given to her by her paramour, "Diamond Jim" Brady, the legendary financier known as the Prince of the Gilded Age.

"**gave her a machine**" "Le Tour du Monde d'une Américaine Sans Argent," *Le Figaro* (Paris), 7 December 1894. Another Paris journal reported, "She entered into an arrangement with a bicycle maker, whereby, provided she rides no other patent, a machine will be given to her, plus $500, at the end of her journey." "An American Lady on Tramp," *Galignani Messenger* (Paris), 10 December 1894. This appears to refer to the Columbia for the account describes the origins of Annie's journey.

35 "**anti-Semitism**" Larry Tye, *Home Lands: Portraits of the New Jewish Diaspora* (Henry Holt, 2001), 105.

36 **"Scarcely a week passes"** Item, *Los Angeles Times,* 29 May 1895, 7.

## Chapter Three: A Woman with Nerve

38 **"A Woman with Nerve"** *Sandusky* (OH) *Register,* 22 October 1894; "A Riding Advertising Agency" *Buffalo Express,* 1 November 1894.

**"a new scheme"** "Among the Wheelmen," *New York Times,* 11 October 1894, 6.

39 **"I was completely discouraged"** "Miss Londonderry Here," *Syracuse Herald,* 5 November 1894, 5.

40 **"to carry the Sterling banner"** "Miss Londonderry," *Buffalo Courier,* 1 November 1894.

**"has advertising contracts"** "Miss Londonderry," *Buffalo Courier,* 1 November 1894. Many Sterlings including Annie's were equipped with Morgan and Wright Tires. The company name is visible on the tires in the photograph Annie had taken of her Sterling in San Francisco in the spring of 1895. It is unlikely Annie's contracts were worth $3,500, however, and later in her trip, when she arrived back in the United States, there were reports that she had, at that point, earned only about one-third of that amount toward the $5,000 required by the wager.

**as one newspaper reported** "On a Long Journey," *Toledo Commercial,* 22 October 1894. Sterling's racing bike, similar in shape to Annie's, weighed 19 pounds. Perhaps Annie's Sterling was something of a hybrid, part racer, part roadster. These weights are given in the 1894 Sterling Cycle Works Catalogue.

**a single gear** There is one report, in the *Singapore Free Press,* that Annie's Sterling was "fitted with two gear-wheels, one for gearing the machine to 68 inches and the other to 63 inches, the latter to be used if the road to be traversed is hilly" ("The New Woman in Singapore," *Singapore Free Press,* 14 February 1895). According to cycling historian David Herlihy, some bikes *were* equipped with two gears, attached to opposite sides of the rear wheel. To "shift" gears the rear wheel had to be removed and flipped around. Thus, the rider would anticipate the general nature of the terrain ahead before setting out, as it was utterly impractical to be switching gears regularly during a ride. But, was Annie's Sterling equipped with two gears? The one detailed photograph of her bicycle known to exist does not appear to show a gear on the left side of the rear wheel, which is the side closest to the viewer.

**the Sterling lacked something** One French cycling journal commented, "It is difficult to believe that a frail young woman would dare to confront such a voyage on such a machine, with no comforts, without brakes or mud guards." (Item, *Le Vélo,* 24 December 1894.)

**compared with the 42-pound bicycle** Annie's decision to switch to a Sterling suggests that either The Pope Manufacturing Company didn't make a substantial financial commitment to Annie or that Sterling made an equally attractive or better offer.

**J. Manz and Company** One of the young apprentices at J. Manz and Company in 1894 was J. C. Leyendecker, who later became famous for his iconic magazine covers for *The Saturday Evening Post.* It is not clear whether Leyendecker had a hand in the image of Annie on her Sterling, but he had done other sketches of young women on bicycles in the 1890s, no doubt a popular subject at the time.

**"an ardent wheel woman"** "Miss Annie Oakley," *The Bearings,* 17 August 1894,

41 **"more posters were created"** Jack Rennert, *100 Years of Bicycle Posters* (Harper & Row, New York, 1973), 3.

42 **"I've cheek enough"** "Wheel Around the World," *New York Herald,* 3 July 1894.

43 **around the world going east** Some newspapers reported that Annie cabled for permission to reverse course and that the bettors agreed. As I doubt there was a wager at all, this, too, is almost certainly apocraphyl.

**"from Bordeaux southward"** "Londonderry, Globe-Girdler," *Cycling Life,* 11 October 1894, 19.

**as far as Pullman** "Miss Londonderry to Start Again," *Chicago Sunday Herald,* 14 October 1894, 8.

43 **"all along the route"** "Miss Londonderry Departs," *Chicago Daily Inter Ocean,* 15 October 1894.

44 **"an admiring friend"** "An Earth Navigator," *Kendallville* (IN) *Weekly News,* 18 October 1894.

**"Miss Londonderry is unusually vivacious"** "Around the World," *Elkhart Daily Truth,* 17 October 1894. It is considerably less than 180 miles from Chicago to Elkhart, so it's not clear how the *Truth* arrived at these figures.

45 **"attracted considerable attention"** Item, *Goshen* (IN) *Democrat,* 24 October 1894, 3.

**"to advertise the wheel"** "A Couple of Transcontinentalists," *Goshen* (IN) *Daily News,* 18 October 1894, 1.

**"on her way around the world"** Item, *Ligonier* (IN) *Banner,* 25 October 1894, 5.

**rode to Wawaka** Item, *Ligonier* (IN) *Leader,* 25 October 1894, 5.

**"a plucky and goodlooking lady cyclist"** "An Earth Navigator," *Kendallville* (IN) *Weekly News,* 18 October 1894.

**if she spoke of her marriage** Though the *New York World* had already reported that Annie was married with three children, there was no reason to emphasize the fact, and news didn't travel in the 1890s as it does today. Few, if any, people along her route knew she was a married mother.

46 **"It seems rather shocking"** Item, *Butler* (Indiana) *Record,* 26 October 1894, p. 5.

**"shot down Jefferson street"** "On a Long Journey," *Toledo Commercial,* 22 October 1894.

47 **"she sells silk handkerchiefs"** "Annie Londonderry in Norwalk," *Sandusky (OH) Register,* 24 October 1894, 1.

**"[A] remarkably good performance"** "Plucky Lady Rider," Unidentified Cleveland newspaper clipping in Goldiner Scrapbook.

**a guest of Mr. Wright** "Miss Londonderry in Cleveland," *The Bearings,* 2 November 1894.

**Mr. Bliss** There was a famous bicycle racer named Bliss active on the racing circuit at this time. Whether this is the same Bliss who accompanied Annie from Cleveland is unknown.

48 **"clever and intrepid"** "Miss Londonderry," *Buffalo Courier,* 1 November 1894. In Toledo, Annie told essentially the same story about a sheriff requiring her to obtain a permit to wear bloomers, but this time she set the story in Fort Wayne, Indiana. See, "On a Long Journey," *Toledo Commercial,* 22 October 1894.

**in nine hours** "Miss Londonderry Continues," *Buffalo Express,* 2 November 1894.

**"nearly dropped dead"** "Miss Londonderry Continues," *Buffalo Express,* 2 November 1894.

**thence to India** "Miss Londonderry," *Buffalo Courier,* 1 November 1894.

49 **"riding at least 15,000 miles"** This is one of the handful of reports that Annie was required to cover a stipulated distance by wheel.

**"$400 for one firm's ad"** On November 29, 1894, *Cycling Life* also reported that parts of Annie's body were for sale. "Fair Annie Londonderry's back is for rent to advertisers. She wants $300 for it while she is scouring the earth on her wheel. For the advertisement that adorns her left breast she gets $400. For her left arm she receives $100. On her left leg she carries another hundred dollars worth of 'business.' All the space on the left side but Annie's blooming cheek is sold. Ribbons she flies for a score of firms until she rivals the rainbow in the hues displayed. The hook and eye sharps ought to lease gentle Annie's upper posterior aspect and blazon it with the stirring words: 'See that Hump!' "

50 **"in barns"** "Miss Londonderry," *Buffalo Courier,* 1 November 1894.

**"exceedingly unfeminine costume"** "A Plucky Wheelwoman," *Illustrated Buffalo Express,* 11 November 1894, 8.

**"Belated pedestrians"** "Another Dead Broke Rider," *Rochester Democrat and Chronicle,* 2 November 1894.

51 **"a bedraggled appearance"** "Around the World," *Rochester Post-Express,* 2 November 1894.

51 **"prepossessing in appearance"** "Around the World," *Rochester Post-Express,* 2 November 1894.

**"a suspicious character"** "Likes Bloomers," *Rochester Herald,* 3 November 1894.

**"the stare of people"** "Likes Bloomers," *Rochester Herald,* 3 November 1894.

**"I'll marry some good man"** "A Globe Girdler," Unidentified Rochester newspaper clipping in Goldiner Scrapbook.

52 **her visit was much anticipated** Item, Syracuse Standard, 30 October 1894, 8; "Cyclets," *Syracuse Courier,* 31 October 1894, 2.

**"a hard struggle"** "Mlle. Londonderry En Route," *Syracuse Standard,* 6 November 1894, 8.

**"the query of pedestrians"** "Is it a Girl?" *Syracuse Courier,* 6 November 1894.

**"laughingly describing her trip"** "Miss Londonderry Here," *Syracuse Herald,* 5 November 1894, 5.

**"an intrepid woman"** "The Woman Globe Girdler," *Syracuse Standard,* 4 November 1894, 6.

**"a horrible nightmare"** "Miss Londonderry," *Syracuse Post,* 2 November 1894, 6.

53 **She left for Utica** The *Syracuse Post* reported on November 8, 1894, that Annie left Syracuse the previous day, paced by Ross French of the Centuries Cycling Club. However, the *Sunday Journal* of Utica reported on November 11 that she arrived in Utica on the tenth, having ridden forty-eight miles *that day* from DeWitt. De Witt is just a few miles east of Syracuse. The *Utica Daily Press* also reported that Annie arrived on the tenth from East Syracuse. Perhaps Annie did leave Syracuse on November 7, only to remain a few miles out of town in De Witt until the tenth, or the *Post* simply got the story wrong.

**announced the arrival** "A 'Dead Broke' Girl," *Utica Sunday Journal,* 11 November 1894, 1. Annie had at least one trunk with her belongings that she shipped from point to point.

**"a tramp"** "Miss Londonderry the Cyclist," *Utica Sunday Tribune,* 11 November 1894.

54 **Frank Lenz** "Where is Cyclist Lenz?" *Utica Sunday Journal,* 11 November 1894, 1.

**Lenz was already dead** David Herlihy, *Bicycle: The History* (Yale University Press, 2004), 255.

**"Everybody ought to be present"** "A 'Dead Broke' Girl," *Utica Sunday Journal,* 11 November 1894, 1.

**boarded a train** "Paragraphs for the Wheelmen," *Utica Observer,* 12 November 1894. Annie's eastbound trip through New York State was one of the last pieces of the puzzle I put together, making a road trip to upstate New York in December 2004 to do some research. I was quite sure Annie had passed through Schenectady because it was on the New York L.A.W. route and though Annie was headed eastbound in November of 1894, I worked my way westbound simply because driving from Boston, Schenectady was the first place I reached. I spent a full morning at the Schenectady County Public Library going through microfilm, and, in the case of the *Schenectady Gazette,* a very fragile volume of original newspapers that crumbled when touched. To my disappointment, I found absolutely nothing about Annie in Schenectady. Around midday, I hit the New York State Thruway going west towards Utica and decided to exit the Thruway near Fonda, a town I knew to be on the main cycling route between New York and Chicago. I was playing a hunch. I followed Route 5 West to Palatine Bridge, then crossed the Mohawk River into Canajoharie, also a name I recalled from the L.A.W. "Tour Book." Canajoharie is a small town on the banks of the Mohawk dominated by a huge Beech-Nut Food plant. At the post office I asked for directions to the public library. At this point, I was primarily in the business of hunting down articles about Annie in the larger city newspapers, but for the fun of it I thought I'd see whether she had managed to find her way into a small town newspaper in Canajoharie, if, indeed, a newspaper was even being published there in 1894. As it turned out, the Canajoharie Public Library had the *Canajoharie Courier* on microfilm for 1894 tucked away in a gray metal filing cabinet. But the library's lone microfilm reader was in a state of advanced disrepair. The film had to be advanced by hand, and the illumination left a lot to be desired.

I knew Annie was likely in the vicinity of Canajoharie in mid-November, and since the *Courier* was a weekly, I only had to examine two or three issues. Within a few minutes I found a small article about Annie and immediately understood why I had come up empty in Schenectady. The article reported she had taken the train from Utica to Albany. When I arrived at the Utica Public Library later the same day, I found articles from the Utica newspapers also reporting Annie had left town by train for Albany. By doing my research on her eastbound trip while traveling west myself, I had unwittingly fallen into a research trap Annie had set for me 110 years ago. Had I gone to Utica first, I could have skipped Schenectady, as she had, because I would have known she had taken the train to Albany. But, then again, I would have missed the thrill of bumping into Annie's ghost in Canajoharie.

## Chapter Four: Le Voyage de Miss Londonderry

55 **"Le Voyage de Miss Londonderry"** *Le Jour* (Paris), 4 January 1895.

**"a piece of France itself"** http://www.greatoceanliners.net/latouraine.html, accessed March 8, 2007.

56 **She regaled everyone she met** "Transatlantic Travelers," *New York Tribune,* 24 November 1894. Mr. Palmer was a partner of Marshall Field's and was largely responsible for the development of Chicago's State Street, including the famous Palmer House Hotel. Mrs. Palmer, the former Bertha Honoré, sometimes called "the Queen of Chicago high society," was a patron of the arts and had been president of the Board of Lady Managers of the World Columbian Exposition, the world's fair that had graced Chicago the year before.

**her ivory and gold Sterling** Annie's journey was reported in the French cycling press at least as early as November 1894. In one report, her white Sterling "with threads of gold" was described as "a veritable work of art." ("Miss Annie Londonderry," *Les Journal de Vélocipédistes,* November 1894.)

**"earned 150 Francs"** "Around the World on a Bicycle," *New York Sunday World,* 20 October 1895, 29.

**arrived at Le Havre** Except for a short time during the Civil War, passports were not required of U.S. citizens traveling abroad before World War I. It appears from indeces maintained by the National Archives that Annie did not apply for a passport.

**listed among the ship's arrivals** "Passengers on La Touraine," *Journal de Havre,* 2–3 December 1894, 3

**impounded her bicycle** "Le Tour du Monde d'une Américaine Sans Argent," *Le Figaro* (Paris), 7 December 1894.

**"in a predicament"** "Around the World on a Bicycle," *New York Sunday World,* 20 October 1895, 29. According to her granddaughter, Mary Levy Goldiner, Annie did not speak French. Several French newspapers also noted that she did not speak French. See, e.g., "Le Tour du Monde à Bicyclette," *Journal de Valence,* 7–8 January 1895, p. 2.

**"printed a large placard"** "Around the World on a Bicycle," *New York Sunday World,* 20 October 1895, p. 29.

**The Paris where Annie arrived** Annie's arrival in Paris was noted in the *New York Times* though it wasn't until December 23 that the *Times* reported: "Miss Londonderry, the round-the-world wheelwoman . . . has reached Paris." *Cycling Life* reported Annie's arrival in Paris on 3 January 1895, almost a full month after her arrival there.

57 **"In a short time"** "All Paris A-Wheel," Arsène Alexandre, *Scribner's Magazine,* August 1895, 195.

**in rode Annie** French roads were generally far better for cycling in the 1890s than American roads. In 1891, there were 328,000 miles of paved roads in France. By 1904, only 154,000 miles of American roads were paved. Of course, a paved road is not always ideal for cycling. For example, cobblestone roads would make for a very uncomfortable ride, far worse than an unpaved road of hard packed dirt. Nevertheless, French roads generally were superior for cycling.

**"is now in Paris"** "Miss Londonderry," *Boston Daily Globe,* 5 January 1895, 4 (quoting the European edition of the *New York Herald*).

**"muscles and nerve"** "24,000 Kilomètres avec un Soul," Unidentified newspaper clipping in Goldiner Scrapbook.

58 **"is not of their race"** "Causerie," *Le Progrès Illustre* (Lyon), 13 January 1895.

58 **"her boyish charms"** "Chronique Lyonnaise," *La Revue Vélocipédique,* 14 January 1895, 33.

**"Mannish"** "Le Tour du Monde d'une Américaine Sans Argent," *Le Figaro,* 7 December 1894.

**"a young boy"** "Le Tour du Monde en Bicyclette," *Le Jour* (Paris), 14 December 1894, p. 1. One cycling journal said nearly the same thing: "Miss Londonderry could easily be taken for, at first sight, a young man rather than a young woman . . ." ("Le Tour du Monde a Bicylette," *La Revue Vélocipédique,* 4 January 1895, 8.)

**"a Herculian build"** "Vélocipédie," *Le Nouvelliste* (Melun), 3 January 1895, 3.

**any interest in romance** "Causerie," *Le Progrès Illustre* (Lyon), 13 January 1895.

59 **"an orphan"** "Le Tour du Monde en Bicyclette," *Le Jour* (Paris), 14 December 1894, p. 1.

**a law student** "Le Tour du Monde en Bicyclette," *Le Jour* (Paris), 14 December 1894, p. 1.

**a doctorate of law** "Le Tour du Monde d'une Américaine Sans Argent," *Le Figaro* (Paris), 7 December 1894.

**a medical student** "Les Aventures de Miss Londonderry," *Le Petit Marsaillais,* 16 January 1895, 2.

**a businesswoman** "Le Tour du Monde d'une Américaine Sans Argent," *Le Figaro* (Paris), 7 December 1894.

**an accountant** "Le Tour du Monde d'une Américaine Sans Argent," *Le Figaro* (Paris), 7 December 1894.

**a reporter** "Le Tour du Monde d'une Américaine Sans Argent," *Le Figaro* (Paris), 7 December 1894.

**a wealthy heiress** Les Aventures de Miss Londonderry," *Le Petit Marsaillais,* 16 January 1895, 2.

**the founder of a newspaper** "Le Tour du Monde d'une Américaine Sans Argent," *Le Figaro* (Paris), 7 December 1894.

**the cousin of a United States congressman** These claims were reported by a French journalist who provided the story to *Le Progrés de Saigon,* 14 February 1895.

60 **"truly a miracle"** *Le Petit Marseillais,* a Marseilles newspaper, reported that Annie "wounded her attacker with two revolver shots" and that the man was arrested and sent to prison for two years. ("Les Aventures de Miss Londonderry," 16 January 1895, 2.)

**"quite the rage"** "Around the World on a Bicycle," *New York Sunday World,* 20 October 1895, 29. See also, "The New Woman on a Tour," *San Francisco Examiner,* 24 March 1895, 8 ("I became the advertising rage in Paris, and was well paid for the work I did.")

**a five day indoor bicycle race** Item, *Echo de Paris,* 8 December 1894.

**The race was cancelled** "Poor Miss Londonderry!" *New York Herald* (Paris Edition), 9 December 1894, 3.

**"Not one in a hundred"** "Around the World on a Bicycle," *New York Sunday World,* 20 October 1895, 29.

61 **"keep that flag"** "Around the World on a Bicycle," *New York Sunday World,* 20 October 1895, 29.

**Annie left Paris** Item, *Le Petit Parisien,* 29 December 1894.

**"Please show her the way"** "Les Aventures de Miss Londonderry," *Le Petit Marsaillais,* 16 January 1895, 2.

**"half-frozen riders"** "Miss Londonderry," *La Bicylette,* 4 January 1895, 4156.

**local cyclists from Melun** "Vélocipédie," *Le Nouvelliste* (Melun), 3 January 1895, 3.

**"known under *the pseudonym*"** Item, *L'Abeille de Fontainebleau,* 4 January 1895, 1.

**"By the bye"** "A Lady Cyclist," *The Egyptian Gazette,* 26 January 1895.

62 **"spattered with mud"** "Voyage à Travers le Monde en Bicyclette," *La Parole de Nemours,* 5 January 1895, 1.

62 **"in a very good state"** "Sur la Route de Chine," *Le Vélo* (Paris), 3 January 1895.

**a box of chocolates** "Sur la Route de Chine," *Le Vélo* (Paris), 4 January 1895.

**"a hospitable family"** "Le Tour du Monde á Bicylette," *Le Cosnois* (Cosne-Cours-sur-Loire), 5 January 1895, 2.

**Velocipedic Union of France** Throughout her trip through France Annie's travel was facilitated by the U.V.F. and its members.

**"the deplorable state of the routes"** "Sur la Route de Chine," *Le Vélo* (Paris), 4 January 1895. None of the eight newspapers publishing in Nevers, one of the major towns before Lyon, mentions Annie's presence there, and *Lyon Vélo,* a cycling periodical, reported, with some sarcasm, that she arrived by train. ("[The train] goes faster and fatigues less," said *Lyon Vélo.*) Why the Lyon dailies didn't mention that Annie had arrived by train is not known; she may well have tried to elide that fact by slipping into town late.

**"She had just enough time"** "Miss Annie Londonderry," *Salut Public* (Lyon), 5 January 1895, 2.

**three Lyon wheelmen** "Sur la Route de Chine," *Le Vélo* (Paris), 8 January 1895, 1.

**well below freezing** "Miss Londonderry," *Lyon Vélo,* 12 January 1895, 2. One presumes the temperature was given in Celsius. Five below zero would be twenty-three degrees Fahrenheit.

63 **on to Vienne** "Sur la Route de Chine," *Le Vélo* (Paris), 8 January 1895, 1.

**arrived in Valence** "Sur la Route de Chine," *Le Vélo* (Paris), 8 January 1895, 1.

**"her valiant enthusiasm"** "Le Tour du Monde à Bicylette," *Journal de Valence,* 7–8 January 1895, 2.

**"Her endurance is remarkable"** "Le Tour du Monde à Bicyclette: Miss Londonderry à Valence," *Journal de Valence,* 9 January 1895, 2.

64 **the Achilles tendon** "Sur la Route de Chine," *Le Vélo* (Paris), 8 January 1895, 1.

**"It is a man's bicycle"** "Miss Londonderry," *Journal de Valence,* 10 January 1895, 2.

**"Pray do wait"** Handwritten note on the back of a business card from *l'Hôtel de la Tête d'Or* in Goldiner Scrapbook.

**"likes French men"** "Le Tour du Monde à Bicyclette: Miss Londonderry à Valence," *Journal de Valence,* 9 January 1895, 2.

**on the morning of January 10** "Miss Londonderry," *Lyon Vélo,* 12 January 1895, 2; "Sport Vélocipédique: Miss Londonderry," *Messager de Valence,* 9 January 1895, 2; "De Valence a Orange avec Miss Londonderry," *Messager de Valence,* 12 January 1895, 3.

65 **"To explain to you"** "De Valence a Orange avec Miss Londonderry," *Messager de Valence,* 12 January 1895, 3. Twenty kilometers an hour would have been an excellent pace even for a rider without an injury.

66 **the Cercle Musicale** Item, *New York Clipper,* 2 February 1895, 771.

"**will pass through Avignon**" Item, *Mistral (Avignon),* 9 January 1895, 3.

**"redoubling their zeal"** "Sport Vélocipédique," *La Semaine Mondaine,* 9 January 1895, 1.

**"Hip! Hip!"** "Voyage Autour du Monde," *L'Echo de Jour,* 13 January 1895, 2.

**"stocked with drinks"** "Sport Vélocipédique," *Le Semaine Mondaine,* 16 January 1895, 2.

**reached Salon de Provence** "Une Bicycliste Qui Fait le Tour du Monde," *Le Petit Marsaillais,* undated newspaper clipping in Goldiner Scrapbook.

**"One night I had an encounter"** "Around the World on a Bicycle," *New York Sunday World,* 20 October 1895, 29.

67 **"the elite of the French nation"** Unidentified Marseilles newspaper clipping in Goldiner Scrapbook.

68 **"When she left for Marseilles"** "Les Adventures de Miss Londonderry," *Le Petit Marsaillais,* 16 January 1895, 2.

**"nothing stops me"** "Miss Londonderry, Distributrice de Prospectus," *Le Petit Provençal,* undated newspaper clipping in Goldiner Scrapbook.

68 **visitation hours** Item, *Le Petit Provençal,* 19 January 1895, p. 2.

**"a huge swarm of ants"** "Le Départ de Miss Londonderry," *Le Petit Provençal,* 21 January 1895, 2.

## Chapter Five: A Girl Globe-Trotter

69 **"A Girl Globe Trotter"** *Washington Post,* 14 April 1895.

**a trip made miserable** "A Tramp to Strauss," *El Paso Daily Herald,* 26 June 1895, 1.

**In India** "Miss Londonderry," *El Paso Daily Herald,* 27 June 1895.

**the company of German royalty** "Around the World on a Bicycle," *New York Sunday World,* 20 October 1895, 29.

**Nearly killed** "Miss Londonderry," *El Paso Daily Herald,* 27 June 1895.

**She rode overland** "She Rides a Wheel," *San Francisco Chronicle,* 24 March 1895, 20.

**to keep from being molested** "Won a $10,000 Purse," *New York Recorder,* 29 September 1895.

**Caught up in the Sino-Japanese War** "Around the World on a Bicycle," *New York Sunday World,* 20 October 1895, 29.

70 **She endured freezing nights** "Around the World on a Bicycle," *New York Sunday World,* 20 October 1895, 29.

**she logged thousands of miles** There was, and is, no governing body to establish guidelines for what constitutes a crossing of the continent by bicycle, or, indeed, a circuit of the earth. No rider of the time literally rode across every inch of the country, or pedaled a continuous circuit. Bicycles sometimes had to be hauled over rough terrain, walked along impassable roads, or carried as the rider waded through water.

71 **After leaving Marseilles** "A Lady Cyclist," *Egyptian Gazette,* 26 Jan-

uary 1895. Nearly two months later, on March 22, *The Referee,* a cycling magazine, would report, "Miss Londonderry, who was last heard from at Alexandria, Egypt, succeeded in raising 1,100 francs ($220) in Marseilles before she embarked for Japan, by selling photographs and souvenirs."

**"A great deal of amazement"** "An Unusual Scene in the Fort," *Ceylon Examiner,* 7 February 1895, p. 3.

**Annie found time** "The New Woman in Singapore," *Singapore Free Press,* 14 February 1895.

73 **"writes a book"** Annie never did write a book.

74 **"Astonishment, curiosity, and amusement"** "The New Woman in Singapore," *Singapore Free Press,* 14 February 1895.

**"the lady cyclist who might have been seen"** "The New Woman in Singapore," *Singapore Free Press,* 14 February 1895.

**the *Sydney* sailed to Saigon** "Une Célébrité va Encore Nous Arriver, Aprés-Demain par le Sydney: C'est Miss Londonderry," *Progrés de Saigon,* 14 February 1895.

**sent a telegraph message** "Une Célébrité va Encore Nous Arriver, Aprés-Demain par le Sydney: C'est Miss Londonderry," *Progrés de Saigon,* 14 February 1895. In a related article on the same date titled "With Miss Londonderry," the writer makes a strange statement about Annie's arrival by steamer: "If Miss Londonderry did not come by bicycle, it is because the Hebrews perspired so much crossing the tropical regions that they [the regions] were transformed into a sea of salt water." Did the writer know Annie was Jewish? Was this an anti-Semitic remark? It's difficult to tell.

75 **On the pedestal** The poem and the sketch are in the Goldiner Scrapbook.

**at the theater the night before** Item, *Le Courrier de Saigon,* 18 February 1895.

**"The Cyclewoman, Miss Londonderry"** "Critique Théâtrale," *Le Courrier de Saigon,* 18 February 1895.

76 **"All who had the good fortune"** "Miss Londonderry," *Le Courrier de Saigon,* 20 February 1895, 1.

**"is hardly a success"** Item, *Pittsburgh Chronicle-Telegraph,* 14 January 1895.

77 **Another sour note** *Cycling Life's* editorial stance was decidedly chauvinistic in any event. For example, it had this to say on September 6, 1894, about the first women's bicycle race held in the United States, at Louisville: "As a drawing card there is no doubt but that the woman's race was a howling success. As an artistic or sporting event, it was a dismal failure. People went to see it for the same reason that they go to see living pictures, or *risqué* burlesques at variety theaters. Anticipated Frenchiness roused the curiosity of the rabble . . . We are famed the world over for the refinement, the gentleness, the beauty, the womanliness of our woman. When they engage in sports that are designed and intended for strong, athletic men, they lose their lovable qualities. It is not a pretty or an inspiring sight to see a crowd of women togged out in picturesque costumes, rushing madly over dusty roads, with eyes sunken, cheeks flushed, hair loose, and lips and tongues dry and parched. Let our wives, our sisters and sweethearts ride their wheels for the pleasure in them, but leave racing for husbands, brothers and beaux. With the advent of the women's race will begin the decline of the bicycle as an exercise and pastime for women. Let us have no more of it." Is it any wonder the audacious Annie, who in addition to racing around the world by bicycle was doing so on a men's bicycle, often in a men's riding suit covered with money-making advertisements, would fall into disfavor with the editors of *Cycling Life?*

**"Glib and vulgar"** Item, *Cycling Life,* 24 January 1895, 14.

**"Did you see the scorching"** Item, *Cycling Life,* 24 January 1895, 14.

78 **arrived in Hong Kong** Item, *Hong Kong Daily Press,* 22 February 1895. ("We had a visit yesterday morning from Miss Londonderry, a young lady in a Bloomer costume who is a bicyclist, traveling around the world. She crossed the Atlantic from that port to Havre, wheeled from Havre to Marseille, took passage by the Sydney at that port *and will go on by her to Yokohama,* where she will tranship to one of the

Pacific liners, and from San Francisco, or whatever her port of arrival may be, she will travel on her machine back to Boston.") [emphasis added]

**"describes herself as a journalist"** Item, *Hong Kong Daily Press,* 22 February 1895.

**"I left Boston last June"** "Got as Far as Shanghai," *Boston Daily Globe,* 30 March 1895, 20. According to the *Daily Globe,* Annie's note was dated February 21, 1895. Either Annie misdated the letter or there was a reporting error, because she had just arrived in Hong Kong on February 21 and wouldn't reach Shanghai for several days.

**Annie wrote a note** "Around the World Without a Cent," *Celestial Empire,* 1 March 1895, 293.

**"at once informed her interviewer"** "Around the World Without a Cent," *Celestial Empire,* 1 March 1895, 293.

79 **"[W]hen I reached Shanghai"** "Around the World on a Bicycle," *New York Sunday World,* 20 October 1895, 29.

80 **"The result proved"** This contradicts later reports that Annie arrived in Chicago $100 shy of the $5,000 needed to win the wager and sold her Sterling back to the company for promotional purposes.

81 **"Admiral Ting sent a flag"** "Weiheiwei Surrenders," *North China and Supreme Court & Consular Gazette,* 15 February 1895, 215.

**arrived in Nagasaki** "Shipping News," *Japan Weekly Mail,* 9 March 1895. Though she traveled under her real name on *La Touraine,* she was listed among the *Sydney's* passengers as "Annie Londonderry."

**the Belgic** The only surviving page of the *Belgic's* manifest, held in the National Archives in San Bruno, California, establishes that the *Belgic* sailed from Japan on this date.

82 **"with a bicycle"** "Around the World on a Wager," *Japan Weekly Mail,* 9 March 1895.

**"The general run of American consuls"** "Miss Londonderry," *El Paso Daily Herald,* 27 June 1895.

83 **was a workhorse** By 1895, laws restricting Chinese immigrants to the United States had been passed, so by the time Annie sailed on the

*Belgic* her fellow passengers would have included many Japanese but probably few Chinese.

83 **"I found out what they liked"** "Around the World on a Bicycle," *New York Sunday World,* 20 October 1895, 29.

## Chapter Six: Annie Is Back

84 **"Annie is Back"** *The Bearings,* 10 May 1895.

**"[W]hen I reached San Francisco"** "Around the World on a Bicycle," *New York Sunday World,* 20 October 1895, 29.

**"Annie Londonderry has proved"** "The New Woman on a Tour," *San Francisco Examiner,* 24 March 1895, 8. The *Examiner* story appeared in its entirety a few weeks later in the *Washington Post* ("A Girl Globe Trotter," 14 April 1895) and, in summary form, in the *Chicago Tribune* ("New Woman on a Tour," 13 April 1895, 16). It was, in effect, Annie's reintroduction to her countrymen and her opportunity to begin building the legacy she hoped to create.

85 **"considerable latitude"** "The New Woman on a Tour," *San Francisco Examiner,* 24 March 1895, 8.

**"buxom young woman"** "She Rides a Wheel," *San Francisco Chronicle,* 24 March 1895, 20. If Annie indeed kept a diary, it has not been found.

86 **ridden across India** "Made Her Way on a Wheel," *San Francisco Call,* 24 March 1895.

**"a long fatiguing journey"** "She Rides a Wheel," *San Francisco Chronicle,* 24 March 1895, 20. A few days after her arrival in San Francisco, *Cycling Life* reported, "Annie Londonderry, who is now in Spain, writes that thus far the Morgan & Wright tires with which her machine is fitted have not yet been punctured. The roads, she declares, are wretched." (Item, *Cycling Life,* 28 March 1895, 20.) The message was apparently contained in a letter; there's no other logical explanation for why it took so long to reach *Cycling Life* in Chicago. But, Annie was never in Spain and we do not know how this information reached Chicago.

**"7,280 miles"** "Made Her Way on a Wheel," *San Francisco Call,* 24 March 1895.

87 **had sent only $1,500** "The New Woman on a Tour," *San Francisco Examiner,* 24 March 1895, 8.

**"She is fully capable"** "Made Her Way on a Wheel," *San Francisco Call,* 24 March 1895.

**"The two men rode on ponies"** "The New Woman on a Tour," *San Francisco Examiner,* 24 March 1895, 8.

**"proposals of marriage"** "A Tramp to Strause," *El Paso Daily Herald,* 26 June 1895, 1. None of these letters, unfortunately, made it into Annie's scrapbook.

88 **"Miss Londonderry, about whose fate"** Item, *Le Petit Parisien,* 29 March 1895.

**"a postal message from Saigon"** "Miss Londonderry Found Again," *Radfahr-Chronik,* 3 April 1895, 1027. Despite the existence of the telegraph, news didn't always travel fast in 1895. A few weeks later, on April 27, the same journal reported that a French cycling journal, *Le Vélo* of Paris, "got sign of life from the courageous American from Yokohama, and. . . . another one from San Francisco." According to the second dispatch from San Francisco, the cyclists of the city organized a concert for Annie's benefit, the proceeds of which "filled her bag and gave new cause that she will win her bet." (Item, *Radfahr-Chronik,* 27 April 1895, 1201.)

89 **"just to learn the road"** Item, *Santa Maria Times,* 11 May 1895.

**"through Morgan Hill"** Item, *Morgan Hill (CA) Sun,* 2 May 1895.

**But the very next morning** The various newspaper accounts of the accident conflict about the date it occurred. But it was either April 10 or 11.

**While riding downhill** Annie's accident near Stockton was reported as far away as Trenton, New Jersey, in the 12 April 1895, edition of the *Trenton Times* ("Accident to a Woman Girdler").

**"The couple were going"** "Bicyclists Hurt," *Stockton Evening Mail,* 11 April 1895, 1. This story suggests the accident occurred the previous day, April 10. However, a story in the 12 April 1895, edition of the *San Francisco Daily Morning Call* suggested the accident occurred on the morning of April 11 ("Injured Near Stockton," 11 April 1895, 12).

89 **"Her bicycle was damaged"** "Bicyclists Hurt," *Stockton Evening Mail,* 11 April 1895, 1.

90 **"[a] black eye"** "Bicyclists Hurt," *Stockton Evening Mail,* 11 April 1895, 1.

**stereopticon views** This is a reference to Annie's lantern slides, which were not true stereopticons.

**"a high fever"** "It Rounds the Form Well," *Stockton Evening Mail,* 13 April 1895, 1.

92 **"almost three-quarters of the journey done"** "Around the World," *San Jose Daily Mercury,* 19 April 1895.

**Asked about her route** "On a Wheel," *San Jose Daily Herald,* 19 April 1895, 8.

**"the longest ride ever undertaken"** "A Long Bicycle Ride," *Salinas Weekly Index,* 2 May 1895.

93 **"Here I met the famous Anna Londonderry"** "Winder's Wendings," *Illustrated Buffalo Express,* 2 June 1895, 11. Winder's book, *Around the United States by Bicycle: Entertaining Sketches of the Fun, Pleasure and Hardships, the Sights and Scenes Incident to 274 Consecutive Days of Riding,* was self-published in 1895.

**"according to her own story"** Well, at least according to *one* of her own stories. Her story had infinite variations.

**had ridden through England** "A Lady Cyclist," *Salinas Weekly Index,* 2 May 1895.

**"Smart girl, Annie Londonderry"** Item, *Cycling Life,* 11 April 1895, 13.

94 **"Folks will pity"** Item, *Cycling Life,* 30 May 1895, 8.

**"she is not elevating"** Item, *Nairn's News of the Wheel* (London), January 9, 1895, 105.

**"What are you giving us"** Item, *Sandusky (OH) Register,* 29 April 1895, 8. This report apparently originated in the *American Cyclist* for the exact same item, crediting the *American Cyclist,* also appeared in the *Watertown (NY) Daily Times,* 18 May 1895, 10, and other newspapers.

**"According to original plans"** "News Notes for the Wheelman," *Chicago Tribune,* 30 April 1895, 11.

**"to girdle the globe"** "A Fair Globe Girdler," *Olean (NY) Democrat,* 3 May 1895. This story was likely picked up from another paper without attribution, most likely the *Chicago Inter Ocean.* Dr. McIrath, who sent regular dispatches about their two-year bicycle trip to the *Inter Ocean,* was determined that his wife earn the title of the first woman to circle the world by bicycle and he was intent on discrediting Annie. A couple of months later a British paper would report that, "[u]p to the present . . . the bicycle hasn't given her [Annie] much trouble—sea trips seem more in her line." "Miss Annie Londonderry," *Penny Illustrated Paper,* 6 July 1895, 19.

95 **expected soon to be in Mexico** Item, *Paso Robles Record,* 4 May 1895.

**According to the *Los Angeles Times*** "The Plucky Girl Who Is Cycling the Globe," *Los Angeles Times,* 15 May 1895, 11.

**Had the cyclists ridden** Annie arrived in Los Olivos with another cyclist named Cox. Mark Johnson had gone ahead to Los Olivos so as not to be late for bicycle races scheduled there.

96 **"the biggest day"** "The Races," *Santa Barbara Daily Independent,* 14 May 1895, 1.

**"nothing less than the earth"** "The Races," *Santa Barbara Daily Independent,* 16 May 1895, 1.

**"nearly exhausted"** Item, *Santa Maria Times,* 25 May 1895.

**"the worst part of her journey"** "The Globe Wheeler," *Los Angeles Times,* 24 May 1895, 7.

97 **When she arrived in San Bernardino** "A Girl Girdling the Globe," *San Bernardino Daily Sun,* 30 May 1895. But the *Daily Sun* also reported Annie had earned more than $2,500 in Paris and Marseilles, though perhaps that was *before* expenses, and we know she earned

money in Boston and en route to and from Chicago. The math is, to coin a phrase, "fuzzy."

97 **"Good looking?"** "A Girl Girdling the Globe," *San Bernardino Daily Sun,* 30 May 1895. By this time Annie was almost always riding in pants. Perhaps she donned a skirt to go about town.

**"Annie Londonderry, who is supposed"** Item, *Los Angeles Times,* 31 May 1895, 11.

98 **"made of cheese-cloth and paper"** "The Globe Girdler," *Riverside Daily Press,* 31 May 1895, 3.

**albeit over short distances** The world record for a flying start quarter-mile at the time was twenty-three seconds by John S. Johnson.

**"The Bearings has always been opposed"** "The Women Again," *The Bearings,* 25 July 1895.

99 **a train engineer named Ziegler** "Around the World on a Bicycle," *New York Sunday World,* 20 October 1895, 29.

**Annie would later say** "Around the World on a Bicycle," *New York Sunday World,* 20 October 1895, 29.

**Multiple reports** See, e.g., "A Woman on Wheels," *Arizona Republican,* 15 June 1895. The *Los Angeles Times* reported Annie had reached Indio, California, about half way between Riverside and Yuma with her bike "badly wrecked." ("Indio," 19 June 1895, 11.) According to the *El Paso Daily Herald,* Annie "nearly perished crossing the Yuma desert" carrying her broken down wheel on her shoulder "all but 18" of the 61 miles she was forced to walk. ("A Tramp to Strauss," *El Paso Daily Herald,* 26 June 1895, 1.)

**"She started from [Indio]"** "Indio," *Los Angeles Times,* 19 June 1895, 11.

## Chapter Seven: Tour on a Bike

100 **"Tour on a Bike"** *El Paso Daily Herald,* 21 June 1895, 1.

**entered Arizona Territory** Item, *Tucson Daily Star,* 13 June 1895.

**"In speaking of her trip"** Item, *Tucson Daily Citizen,* 19 June 1895.

**"She has had an exciting time"** "A Woman on Wheels," *Arizona Republican,* 15 June 1895.

101 **"threw her hands up"** Item, *Arizona Daily Gazette,* 16 June 1895.

**An ad in the *Arizona Daily Gazette*** *Arizona Daily Gazette,* 15 June 1895, 5.

**"clever exhibition"** Item, *Arizona Daily Gazette,* 16 June 1895.

**After she left Phoenix** "Miss Londonderry Arrives," *Tucson Daily Star,* 19 June 1895, 4.

102 **So anticipated was Annie's arrival** Miss Londonderry Arrives," *Tucson Daily Star,* 19 June 1895, 4.

**"Quite a little party"** Item, *Tucson Daily Citizen,* 18 June 1895.

**"All the Tucson riders"** "Miss Londonderry Arrives," *Tucson Daily Star,* 19 June 1895, 4.

**One of the riders remarked** "Miss Londonderry Arrives," *Tucson Daily Star,* 19 June 1895, 4.

**"Annie Londonderry, Globe Girdler"** "Hotel Arrivals," *Tucson Daily Star,* 20 June 1895.

**"Miss Londonderry, the lady of the bike"** "Miss Londonderry Arrives," *Tucson Daily Star,* 19 June 1895, 4.

**"fancy riding"** Item, *Tucson Daily Star,* 20 June 1895; Item, *Tucson Daily Citizen,* 20 June 1895.

**She also spent the day** Item, *Tucson Daily Star,* 21 June 1895.

105 **the party passed through tiny Vail's station** Item, *Tucson Daily Citizen,* 21 June 1895. Bert got a bit lost on the way back and his friends grew worried until he finally returned about 6 P.M. ("The City in Brief," *Tucson Daily Star,* 22 June, 1895, 4.)

**Annie reached Wilcox** Item, *Lordsburg Western Liberal,* 28 June 1895, 2. The *Liberal* reported that Annie had arrived there by train from Wilcox and left on a train for Deming.

**During her stopover** "Miss Londonderry Interviewed," *El Paso Daily Herald,* 25 June 1895, 1.

103 **"What make of bicycle"** Item, *El Paso Daily Herald,* 25 June 1895, 1. Annie probably told the reporter she had ridden but one bicycle on her journey because she was now engaged to promote the Sterling brand. But it is also possible she said so because her circuit of the earth, for the purposes of the "wager," had now begun in Chicago where she acquired the Sterling.

**had now earned $3,000** "The New Woman," *Deming (NM) Headlight,* 28 June 1895.

104 **"the El Paso cyclists are preparing"** "Tour on a Bike," *El Paso Daily Herald,* 21 June 1895, 1. From other stories in the El Paso press, it appears Mr. Williams may have been a journalist who was involved in organizing Annie's El Paso visit.

**"Preparations are now being made"** "Tour on a Bike," *El Paso Daily Herald,* 21 June 1895, 1.

**"Say reader"** "A Tramp to Strauss," *El Paso Daily Herald,* 26 June 1895, 1. Before retiring for the evening Jim Williams sent a telegram to the *Herald's* competitor, the *El Paso Daily Times* saying "Met Miss Alice Londerery [sic] here at 10:45. Found her tired, but will leave here early morning for El Paso." ("Miss Londonderry this Morning," *El Paso Daily Times,* 26 June 1895.) This suggests Williams worked for the *Daily Times.*

105 **"She is a bright, vivacious woman"** "A Tramp to Strauss," *El Paso Daily Herald,* 26 June 1895, 1.

107 **"horrified city fathers"** Item, *Los Angeles Times,* 5 July 1895, 6.

**"against the law of Texas"** "A Tramp to Strauss," *El Paso Daily Herald,* 26 June 1895, 1.

**"She says the native princes"** "Miss Londonderry," *El Paso Daily Herald,* 27 June 1895.

109 **"The impression is prevalent"** Item, *El Paso Daily Herald,* 27 June 1895, 1.

110 **"such a sweet . . . smile"** Item, *El Paso Herald,* 2 July 1895, 4.

**"But in eighteen days"** This may have been what Annie said but she left Chicago on October 14, 1894, and eighteen days later, on

November 1, she was in Buffalo. She didn't reach New York City for another two weeks.

**"the hold-up racket"** This is a reference to Annie's story about being robbed by highwaymen north of Marseilles. Also, it took Annie more than two weeks to reach Marseilles, not six days.

111 **"Thence she went"** The reporter's grasp of geography was a little loose.

**"a doctor of divinity"** Probably a reference to a missionary. Annie later write that she was accompanied at times in China by newspaper correspondents and a missionary.

**"the stereopticon exhibition"** Unless there are images that I have not found, it is doubtful Annie took any of the photographs she used in her lecture. For one thing, how would she have carried a camera? There were no miniature cameras at the time. Of the seventy-five lantern slides, referred to in this article as "stereopticons," located at the home of Annie's granddaughter, many bear the logo "G.W.W." for George Washington Wilson, a Scottish photographer who sold popular travel images. Many of the others are meticulously hand-tinted color images.

112 **the desperado Martin Mrose** Professor Dennis McCown, of Austin Community College, who has extensively researched the life of John Wesley Hardin, provided this account.

**Selman's son** Coincidentally, Selman, too, was a cyclist, "the only police officer so far that has attempted to ride the steel horse." (Item, *El Paso Daily Herald,* 27 June 1895, 1.)

**"I am opposed to the bicycle"** Item, *El Paso Daily Times,* 30 June 1895, 6.

113 **"All those who have ridden"** Item, *El Paso Daily Herald,* 2 July 1895.

**"the pace was too much"** Item, *El Paso Daily Herald,* 2 July 1895.

**"make the pace"** Item, *El Paso Daily Herald,* 2 July 1895.

**"pulled Bart Allen"** Item, *El Paso Daily Herald,* 5 July 1895.

**"to cover herself"** Item, *El Paso Daily Herald,* 2 July 1895.

113 **She cleared $52** Item, *El Paso Daily Herald,* 5 July 1895.

**"look over her freight train load"** "A Tramp to Strauss," *El Paso Daily Herald,* 26 June 189, 1.

**"as far as their nerves"** Item, *El Paso Daily Herald,* 5 July 1895.

**she headed north** Item, *El Paso Daily Herald,* 6 July 1895.

## Chapter Eight: A Whirl 'Round the World

114 **"A Whirl 'Round the World"** *Omaha World Herald,* 25 August 1895, 5.

**A repair kit** Item, *El Paso Daily Herald,* 8 July 1895, 1; "She is Coming! Miss Londonderry on Her Famous Bicycle Trip," *Albuquerque Daily Citizen,* 11 July 1895.

**"went on her way"** "She Is Coming!" *Albuquerque Daily Citizen,* 11 July 1895.

**the thirty-mile trip to Las Cruces** It seems most likely that Annie rode her bicycle, the tire now repaired, to Las Cruces. However, the *Rio Grande Republican* of Las Cruces reported that she walked from El Paso to Las Cruces "as her bicycle was out of repair." See, "She's Winning the Wager," *Rio Grande Republican,* 12 July 1895, 1.

**"blinding rain"** "She Arrives!" *Albuquerque Daily Citizen,* 15 July 1895.

**compelled to remain in the city** "She's Winning the Wager," *Rio Grande Republican,* 12 July 1895, 1.

**She sold photographs** "She's Winning the Wager," *Rio Grande Republican,* 12 July 1895, 1.

**While in Las Cruces** I have been unable to locate a copy of Kelly's denunciation of Annie. The microfilm of the *Las Cruces Independent Democrat* held by New Mexico State University at Las Cruces is missing many editions of the paper, including all of the July 1895 editions. According to an e-mail I received dated June 22, 2006, from Faith Yoman, librarian at the New Mexico State Library, all of the microfilm of the *Independent Democrat* came from the same original source and "there are no [other] known copies of the 1895 *Independent Democrat.*" The paper was a weekly.

115 **"was on a whiz"** Item, *Santa Fe Daily New Mexican,* 2 August 1895, 1.

**Her grievance** Item, *Santa Fe Daily New Mexican,* 1 August 1895, 2.

**"With the usual disregard"** "One of the Many," *Rio Grande Republican,* 19 July 1895, p. 1.

**"The alleged female person"** "Editor Kelly Makes His Point," *Las Cruces (NM) Independent Democrat,* 14 August 1895.

**"a stupid slander"** "Editor Kelly Makes His Point," *Las Cruces (NM) Independent Democrat,* 14 August 1895.

**"sloshing around in his editorial mudhole"** "Editor Kelly's Complaint," *Santa Fe New Mexican,* 5 August 1895, 2.

116 **"had been spread all over town"** As quoted in "Two Journalistic Types," *Las Cruces (NM) Independent Democrat,* 14 August 1895. I could not locate the original *Optic* story.

**"the valley of death"** "She Is Coming!" *Albuquerque Daily Citizen,* 11 July 1895.

117 **She arrived in Socorro** Item, *Socorro Chieftain,* 19 July 1895, 1.

**"Annie Londonderry, Round the World on a Wheel"** "Miss Londonderry Here," *Albuquerque Morning Democrat,* 16 July 1895, 3.

**traveled exactly 17,432 miles** "Miss Londonderry Here," *Albuquerque Morning Democrat,* 16 July 1895, 3.

**"I have gone hungry"** "She Arrives!" *Albuquerque Daily Citizen,* 15 July 1895.

**"I started on account of a bet"** "Miss Londonderry Here," *Albuquerque Morning Democrat,* 16 July 1895, 3. It's not clear why Annie said she had to reach Boston. She had only to reach Chicago to have made the circuit. And, according to most reports, she stood to gain $15,000–$10,000 in prize money and the $5,000 she was earning en route—not $30,000. This could be a reporter's mistake or another example of Annie's conversational impulsiveness. (The *Rio Grande*

*Republican* also reported she stood to gain $30,000. "She's Winning the Wager," *Rio Grande Republican,* 12 July 1895, 1.) This is one of several places where publication of a book about Annie's adventures is mentioned. For example, the German cycling journal *Radfahr-Chronik* reported on April 27, 1895, "After her homecoming the resolute sporting comrade wants to publish a description of her circumnavigation of the globe and her many interesting adventures in a book that will surely find customers." As earlier noted, if Annie kept a diary, it hasn't been found and it appears she never wrote the book.

117 **"the royal Bengal tiger"** "Miss Londonderry Here," *Albuquerque Morning Democrat,* 16 July 1895, 3

**"Since she has been on the road"** "Miss Londonderry Here," *Albuquerque Morning Democrat,* 16 July 1895, 3. The *Albuquerque Daily Citizen* gave Annie's age as 23, her height as 5 feet 2 inches, and her weight also at 136 pounds ("She Arrives!" *Albuquerque Daily Citizen,* 15 July 1895.)

**"She is a charming, vivacious talker"** "She Arrives!" *Albuquerque Daily Citizen,* 15 July 1895.

118 **Annie earned $400** Item, *Raton Reporter,* 27 July 1895, 2. This would be more than $8,000 dollars today and seems improbable.

**"It looks a little worse for the wear"** "She Arrives!" *Albuquerque Daily Citizen,* 15 July 1895.

**"[I]f no accident happens"** "Miss Londonderry Here," *Albuquerque Morning Democrat,* 16 July 1895, 3.

**She reached Cerillos** Item, *Las Vegas (NM) Daily Optic,* 19 July 1895, 4.

**"easily ran away"** Item, *Santa Fe Daily New Mexican,* 20 July 1895, 4.

**she pedaled towards Las Vegas** Item, *Las Vegas (NM) Daily Optic,* 22 July 1895, 4. The chronology of the next two days is confusing because reports in the *Optic* are inconsistent. On Monday, July 22 the *Optic* reported Annie had reached Fulton (population 27) at 1:15 P.M. that afternoon "looking like a drowned rat," and saying she would remain at Fulton until five A.M. the next day before leaving for Las Vegas, some thirty-three miles further up the line. On Tuesday, July 23, the *Optic* reported Annie had left Bernal, a tiny outpost between Fulton and Las Vegas, a little after two P.M. and that three cyclists from Las Vegas—Boyce Brash, W. G. Haydon, and G. M. Birdsall—headed down the road towards Bernal to meet her and escort her to the city. (This was desolate country. Bernal, with a population of forty-nine was the largest of the towns between Lamy and Las Vegas.) Yet, on Wednesday, July 24, the *Optic* reported her arrival in Las Vegas the previous day, saying she had "ridden and walked—largely walked—from Rowe, since breakfast, a distance of 41 miles." But Rowe is west, and more distant from Las Vegas, than both Fulton and Bernal. If she had already reached Fulton on the twenty-second, she didn't begin her day on the twenty-third at Rowe.

**"a rather forlorn looking object"** "She Cycles into the City," *Las Vegas (NM) Daily Optic,* 24 July 1895, 4. The Gallinas River runs through Las Vegas, New Mexico.

119 **Charles Ilfeld** There are Ilfeld descendants today in the Albuquerque area and even a town in New Mexico by that name.

**Whether Annie revealed herself as a Jew** One undated article from a French cycling journal did refer to Annie, traveling without money, as "poorer than the wandering Jew," but it is unlikely that this was a veiled reference to her heritage. (Item, *Revue Mensuelce,* undated.)

**"she is a drawing card"** "Clearly She Draws," *Las Vegas (NM) Daily Optic,* 27 July 1895, 4.

**"sharp as a tack"** Item, *Las Vegas (NM) Daily Optic,* 24 July 1895, 4.

**"jocularly referred to as Miss Bostonberry"** "She's Gone from Us," *Las Vegas (NM) Daily Optic,* 29 July 1895, 4. The *Optic* also reported that "[f]our of her escort turned back at the northern edge of town, two of them being ladies and two of them business men who did not care to go further. The remaining seven, consisting of Boyce Brash, Jacob Graaf, George Hayward, Ira Hunsaker, Arthur Holzman, W.A. Therault and Earl Tyler, made the trip to Watrous, whence six of them returned by rail, the seventh, Therault, continuing the escort business as far as Wagon Mound."

120 **"A map of her route"** The map actually shows a line from Chicago to New York, and that she sailed to France.

**"in the neighborhood of Siberia"** The exact boundaries of Siberia are not defined and many would consider Vladivostok, just north of the Korean border to be part of Siberia. Annie claimed to have cycled in Korea and did collect a lantern slide of the port of Vladivostok. That isn't proof that she reached that point, but it could be argued she was "in the neighborhood."

121 **From Las Vegas** "Miss Londonderry," Trinidad *(CO) Weekly Advertiser,* 1 August 1895, 1.

**arrived in Raton** Item, *Raton (New Mexico) Reporter,* 30 July 1895, 3; Item, *Trinidad (CO) Daily News,* 30 July 1895; "Miss Londonderry," *Raton (NM) Reporter,* 1 August, 1895, 3.

**a trip "full of adventure"** "Miss Londonderry," *Raton (NM) Reporter,* 1 August, 1895, 3. Consistent with other reports, the *Reporter* described Annie as 5 feet 2 inches and 136 pounds. It described her gear as comprising a skirt, a blanket, a change of underclothes, and a canteen. No mention was made of a revolver.

**a bicycle-riding exhibition** "Miss Anna Londonderry," *Raton (NM) Range,* 1 August, 1895, 2.

**"She stated that Japan won"** "Miss Anna Londonderry," *Raton (NM) Range,* 1 August, 1895, 2.

**Annie left Raton** "Miss Anna Londonderry," *Raton (NM) Range,* 1 August, 1895, 2.

**twenty miles from there to Trinidad** "Arrives at Trinidad," *Rocky Mountain News,* 1 August 1895.

122 **"thronged with people"** Item, *Trinidad (CO) Daily News,* 31 July 1895.

**"[E]laborate preparations"** "Arrives at Trinidad," *Rocky Mountain News,* 1 August 1895.

**The charge for admission** Item, *Trinidad (CO) Daily News*, 1 August 1895.

**On the same page** Item, *Trinidad (CO) Daily News*, 31 July 1895.

**reprinted an article** "Wheeling 'Round the World," *Trinidad (CO) Daily News*, 2 August 1895.

**spent one night there** Item, *La Junta Semi-Weekly Tribune*, 10 August 1895.

**to Colorado Springs** "Courageous Woman Cyclist," *Colorado Springs Gazette*, 10 August 1895.

123 **"broken machine"** "Annie Londonderry To-Day," *Denver Daily News*, 12 August 1895, 3.

**sent two telegrams** "Annie Londonderry To-Day," *Denver Daily News*, 12 August 1895, 3.

**"found to be a young lady"** "Around the World on a Wager," *Rocky Mountain News*, 13 August 1895.

**contracted pneumonia** "Miss Londonderry Wins," *Omaha World Herald*, 14 September 1894, 1

**"followed the Union Pacific"** "A Whirl 'Round the World," *Omaha World Leader*, 25 August 1895, 5.

**"left the city before daylight"** Item, *Cheyenne Daily Sun-Leader*, 20 August 1895.

**isn't a single report . . . until Columbus** Item, *Columbus Journal*, 28 August 1895, p. 3. Though the report appeared on Wednesday, August 28, the story said Annie had arrived "Thursday last," which would have been August 22.

**"The wager made"** "A Bicycle Globe Trotter," *Fremont Daily Tribune*, 24 August 1895, 1. Interestingly, the *Tribune* also reported that the war in China had forced Annie to ride several hundred extra miles "going as far north as Siberia. She had traveled nearly 27,000 miles when she reached Fremont."

124 **"France, Italy, Turkey"** "Tells Large Stories," *South Sioux City (NE) Star*, 25 August 1895, 3.

126 **"the greatest lady bicycle rider"** *Omaha Evening Bee*, 26 August 1895, 8.

**"sensible wheel talk"** Item, *Omaha World Herald*, 31 August 1895.

**"quietly wheeled into our city"** "Around the World," *Missouri Valley (IA) Times*, 5 September 1895, 2.

127 **"The people of the peerless state of Iowa"** "Circling the Globe," *Marshalltown Evening Times Republican*, 4 September 1895,

**"while riding on the C. & N.W."** "Circling the Globe," *Marshalltown Evening Times Republican*, 4 September 1895.

**"my fall near Tama"** " 'Round the World," *Clinton Herald*, 10 September 1895.

128 **"a drove of pigs"** "Won a $10,000 Purse, *New York Recorder*, 29 September 1895.

**That she broke her wrist** "Miss Londonderry's Trip Ended," *New York Times*, 25 September 1895, 6.

**"the farmer responsible"** "In the City," *Cedar Rapids Evening Gazette*, 7 September 1895.

**"[I]f I had broken my arm"** "Woman 'Globe Trotter,' " *Davenport Daily Leader*, 1 October 1895. In this story, Annie also claimed she was American born, and that her husband, Max, was a Pole and a nobleman. She was not American born and he was not a nobleman, though given his patient wait for Annie's return he was a noble man.

**"She was walking"** "In the City," *Cedar Rapids Evening Gazette*, 7 September 1895.

**her cyclometer now read** " 'Round the World," *Clinton (IA) Herald*, 10 September 1895.

129 **precisely 9.604 miles** "Around the World on a Bicycle," *New York Sunday World*, 20 October 1895, 29.

**"talked most entertainingly"** " 'Round the World," *Clinton (IA) Herald*, 10 September 1895. One presumes "Sagon" is a reference to Saigon, now Ho Chi Minh City, in Vietnam. However, Saigon is about ten degrees *north* of the equator, not two degrees south of it.

130 **"an ordinary stock wheel"** This is at variance with the report in 22 October 1894, edition of the *Toledo Commercial* that Annie's Sterling was "manufactured expressly" for her.

**"with a thankful sigh"** Item, *The American Wheelman,* 19 September 1895, 23.

131 **though the *Omaha World Herald*** "Miss Londonderry Wins," *Omaha World Herald,* 14 September 1895, 1. More than a week after she finished her ride in Chicago, The *Chicago Saturday Blade* did report that Annie's round the world jaunt had come to an end in the city. "A Woman Globe-Trotter," *Chicago Saturday Blade,* 21 September 1895, 5. Annie added some colorful details to her accounts of the war between China and Japan. "I was an eye-witness to a great deal of the war," she told the *Blade,* "and I have in my trunk photographs that will appear in my forthcoming book to prove what I say. After taking the forts at the battle of Pahsto Island the Japs actually drank the warm blood. The heads of the Chinamen who were only wounded were cut off and flung in the air."

**"a rousing reception"** "Has Circled the Globe," *Rochelle Register,* 13 September 1895, 1.

**"because of Miss Londonderry's fame"** "Bikeology: Messrs. Upton and Rumble with Miss Londonderry," *Clinton (IA) Semi-Weekly Age,* 17 September 1895.

**raffle her Sterling** The *Chicago Times-Herald* reported Annie was thinking of raffling off the Sterling. ("Her Task Is Finished," *Chicago Times-Herald,* 13 September 1895.)

**given a new wheel** "Bikeology: Messrs. Upton and Rumble with Miss Londonderry," *Clinton (IA) Semi-Weekly Age,* 17 September 1895.

**her first stop was New Brunswick** "A Globe Rider," *Rochester* (NY) *Democrat and Chronicle,* 18 September 1895, 1. According to the *Fort Wayne Times-Post,* Annie cycled into New Brunswick claiming to have cycled around the world and burst into tears when people did not believe her and produced an album with "the autographs of kings and queens she had met. She threatened also to write a book." "Female World Girdler," *Fort Wayne Times-Post,* 20 September 1895, 1. However, the *New York Times,* which also reported on Annie's visit to

New Brunswick, said, "She has not ridden her wheel since leaving Chicago." "Miss Londonderry Coming Back," *New York Times* 19 September 1895, 6.

**"With her left arm in a sling"** "Won a $10,000 Purse" *New York Recorder,* 29 September 1895. Annie often told the newspapers of her plans to write a book about her adventures, but she never did.

132 **as far away as Milan** "Il Viaggio di Miss Londonderry," *Il Ciclista,* 31 October 1895; "Miss Annie Londonderry," *La Bicicletta,* 3 November 1895.

132 **and Honolulu** "Miss Annie Londonderry's Tour of World," *Hawaiian Gazette,* 18 October 1895.

**"[won] her race"** Item, *Tama (IA) Free Press,* 19 September 1895, 5.

**"not her real name"** Item, *El Paso Daily Herald,* 2 October 1895, 1.

**"the globe-girdling sign board"** As reported in "Around the World on Wheels for the Inter Ocean," *Chicago Inter Ocean,* 29 December 1895, 16. The American consul in Yokohama about whom Annie complained to the *El Paso Daily Herald* was John McLean, not a Colonel McIvor.

## Chapter Nine: Capture of a Very Novel "Wild Man"

134 **"Capture of a Very Novel 'Wild Man' "** *New York Sunday World,* 3 November 1895, 36. This chapter originally appeared, in substantially the same form, as an article titled "The Mystery of the New York Reporter and the Massachusetts 'Wild Man,' " in the *New England Quarterly* 77, no. 4 (December 2005).

**It all began** This account is drawn from the following newspaper stories: "Life in Danger," *Boston Daily Globe,* 24 October 1895; "Wild Man in Royalston," *Fitchburg Daily Sentinel,* 24 October 1895; "Royalston's Mystery," Fitchburg Daily Sentinel, 25 October 1895; "Kept in Fear," *Boston Daily Globe,* 25 October 1895; "Is He a Dime Store Victim?" *Springfield Daily Republican,* 26 October 1895; "The Royalston Sensation," *Athol Transcript,* 29 October 1895. The dates of the various events described differ slightly in different accounts, so the timeline presented here is approximate.

135 **"blazed fiercely"** "Wild Man in Royalston," *Fitchburg Daily Sentinel,* 24 October 1895.

**"I thought the man"** "Wild Man in Royalston," *Fitchburg Daily Sentinel,* 24 October 1895.

**Roswell L. Doane** There is a photograph of Doane in *Athol Past and Present* by Lilley B. Caswell (self-published, 1899).

136 **"little gray-bearded man"** "Life in Danger," *Boston Daily Globe,* 24 October 1895; "Kept in Fear," *Boston Daily Globe,* 25 October 1895, 1 (this story was signed "The Globe Man"). Though Richardson described the man as six feet tall, the *Globe* described him as "little."

**The Western Union telegram** Telegram in the Goldiner Scrapbook. "Sanger," who might also have been the "Globe Man" who wrote the story for the *Boston Globe,* could have been William H. Sanger, whose occupation is listed in the Boston City Directories for 1895 and 1897 (published by Sampson, Murdock, & Co., Boston) as "correspondent and asst. clerk of [the Massachusetts] Senate"; "correspondent" suggests that he was a newsman. Another possibility is Elizabeth C. Sanger, no relation to William H., who, for thirty-six years, beginning in 1903, was the *Boston Globe*'s society editor. (See the "Who's Who on the Boston Globe" form completed by Ms. Sanger and on file at the *Boston Globe* archives, Boston.) Sanger began her *Globe* career as a "special story writer" in 1900. In 1895, she would have been thirty years old, perhaps trying to build her journalism credentials by freelancing for the *Globe* and the *World*. Or there could be another Sanger altogether.

**Postal Telegraph Cable Company** Telegram in Goldiner Scrapbook. A number of wild man stories circulated around New England in 1895. On 13 September 1895, the *Boston Daily Advertiser* and the *Boston Daily Globe* carried identical stories headlined "The 'Wild Man' Coming," datelined West Hartford, Connecticut. "The wild man has left Colebrook and is now traveling towards Massachusetts," the stories began. They described a wild man in the vicinity of Colebrook, Connecticut, who was stealing chickens and onions from local farms and chased a farmer for two miles through the woods. Another farmer reported seeing the wild man, described as a "crazy freak," in his brother's barn, but the wild man escaped through a small window and headed "to the mountain."

**"to capture the desperado"** "Capture of a Very Novel 'Wild Man,' " *New York Sunday World,* 3 November 1895, 36. In November 2003, I called the Athol Public Library looking for information about the wild man of 1895 and was referred to a local historian, Richard Chaisson, a retired journalist from the *Worcester Telegram & Gazette.* When I phoned Chaisson, he immediately recognized the story I was talking about. "Oh, yes!" he said, "The *New York World* even sent Nellie Bly up here to investigate." When I explained that it wasn't Nellie Bly but Annie Kopchovsky who had been sent by the *World,* Chaisson was astonished. We met a few days later at the Athol Public Library and drove up the road to Royalston to the vicinity where the search for the wild man took place.

137 **"One has a strange feeling"** "Capture of a Very Novel 'Wild Man,' " *New York Sunday World,* 3 November 1895, 36. All quotations from this point to the subsequent footnote are from this same source.

138 **"the difficulty in [the] situation"** Item, *Worcester West Chronicle,* 31 October 1895.

139 **"There are . . . Royalston people"** "Royalston's Mystery," *Fitchburg Daily Sentinel,* 25 October 1895.

**"the 'Wild Man' turns out"** "Latest, the Boy Confesses," *Athol Transcript,* 29 October 1895.

**after being questioned "sharply"** "The Royalston Sensation," *Athol Transcript,* 29 October 1895.

**"who early formed the opinion"** "Richardson Was the 'Wild Man,' " *Fitchburg Daily Sentinel,* 29 October 1895.

140 **"The Royalston 'wild man'"** "Fake Reporting," *Athol Transcript,* 5 November 1895.

**"Received of A. Londenery"** Handwritten note in Goldiner Scrapbook.

**"can't you get"** Telegram in Goldiner Scrapbook.

**a "brazen capacity"** Brooke Kroeger, *Nellie Bly: Daredevil, Reporter, Feminist* (Times Books, 1994) 145.

141 **"Young Richardson was released"** "Capture of a Very Novel 'Wild Man,'" *New York Sunday World,* 3 November 1895, 36.

**article on women farmers** "New York's Tenement-House Farmers," *New York Sunday World,* 27 October 1895.

**never charged with a crime** "Capture of a Very Novel 'Wild Man,'" *New York World,* 3 November 1895, 36. In March 2005, with the help of Richard Chaisson, I located Charley Richardson's great-grandson, Jim Richardson, living in Royalston. He had never heard of the wild-man escapade, though he did report that he had heard his great-grandfather was "a little off." We met in early April, and, with the help of family records, Jim Richardson provided this information about Charley Richardson's later life.

# Epilogue

142 **"The moment she takes her seat"** Quoted in Lynn Sherr, *Failure Is Impossible: Susan B. Anthony in Her Own Words* (Times Books, 1995), 277.

143 **"one of the biggest frauds"** Item, *Omaha World Herald,* 14 November 1897, 24.

**or pushing wagons** An excellent collection of photographs of some of these adventurers can be found at *www.xoomer.virgilio.it/globetrotters/* (accessed on February 8, 2007). One was "The Man with the Iron Mask," a walker wearing an iron mask attached to which was a sign saying "$21,000 wager." The man was Harry Bensley of the United Kingdon and the wager was whether Bensley could walk around the world without being identified.

**"should meet with appreciation"** "Plays and Players," *Boston Globe,* 1 September 1895, 17. *The Globe Trotter* first premiered in Philadelphia in May 1894, the month before Annie's trip began.

**"Theirs were the glow"** Irving A. Leonard, *When Bikehood Was in Flower* (Seven Palms Press, 1983), 20.

144 **Margaret Valentine Le Long** "From Chicago to San Francisco A Wheel," *Outing Magazine* 31, no. 5 (February 1898), 497–501.

145 " 'Every once in a while' " "Around-the-World Wagers," *Washington Post*, 10 February 1901, 19.

147 a self-proclaimed Messiah "A Modern Christ and His Flock," *New York Sunday World*, 24 November 1895.

a New York City matchmaker "Wellman's Matrimonial Spider-Web," *New York Sunday World*, 26 January 1896, 17.

147 the New York mail train "A 'New Woman' Mail Clerk," *New York Sunday World*, 10 January 1896, 36.

women-only stock exchange "Private Rooms for Women Stock Gamblers," *New York Sunday World*, 17 November 1895.

among others See, e.g., "New York's Tenement House Farmers," *New York Sunday World*, 27 October 1895, 29. "Inside the Door of Hope Where Barbara Aub First Confessed," *New York Sunday World*, 22 December 1895; and "The Poor Aid the Poor Sick," *New York Sunday World*, 2 February 1896.

three letters from the wife of Victor Sloan These letters are in the Goldiner Scrapbook.

149 in a boarding house According to Annie's granddaughter, Mary Levy Goldiner, Annie went to California to recuperate from a likely bout of tuberculosis.

# Afterword

151 I first learned about my great-grandaunt My great-grandfather, Bennett Cohen, was the brother who did not come up to say goodbye to Annie the day she left the Massachusetts State House to begin her journey.

153 date and place of birth Based on all the evidence I eventually uncovered, I believe Annie was born in 1870 or 1871 in or near Riga, Latvia.

154 living, biological descendant Mary and Paul have two adopted children, Howard and Libby.

156 all the girls Mount Saint Mary's is now Marymount College. The

school provided me with transcripts, complete with grades, for Annie and Max's three daughters.

157 **Sister Thaddea**  Thaddea, derived from St. Jude Thaddeus, the patron saint of lost or impossible causes. Sion, or Zion, refers both to both Jerusalem and to the religious aspirations of the Jewish people.

**a profoundly bitter letter**  Though the letter begins "Dear Mollie," Simon often uses the spelling "Molly" throughout the letter. To avoid any confusion, I have changed all spellings to "Mollie."

158 **Why an American girl**  "Many Tributes to Sister Thaddea, New York Jewess Who Became Nun," *Saskatoon Star Phoenix,* 29 November 1961, 16. Sister Thaddea's doctoral thesis—she earned her Ph.D. from The University of Ottawa—was dedicated to "the sacred memory of my beloved Father, a true Israelite in whom there is no guile, who left this earth on May 9, 1946, and to my sorrowing mother . . ." Her thesis topic was "The Economic and Social Conditions in the Ghetto, Together with the Aspirations of the Jews as Described by Ghetto Writers."

159 **the secret of their eldest daughter**  Ironically, though my mother knew nothing about Annie or her bicycle trip, she *did* know that her father, Harry, had a first cousin who had become a nun.

# Acknowledgments

I could never have unearthed the story of my great-grandaunt, Annie Cohen Kopchovsky (a.k.a. Annie Londonderry), without the help, large and small, of countless people, many of whom I have never met but who helped nonetheless, typically with great enthusiasm.

I met Annie's granddaughter, Mary Levy Goldiner, my second cousin once removed, through this project. Mary was enthusiastic about my interest in Annie from the start. I can't begin to express my gratitude to Mary, and her husband, Paul, for all they have done to make this book possible. I found Mary, and much else, with the indispensable help of genealogist Nancy Levin Arbeiter.

David Herlihy, the author of *Bicycle: The History* (Yale, 2004), is one of the world's foremost experts on the history of the bicycle. David helped me with invaluable research, especially in France, research I never could have undertaken on my own, and his encouragement and support were generous, continuous, and enthusiastic. I cannot overstate David's contribution to this book.

My editor, Danielle Chiotti, showed exceptional editorial instincts in her review of the manuscript and made this a better book than I could possibly have written on my own. I am very grateful to her and her colleagues at Citadel Press for bringing this book to life.

My agents, Melissa Grella and Elisabeth Weed of Kneerim and Williams (Elisabeth has since moved on to another agency), loved Annie's story from the start. Thanks also to Elaine Rogers and Patricia Nelson of Kneerim & Williams.

Eva Murphy, a librarian at the Massachusetts State Library, has a keen memory, and it was thanks to Eva that I encountered historian Dennis McCown of Austin, Texas, who was also on Annie's trail. Dennis generously provided old newspaper articles he had collected about Annie as well as encouragement and insight throughout.

I first heard about Annie from Michael Wells of Cape Cod, Massachusetts, who provided the first handful of articles I ever saw about her. John Weiss, another researcher on Annie's trail, generously shared his finds with me and provided invaluable guidance, as well. I am indebted to them both.

Gillian Klempner and Meghan Shea of Spokeswoman Productions are working to bring Annie to life in a documentary film. My thanks to them and to Mike Rogers and Ben Willman, their partners in crime and in life. Thanks to old-timey wheelman Gary Sanderson for leading us safely to New York from Boston on his high wheeler when Gillian and Meghan suggested we re-create the first leg of Annie's journey.

Sister Catherine Seeman of St. Mary's Parish in Saskatoon, Saskatchewan, helped me with a very important and stunning piece of the puzzle. I am deeply in her debt for her kindness.

Bill Strickland of *Bicycling* magazine published my first piece about Annie in May 2005. It was the first account of her trip to appear since Annie's first person account appeared in *The World* newspaper of New York on October 20, 1895. Thanks, too, to Linda Smith Rhoads and Louise E. Robbins of the *New England Quarterly* for publishing the piece I wrote about Annie's search for the Massachusetts wild man, which became the last chapter of this book.

Dick Rath brought an important part of Annie's legacy to life when he restored for me an 1897 Sterling bicycle nearly identical to the 1894 Sterling Annie rode for most of her trip.

I also owe thanks to Thomas LeBien, publisher at Hill and Wang. Although Thomas did not publish this book, he looked at the project early on and provided invaluable feedback and encouragement.

Special thanks to the very patient staff of the Needham, Massachusetts, Public Library, especially April Asquith and Cathy Stetson, who probably thought my requests for interlibrary loans of microfilm would never cease. Public libraries—many of them are listed below—are often taken for granted, but they are the cornerstone of a society that values the free flow of information and freedom of thought.

My sister-in-law, Ceci Ogden, helped enormously with research assistance on the California portion of Annie's journey, and thanks to my brother-in-law, Andy, for running up to the National Archives in San Bruno to chase down a lead.

Many thanks to the people behind USGenNet of Rio Vista, California, and the Livingston County History and Genealogical Project of Michigan. Together they compiled and hosted the 1895 U.S. Atlas online at www. livgenmi.com/1895/. This atlas was an invaluable resource. I found myself returning to the site repeatedly trying to locate information about various cities and towns as they existed in 1895 and for maps that helped me track Annie's progress.

Thanks to Glenn Rifkin and Eric Fettmann, longtime friends from Paramus, New Jersey, and David Minard who gave unstintingly of his time and talents as a graphic and web designer. David, thank you for *everything*.

In no particular order I also want to acknowledge the veritable army of people who provided assistance of one kind or another along the way. With apologies to those I have inadvertently overlooked, my heartfelt thanks to my mother, Baila Zheutlin, and John Coleman and Robert Smith, my first cousin once removed and my second cousin once removed, respectively; Seth Bauer, who read and commented incisively on an early draft of this book (he said it was perfect as written); Sally Sims Stokes; Nancy Cott; Janet Edwards; Linda Lawrence Hunt; Clara Silverstein; Roger Kennedy, director emeritus of the Smithsonian Institution; Ellen Smith of Brandeis University; Kay Cahill Allison; Bill Pryor; Judy Safian-Demers; Ed Shaw; Monique Fischer and the staff of the Northeast Document Conservation Center in Andover, Massachusetts, for helping with the physical preservation of the artifacts of Annie's life; The Jewish Cemetery Association of Massachusetts; Richard Chaisson of Athol, Massachusetts, for helping me explore a fascinating chapter in Annie's journalistic life; Ken Fletcher, volunteer at the Carnegie Public Library, Trinidad, Colorado; Char Sidell, librarian at the Broadmeadow Elementary School in Needham, Massachusetts; Alison Barnet; Gail Hedges, president of the Foundation for Children's Books; the Kenosha, Wisconsin Public Library; Karen K. Schmiege of the Albuquerque Public Library; Kevin Davey of the Chicago Public Library; Debbie Newman and Leslie Broughton of the Arizona Historical Society; Jennifer Albin of the Arizona State Library; Luke Jasprzebski of the University of Texas at El Paso Library; the Special Collections department of the Penmore Library, Colorado Springs, Colorado; Kristin Bickel, of the La Junta, Colorado

Woodruff Memorial Library; Bob Ilfeld of Albuquerque, New Mexico; Robert Shindle of the University of Baltimore Educational Foundation Special Collections/Steamship Historical Society of America Collections; Duncan R. Jamieson, professor of history at Ashland University: Noreen Riffe, Special Collections Librarian, at the Pueblo, Colorado, Public Library; Jack Austin, genealogy volunteer at the El Paso Public Library; the staff of the Riverside Cemetery, Saddle Brook, New Jersey; Emelen Brown of the University Archives at New York University; Bob Sullivan of the Schenectady County Public Library, New York; Don Biecker of the Columbia Bicycle Co. of Westfield, Massachusetts; Paul Beck of the Kendallville, Indiana, Public Library; the Information Desk Staff of the Cedar Rapids Public Library, Cedar Rapids, Iowa; Betty Collicott of the Cozad, Nebraska, Public Library; Celine Stahlnecker of the Grand Island, Nebraska, Public Library; Marc Shectman of *The Boston Globe* library; Carl Hallberg, reference archivist at the Wyoming State Archives in Cheyenne; Julie Habjan Boisselle of the Mount Holyoke College library, South Hadley, Massachusetts; Mary Beth Sancomb-Moran, of the Sidney, Nebraska, Public Library; Vince Begley of Marymount College, Newburgh, New York; Sara Aden of the North Platte, Nebraska, Public Library; Carl F. Burgwardt of the Pedaling History Bicycle Museum, Orchard Park, New York, who answered many questions about bicycles of the 1890s; Tom Farley of West Sacramento, California, for helping me understand the state of the U.S. telephone system in the mid-1890s; David Siegenthaler, of the Elgin, Illinois, Area Historical Society; the staff of the Iowa City, Iowa, Public Library; Lorna Caulkins of the Grinnell, Iowa, Public Library; Wilma Parezek of the Tama County, Iowa, Historical Society; Claire McKibben of the Kearney, Nebraska, Public Library; Shirley Garrett of the Mount Vernon, New York, Public Library; Raymond Lum, librarian for Western languages at Harvard University's Harvard-Yenching Library; Ross Petty of Babson College, Wellesley, Massachusetts, for his help with the history of women and cycling; Pryor Dodge, author, collector, and cycling historian of New York, New York; Gail Hall of the Lordsburg-Hidalgo Library in Lordsburg, New Mexico; Judy Behm of the Carroll, Iowa, Public Library; the staff of the Utica, New York, Public Library; the staff of the Silver City, New Mexico, Public Library; Judy Dominici of the Nashua, New Hampshire, Public Library; Larry Tye, author of *Home Lands: Portraits of the New Jewish Diaspora;* Jean Palmer of the Onondaga, New York, County Public Library; Ira Ward, volunteer at the Marshalltown, Iowa, Public Library; Professor Jonathan D. Sarna, Joseph H. and

Belle R. Braun Professor of American Jewish History at Brandeis University, Waltham, Massachusetts; Rachel Sagan and Karla Goldman of the Jewish Women's Archive, Brookline, Massachusetts; Monica Staley; the staff of the Pottawattamie County Genealogical Society, Council Bluffs, Iowa; Dale Kreiter of the Santa Maria, California, Public Library; Ken Warfield of the Santa Barbara, California, Public Library; Ann Billesbach, Scott Argabright, and Matt Pierzol of the Nebraska State Historical Society, Lincoln, Nebraska; the staff of the Mount Auburn Cemetery, Cambridge, Massachusetts; Mary Grein of the Melrose, Massachusetts, Public Library; Bruce Epperson and Stephen Goddard for their expertise on the Pope Manufacturing Company; William Steele, professor of history at International Christian University in Tokyo; Beth Williams of the Nevada, Iowa Public Library; Drs. Tom Piemonte, Brooks Watt, and Lawrence Shields for helping to arrange access to the archives of the Algonquin Club, Boston, Massachusetts; Larry Adams, curator, Mamie Doud Eisenhower Birthplace, Boone, Iowa; Karen Ramos of the Stockton, California, Public Library; Sue Payne of the San Bernardino, California, Public Library; Judy Brown and Coi Drummond-Gehrig and the staff of the Denver, Colorado, Public Library; the Information Services staff of the Erie County Public Library, Erie, Pennsylvania; Jeanine Rhodes of the Elkhart, Indiana, Public Library; Kim Limond, reference librarian at the Clinton, Iowa, Public Library; the staff of the Canajoharie, New York Public Library; Pat Worthington of the El Paso County Historical Society, El Paso, Texas; Pat O'Hanlon of the Truth or Consequences, New Mexico Public Library; the staff of the State Library of New York in Albany; Jennifer Lee of the Columbia University Library; Daryl Morrison, head of Special Collections at the University of California at Davis; Shan Sutton, head of Special Collections at the University of the Pacific Library, Stockton, California; Céline Hirsch, Archivist at the Nostra Signora di Sion in Rome, Italy; Ron Erickson; Beverly Sierpina; Dana McNair; M. Susan Barger; Michelle Kaminga, Eric Frere, Sharon Klempner, and Jennifer Pinto Safian and Chet Safian for French translations; Linda Grahn and Renate Franz for German translation; Lisa Mullins and David Leveille of Public Radio International's *The World;* and the folks at Warehouse Picture Framing.

Last, but most assuredly not least, heartfelt thanks to my wife, Judy Gelman, and my sons, Danny and Noah. I love them dearly.

# Index